THE ROAD FROM EMPIRE TO ECO-DEMOCRACY

The Road from Empire to Eco-Democracy

Gene Marshall
lead author

with coauthors
**Ben Ball, Marsha Buck,
Ken Kreutziger, and Alan Richard**

The authors are members of
The Research Symposium on Christian Resurgence
for Century Twenty-One,
a project of Realistic Living,
a nonprofit organization focusing
on religion and social ethics.

www.RealisticLiving.org

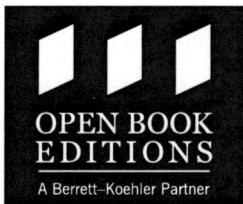

**OPEN BOOK
EDITIONS**
A Berrett–Koehler Partner

The Road from Empire to Eco-Democracy

Co-authors

Gene Marshall
lead author

with coauthors
Ben Ball, Marsha Buck,
Ken Kreutziger, and Alan Richard

iUniverse books may be ordered through booksellers or by contacting:

iUniverse
1663 Liberty Drive
Bloomington, IN 47403
www.iuniverse.com
1-800-Authors (1-800-288-4677)

ISBN: 978-1-4620-8364-0 (sc)
ISBN: 978-1-4620-8365-7 (e)

Library of Congress Control Number: 2011962928

Printed in the United States of America
iUniverse rev. date: 12/22/2011

Cover Design by Paula Brennecke

Table of Contents

About the Authors

The coauthors of this book are members of the Research Symposium on Christian Resurgence for Century Twenty-One, a program of Realistic Living, a nonprofit organization on ethics and religion. As the following biographical summaries indicate, each of us comes to this project with many years of experience both in book learning and practical work in social change movements. Our experience and knowledge is various; so many chapters have arrived at their final form after many (sometimes tense) exchanges. We believe that the final product is better because of this intense interaction during the four years of work on this project. We wish to introduce ourselves at the beginning of this book and invite your also passionate and continuing discussion of these controversial and urgent topics.

Gene Marshall began his education as a mathematician and physicist. In 1953 he decided to leave a mathematics career and attend seminary at Perkins School of Theology in Dallas, Texas. He has served as a local church pastor, a chaplain in the army, and in 1962 joined a religious order of families (the Order:Ecumenical), and traveled across the United States, Canada, Latin America, Europe, and Asia as a teacher and lecturer of religious and social ethics topics. These trips included an in-depth study of world cultures and a vivid sense of the social conditions of the world's peoples. He was an active participant in the civil rights revolution, serving for one year as the Protestant executive of The National Conference on Religion and Race. For six years he served as dean of an eight-week residential academy that trained leadership for religious and social engagement work throughout the world. In 1983 Gene and Joyce Marshall organized a nonprofit educational organization, Realistic Living, and began publishing journals, books, and essays. This book is his seventh book-length project. In 1999 Gene became a founding member of the Research Symposium on Christian Resurgence for Century Twenty-one. As a member of this organization he has headed the team of coauthors of this book.

Ben Ball received BS and MS degrees in chemical engineering from the Massachusetts Institute of Technology and completed Harvard Business School's Advanced Management Program. After thirty years' service with Gulf Oil Corporation, he retired as corporate vice president. He then held for twenty-five years various teaching and research appointments at MIT and their Energy Laboratory and Institute for Advanced Studies, including that of adjunct professor of management and engineering. For twenty-eight years he served as a management consultant to dozens of corporations and governments worldwide; gave expert testimony in many more dozens of cases in state and federal courts and before the US Congress and the United Nations; and served on committees of the National Academy of Engineering, the UN, and the University of Texas Energy Laboratory. He authored or coauthored more than one hundred publications, mostly dealing with strategy and energy issues. He was a senior faculty member of the Ecumenical Institute, is a founding and active member of the Research Symposium on Christian Resurgence for Century Twenty-One, an active member of Realistic Living, and a member of their international advisory board. He is also an active member of the Foundation for Contemporary Theology.

Marsha Buck has spent most of her adult life in Alaska, working first as a teacher of the blind, a bush pilot, and a music therapist, and then later serving as a special education teacher and administrator and as an elementary school principal. She received undergraduate degrees in music education, music therapy, and special education at Michigan State University prior to moving to Alaska. She received graduate degrees in school administration from the University of Alaska. When Marsha financially had "enough," she retired from working for money and began serving as an advocate for civil equality for women and LGBT people, as the co-manager of a women's chorus, as an editor for lead author Gene Marshall, and as an organic vegetable gardener within two miles of a glacier. She is a musician who has performed as an oboist in several symphony orchestras and currently sings soprano with the Juneau Pride Chorus. Marsha is a founding and active member of the Research Symposium on Christian Resurgence for Century Twenty-One, as well as an active member of Realistic Living and a member of their board of directors.

Kenneth Kreutziger has been a "political junky" all his life following local, national, and international political personalities and issues. His political tendencies started in high school as a boy's state candidate elected to secretary of state, and he is currently an elected official in his community as a town meeting member in a representative town meeting form of local governance. Mr. Kreutziger had a professional career of nearly forty years in urban planning and urban design, first as a consultant in an international multidisciplinary firm where for the last five years he was a partner, and then in his own firm, providing services primarily to cities and towns in eastern Massachusetts. In 2000 he was designated a "fellow" of the American Institute of Certified Planners by his colleagues for his contributions to the profession. His undergraduate degree is in architecture, his graduate degree in urban planning. Mr. Kreutziger's wide range of interests and work cover the topics for this book, but he focuses on care of the environment and on the nature and strength of our democracy, where there is social justice for all, and on enhancing the development of a common wealth for all citizens. For more than a decade he has been an active member of the Research Symposium on Christian Resurgence for Century Twenty-One.

Alan Richard, Ph.D. has twenty years' of experience as an activist and community organizer, fifteen years' of experience as a published behavioral health researcher, and ten years' of experience managing large behavioral health programs. He holds a doctorate in religion from Syracuse University. His work has appeared in a broad range of peer-reviewed scientific journals in the fields of psychology, sociology, public health, economics, substance abuse, and religion. Dr. Richard has developed a number of effective social interventions including a multi-session, school-based substance-abuse curriculum, a continuum of care for homeless youth, and a combined HIV and mental health intervention for youth in detention. He has served as peer reviewer for *AIDS Education and Prevention, Journal of Acquired Immune Deficiency Syndromes, American Journal of Public Health*, and *Journal for the Scientific Study of Religion*. He has also served as grant reviewer for the federal Department of Health and Human Services. He is currently research director for The Center for Success and Independence, senior scientist for RTH Research Group, and vice president of Communities Organizing for Resources and Environment. In 2004 he became active in the Research Symposium on Christian Resurgence for Century Twenty-One, and he joined the staff of Realistic Living in 2010.

Acknowledgments

We are grateful to Joyce Marshall, who has made many additions to this manuscript, especially on Chapter 5: The Continuing Drag of Patriarchy. We are also grateful to Irma Hudson, who worked with the coauthors as another proponent of feminist and cultural concerns. The members of the Research Symposium on Christian Resurgence for Century Twenty-One have been a constant support of this work, hearing reports and making suggestions during the four years of work on this project. The authors of this book are a task force of that organization.

Introduction
Toward a Unified Progressive Vision

This book is not about making piecemeal repairs on understandable problems. It is about contributing to a massive social transition that we will never fully understand in our lifetimes. We who call ourselves "progressives" tend to each be doing our own good things, but in the main we lack a comprehensive overview of how we exit the deathtrap into which humanity has cornered itself and how we construct a social vehicle within which humanity can survive and thrive.

We see a fully progressive vision as an intimation of a much better future but also as a fight against a set of illusions that characterize our age. Our fight is against a set of lies that are given "sacred" standing in the hearts and minds and commitments of most people, resulting in a set of compulsions that enslave rich and poor alike. It is a fight against a matrix of malice toward realism, toward real people, toward the real Earth—a malice that sickens the whole of humanity and undermines the wider community of Earth life. What are some of these illusions?

Illusion 1: *The notion that our species can survive more centuries of the top-down means of organizing human society—that kings-over-peasants, rich-over-poor, and society-over-nature is a means of organization that can be continued without ecological doom and sociological chaos.*

The truth is the last fifty-four hundred years of hierarchical organization, that period of history we call "civilization," or "empire," is drawing to a close. (More on this later.) Our options are: (a) Will the end time of civilization be entirely catastrophic? or (b) Will it be the birth time for something better than civilization?

Illusion 2: *The notion that a society can be called "succeeding" if it allows some players to have millions of units of economic power while others have next to none.*

    The truth is rich and poor alike are faced with abandoning their customary class attitudes if we are to overcome the trap into which being civilized has led us. Unless we can overcome the extreme gulf between rich and poor and establish something like a moderate middle-class living for everyone, our species is doomed.

Illusion 3: *The notion that a market economy is a natural process rather than a government-supported function that requires appropriate regulation in order to remain effective.*

    The truth is only wise governmental regulation makes the market creative, fair, competitive, safe, and ecologically sound.[1] Expecting economic well-being for all people to happen through the volunteer goodness of for-profit institutions is a delusion. Public corporations only volunteer things that fit within their mandate to please customers and to reward managers and investors. That is their job, to which they are legally bound; we cannot expect something more noble from corporations. We cannot expect good public policy from corporations.

Illusion 4: *The notion that corporation managers using other people's money (investors' money) to lobby and campaign for narrow corporation interests is in accord with free speech as intended by the US Constitution. (Other nations may have their own versions of this.)*

    The truth is: Both our Constitution and our common sense advise otherwise. Five misguided U.S. Supreme Court Justices

---

[1] This fact is not a new insight. It was clearly understood and articulated by Adam Smith, the inventor of the market economy (see *Adam Smith and the Wealth of Nations: 1776–1976 Bicentennial Essays* by Fred R. Glahe).

recently ruled to allow unlimited amounts of corporation money to influence—if not determine—political elections. A corporation is not a person and should not be treated as one. A corporation should be treated as the artificial, impersonal fiction that it is. It is nothing more than a contract with a democratic government to do something useful for the citizenry of that government. In principle, in fact, and in law, a corporation can be de-licensed if it does not comply with these obligations. If government does not reclaim this appropriate power over the economic system, we slide into full-blown oligarchy—a government of, by, and for the wealthy few. Let us state this principle as strongly as possible: a corporation must be legally prohibited with severe penalties if it spends one penny lobbying or financing the campaign of any public official. That penny belongs to its workers and investors. The government belongs to the people, not to the corporations. Until we the citizenry insist upon this, our "democracy" is a joke.

Illusion 5: *The notion that an economy needs to grow if there is to be prosperity for all its citizens.*

　　The truth is perpetual growth is a formula for ecological and economic ruin. Instead, it is possible to have a steady-state economy, one based on a love of the Earth and a devotion to its flourishing. Every mature ecosystem has a steady-state economy. Perpetual growth on a finite planet is a disaster. Most conservatives and many liberals do not grasp this. Some parts of an economy may need to grow, but ever continuing overall growth has become a prescription for ecocide, genocide, and final burial.

* * * * * * * *

These five illusions and their truthful alternatives may not strike every progressive-leaning person as true, or fully true. In these abbreviated statements, key words have not been carefully defined, and supporting evidence has not been supplied. If questions have been raised about these assertions, our purpose for now has been met. In the chapters ahead, we will further elaborate on these topics.

But even when such topics are fully elaborated on, progressives will continue to disagree about many things; they will emphasize different aspects of the whole picture; and they will conduct vigorous discussions among one another. This is so because being a progressive means facing a future that cannot be fully envisioned. The future is always a surprise, and when we are anticipating a major historical turning point, the surprises are even deeper. Reactionaries have it easier; they know the established patterns they are defending or the obsolete patterns to which they want to return. Reactionaries have their disagreements too, but it is easier for them to come together in opposition to progressives than it is for progressives to come together in opposition to reactionaries. Nevertheless, we progressives need to do the hard work it takes to come together; otherwise, we will not win what we dearly want to win (more on that later). We need to find a common vision of the future and a common strategy for getting there.

The authors of this book believe that being a true progressive means more than having a set of platitudes or a set of ideals that we impose upon our times. Rather, the progressive vision is a search for truth. It is not just one more set of arbitrary opinions placed alongside other sets of arbitrary opinions. It is a quest to countermand the lies of our society, to tell the truth and be honest about what the actual events of our history are calling us to do. So how do progressives think together toward a unifying consensus about what deeply matters to us and our planet?

In this book we will recommend an open-ended approach to social truth that rejects any sort of final solidification. Nevertheless, (1) we reject the thoroughgoing relativism that implies that every social opinion is as good as any other. We believe that a valid discussion on social truth implies a full honoring of scientific factuality. And (2), we believe that the competent inward contemplation of human nature can result in insight into what is actually true rather than simply more arbitrary opinions. The truth of our existence challenges us to improve our opinions, however humiliating this may be. And (3), our third approach to social truth has to do with workability. We consider this a key insight into social change, especially when facing a hugely different future, the anticipation of which is vulnerable to all kinds of illusory idealisms. We see "what works" as a down-to-Earth test of "truth" that any responsible vision of the future requires.

Following is an elaboration of each of these three approaches to truth:

(1) Finding Consensus in Scientific Knowledge

Our progressive consensus building begins with the plain facts of scientific research. In US society we are facing a revolt against science. As Al Gore pointed out, the facts of global warming are an "inconvenient truth." The truth about this mounting climate crisis is inconvenient to oil companies, coal companies, conservative ideologues, wasteful energy users, and so on. The facts of evolution and the Big Bang cosmology of contemporary physics are inconvenient truths to biblical fundamentalists. Business-friendly politicians feel justified in favoring profit-making tree harvesters over the wisdom of the scientific forestry community. And on it goes. Progressive consensus building needs to counter this fact-hating trend in our society. We need to allow our lives and thinking to be limited by the facts and our proposals grounded in what is factually confirmed. Though scientific knowledge is a progressive process that never arrives at absolute certainty, it does provide strong relative certainty that needs to be fully honored.

(2) Finding Consensus in Inward Inquiry

Our creative consensus building also needs to honor what we know about humanity from our inward inquiry into our own consciousness of being human. We need to root our social thought in our awareness that beneath all the escapes and misinformation our species has invented, we are truly a very deep wonder and we have a capacity for goodness. We also need to notice the horrific capacity of our species for perverting our natural openness, love, and freedom into defensiveness, malice, and compulsions. And we need to observe how profoundly humans can change. Valid change toward personal maturity is not a matter of becoming superhuman, but a matter of giving up our self-created substitutes for being human, and allowing our true nature to bloom.

(3) Finding Consensus in Social Workability

Our creative consensus building needs to combine our scientific knowledge and inward wisdom into workable patterns of social life. We need to take note that our modes of social life are not determined by our biology but are invented by human beings as we strive to adapt to the diverse environments in which we emerge as functioning societies. Certainly our biological limits and possibilities enter in as factors in our discernment of what is workable; but we, our species, invented the tribal mode of social organization, the civilization mode of social organization, and all the many varieties of each. Though the tribal mode and the civilization mode of social organization have proved workable for long periods of time, we will show that both modes of social organization have become unworkable as solutions to the challenges now faced by our species. Further, we are not biologically determined as a species to ride our obsolete social vehicles into the abyss. We have a capability for discerning what new social modes of organization are workable. We can dismantle the old modes and construct the new. This is the hope on which the authors of this book will elaborate.

We do not claim perfection. Some of our conclusions may be proven wrong as history unfolds. Nevertheless, we are attempting to serve the truth—the sort of truth that cuts through the maze of misunderstandings, misinformation, rigid biases, and downright lies that characterize so much of our public discourse. The authors of this book live in the United States, and most of our illustrations will focus on the United States, but the topics of our concern are planet-wide in their importance. Wherever readers of this book may live, similar awakenings and similar strategies for action may apply. We are interested in dialogue with all these many places and their perspectives. We understand that we live on a single planet and that every issue is international in many of its aspects. Nevertheless, we will begin in the United States.

What does it mean to be socially awake in the United States in this moment of planetary history? How can the awakening portion of humanity living in the United States awaken a majority of the US citizenry and organize these awakening multitudes in public actions that are socially transforming? These are the questions that drive the chapters of this book.

We understand that progressives need to come together in a rough sort of unity that enables a successful fight against the taken-for-granted illusions of our social systems. Our fight is not with the rich or the poor or with any particular group of humans. To win the changes needed to avoid planetary doom, we will need half the rich to abandon their mostly conservative illusions and become progressives who assist the middle classes and the poor in building a society based upon factual knowledge, true humanness, and workability. We will also need half the poor and many more than half of the dwindling middle class to join this progressive fight against the illusions of civilization and for the truth that supports a workable future. Progressives will need to work toward everyone becoming middle class, putting an end to poverty and unlimited wealth forever. Our fight is not with one another; our fight is with the illusions that have taken all of us captive.

If we wish to participate in building a viable future for our species, we need to choose our audiences and reveal to them the inconvenient and often distressing truths that citizens have to accept in order for our species to survive. Then we need to forgive everybody and welcome everybody home to a post-illusion journey toward a viable human presence on planet Earth.

An Overview of the Book

We have titled this book *The Road from Empire To Eco-Democracy* because we seek to illuminate a viable path from the imploding social mode we call "civilization" to a workable alternative mode of social organization. We will show that every civilization is an empire, and that empire and civilization are two words for the same thing. We are naming the post-civilization mode of social organization "Eco-Democracy" because ecological responsibility and democratic processes are foundational elements in our vision of the future.

We have titled **Part One** of this book "**Ten Wake-up Calls to Civilized Sleepers.**" The awakenings are in these ten arenas: Ecology, Democracy, Fossil Fuel, Population, Patriarchy, Racism, Theocracy, War, Money, and Poverty. Awakening is already happening, but not to everyone. Among those who are waking up, many are not fully awake to all ten awakenings. Some may be awake to the sad state of democracy, but still unfamiliar with the full extent of our ecological crisis. Some may be awake to the continuing subjugation of women, but still confused about the tyranny of our money system. Some may be awake to the horror of poverty, but unaware of how poverty is related to all these other grim topics and how poverty is the clearest sign that civilization is failing as a viable mode of social organization for the future. When taken together these ten awakenings make it clear that we must move beyond empire/civilization. In order to avoid a trip to the cliffs of ecological and social collapse, humanity cannot continue to tolerate the mode of social organization we call "civilization."

In **Part Two, "Taking the Long View,"** we explain how seeing the corrective action as moving "beyond empire" is a radical step in the entire history of the planet. The needed transition is not about creating a better form of civilization; it is about "getting beyond civilization." This does not mean going back to a form of "tribal society."[2] It means creating a third basic mode of social organization. We maintain that every civilization has been imperial in its basic quality. Being an empire and being a civilization turns out to be one and the same thing.

---

2 Tribal society is our name for the forms of society that existed before civilization and that in modified forms still exists in some places to this day. "Tribal" is not a term of derision but an acknowledgement of a vibrant social mode that served humanity well for at least one hundred thousand years.

Some civilizations have been more expansive than others, more brutal than others, or more oppressive toward their citizens than others, but a civilization is a form of social order that uses military power to favor its elite citizens, to expand its influence in the world, and to coerce its commoners into the chore of accomplishing these imperial tasks. Part Two focuses on the origin and demise of civilization and the coming into being of what we will call "Eco-Democracy," which is our working title for getting "beyond empire." This post-imperial, post-civilizational mode of social organization is still a consensus being formed by future-oriented humans, but two qualities of that future stand out above all others: (1) a new form of society must live in harmony with the ecological limits and possibilities of planet Earth; and (2) its governmental structures must be democratic rather than wealth-driven. The name "Eco-Democracy" maintains these two insights. There can be no ecologically successful society that is not democratic. And there can be no lasting democracy that fails to resolve the ecological crises.

Part Three, "Seeing Society Whole," focuses on defining what we mean by economic, political, and cultural processes. Most US citizens have little grasp of what comprises the basic processes that characterize every society—every past, present, and future society. Part Three helps remedy this lack of tools for social thought. It also helps us see how deeply imbalanced our society is toward the economic processes. Robert Reich, in his book *Supercapitalism*[3] points out how many US adults have become competent consumers and investors, but have ceased to be informed citizens. Further, many of those who are enthusiastic citizens concern themselves almost entirely with economic values and far less with overall well-being of society. To restore balance we must enrich culture, especially citizen education and planetary realism. Such an enriched culture will strengthen the political structures and thereby empower the political to restrain our runaway economy.

---

3 Reich, Robert B; *Supercaptialism: The Transformation of Business, Democracy, and Everyday Life* (New York: Alfred A Knopf, 2008) Chapter Five: Politics Diverted.

Part Four, "Eco-Democracy: How Do We Get There from Here?" focuses on the core questions of this book. How do we get beyond empire? How do we move toward Eco-Democracy? What are the effective strategies for accomplishing this transition? What is the "Road" from our doom-threatened "here" to a viable "there" for the human species on planet Earth?

These questions are informed by the visionary clarifications introduced in Parts One, Two, and Three. But knowing where we are and where we want to go is only the beginning. We need to inquire into how our experience gives us a sense of what could be a plausible path toward this huge and radical change. Further, who among our species will lead this movement for change; how are they to arouse the masses; and who will be the enemies of this arduous journey? What basic strategies of action will be required—not necessarily by each person but by the whole body of change agents? We need this big strategic picture in order to be motivated to do our small part and to sense how we each fit into the master drama of change that can actually get us *there* from *here*. Without such plausible strategies, our hope for a viable alternative future vanishes. If our minds are not filled with such a vision of hope, then our minds are occupied with visions of hopelessness or sheer denial. Getting there from here requires building in ourselves and others this down-to-Earth, practical, flexible, hopeful mind. As we take this road we know that we will be surprised by the difficulties as well as the opportunities. Nevertheless, we build hope year after year until the task is done. Such hope building is a core power within our species. We only need to open ourselves to this power.

* * * * * * * *

Our entire book, though brief for such huge topics, aims to provide an inclusive outline for the thinking and action that we ordinary citizens of the United States and elsewhere need if we are to win what can be won for humanity and for planet Earth in century twenty-one.

Part One:

Ten Wake-up Calls to Civilized Sleepers

Human beings are becoming aware of the ways reality is challenging our species in this historical present. In this sense, Part One is about what *is* and how civilized humanity is asleep—asleep to the possibilities for deep and necessary change and to the impossibilities we must face and accept. Most of the time we flee from being aware of our limitations and challenges; nevertheless, these realities are unavoidable. We begin by facing reality.

The ten wake-up calls discussed in the chapters of Part One are controversial because each of us approaches our experience of these topics with old pictures of reality that these awakenings are undermining. These awakenings are also controversial because they are not yet fully known. Humanity is still awakening to them.

Our description of these ten wake-up calls is a mere summary, and less than a full summary considering the hundreds of books and essays written on these topics. Our aim is to remind us of ten basic sociological awakenings that are shared by the awakening portion of humanity. Any one of us may not be equally alert to each of the ten. Yet all ten are important, and they reinforce each other. We will not enter the promised land of a viable human presence on this planet until a full majority of us are fully awake to all ten of these basic challenges and until we adequately deal with them.

Chapter 1
The Primacy of the Ecological Crisis

In his book *Person/Planet*[4] Theodore Roszak pictures society as a human creation supported and limited by the planet on one side and by the person on the other.

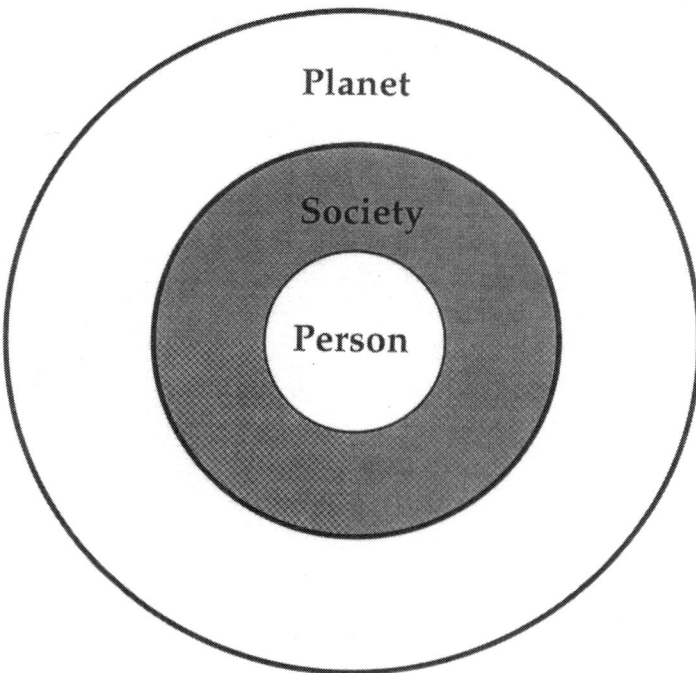

---

[4] Theodore Roszak, *Person/Planet* (Garden City, New York: Anchor Press/Doubleday, 1978)

Roszak's main point was that those of us who are defending human persons from becoming a mere cog in the social machinery and those of us who are defending the planet from becoming devastated by the "progress" of society are on the same team. Society is destructive unless it fully honors the person and the planet. Industrial civilization, in spite of all its obvious benefits, has proved to be out of sync in both ways. Any vision of an alternative future society that can be considered wholesome, sustainable, worthy, workable, or sane must fashion economic, political, and cultural changes—new practices and institutions that honor both the person and the planet.

This is a realization that the architects and managers of industrial civilization do not—perhaps cannot—fully acknowledge while remaining managers of the current form of society. The ecological perspective requires an end to the prospect of unending economic growth. It requires a whole new way of defining "progress." When the ecology of the planet enters our scope of consideration, we can no longer define progress as more money flow, more buying, more selling, more producing, more distributing, more consuming, more employing, more accumulating, more investing. "Are we all more-titions?" asked e. e. cummings in one of his poems. Indeed, we are killing ourselves with more people and more resource use. If we do not reverse the size of our human footprint upon the planet we will cause a die off—not only of birds and frogs, pandas and wolves, forests, grasses, and rare medicinal plants but of our own species due to ecological collapse.

Ecology must be our first priority. "Earth first" is more than a slogan; it is a necessity for human survival. And "Earth first" need not mean animosity toward the human species. The human species is part of the glory of Earth; it is a portion of the planet that is conscious of being conscious and thereby aware of the entire history of the planet and of the possibility of shaping the beauty and joy of Earth's future. Business success is secondary to Earth success. Economics is secondary to ecology. Economics must first promote the well-being of the entire planetary system, and only then can a business be allowed to make a profit and handle other matters that the business community emphasizes.

Such a shift in values does not mean devaluing the human person. Indeed, valuing the natural planet includes valuing the human person as part of that planet. Like frogs, we have blood flowing in our veins; we breathe oxygen; we require space; we eat; we die. Humans are part of the planet. Humans are the intense awareness of this planet, the consciousness that is conscious of being conscious. Life and human life make this planet unique among all the planets we know. But valuing the human person does not mean allowing unlimited population growth or extending unlimited wealth to any of these persons. And it certainly does not mean the extension of unlimited indulgence to an ever-narrowing few at the expense of an ever-expanding many.

Ecology has become the first principle of a viable economics, a viable politics, and a viable culture for continued human life on this planet. Earth is the necessary foundation for human society; fully acknowledging this truth requires a total transformation of values for every political body, every business organization, every educational institution, and every religious institution. The institutions of society are human made. We made them; we can remake them. We constructed them; we can dismantle them and construct others. The devastation of this planet is not a done deal. We can choose instead to dismantle the present forms of industrial civilization and construct something better. And we need not call this new something "civilization." We may need to shock our minds into the realization that we are challenged to do something as drastic as that ancient shift from tribal societies to the dawn of large complex hierarchical civilizations. It is meaningful to say we need to move toward a third basic mode of human society. Shall we call it "post-civilization"? Shall we call it "Earth community"? Whatever we call it, it has never existed before. As a species we have never before been challenged to consciously build a human society in which the entire ecology of the planet (including humans) is first priority.

This dawn of the priority of ecology requires a consideration of the fact that the planet has regions, eco-regions, and bioregions. We all live on the same planet, but we each live in our own region of the planet. Some eco-region or bioregion is our home. The bioregional perspective is so important that we must all learn to consider ourselves "bioregionalists." This is not hard to do. Here is how you become a bioregionalist: you leap up out of your county, state, province, and nation, and then as you come back down to the same spot, you envision landing on Earth in your region of Earth. You land on your valley, mountain, forest, prairie, or ocean shore. That leap makes you a bioregionalist. This region of Earth becomes your home. Your political districts are now secondary. This bioregional leap is a simple shift in perspective, but its consequences are revolutionary in a deep and primary way.

Following is a further elaboration of the bioregional perspective:

> The term "bioregional" points to human beings living in committed relationships with local regions of the natural planet. A person or a group enters into the bioregional family of society-builders when that person or group subscribes wholeheartedly to these statements:
> **Earth is my home: I am an Earthling.**
> **A continent of Earth is my home.**
> **A region of Earth is my home.**

This fresh sense of home is simple, but it has implications:

> The United States, Canada, Mexico, or some other nation is not my home; it is just my nation.

> My state or province is not my home; it is just my state or province.

My zip-code district is not my home; it is just my zip-code district.

Western civilization is not my home. No civilization is my home; it is just my civilization.

My tribe is not my home (if you are a tribal person); it is just my tribe.

> Tribal people have been bioregionalists compared to civilized people, but they are not bioregionalists because they are tribal. They are bioregionalists because they have honored both the living and the non-living in a specific region of the planet.

When we apply the bioregional sense of home to envisioning the future of human society, we do not see tribes or civilizations. We see a planetary confederation of semiautonomous Earth-regions.

When we apply the bioregional sense of home to envisioning the future of political and economic systems, we do not see a global economy ruled by global wealth and power, with little or no possibility for local self-governance. We see popular consensus building beginning in each local region and extending into an Earth-sensitive governance of the entire economic playing field for all players across the whole planet.

When we apply the bioregional sense of home to envisioning the future of human cultures, we do not see planet-wide uniformities conceived by product advertisers. We see local families of plants, animals, and humans forming unique expressions of aliveness in each region of the planet.

Such a vision is basically simple, but it has far-reaching implications. It means shutting down in our own

minds the dream of building a better civilization or
the dream of returning to some new sort of tribal
life. It means dreaming a new dream. This new
dream is not something grandly idealistic; it is a
realistic direction for avoiding untenable ecological
disaster. While we may learn many lessons from a
thousand centuries of tribal society and fifty-four
centuries of civilization, *we must now create something
new*. We must see civilizational hierarchy and tribal
intimacy as obsolete patterns of living that are no
longer appropriate for the real situation in which we
dwell. We must dream a new dream. *"Bioregionalism"
is a name for that new dream.*[5]

Unless citizens of the United States and every other nation
dream this new dream and see their nation in this context,
the hope for human well-being on this planet is nil. Nations
battling one another for the last oil field or the last body of fresh
water is not a pretty picture. Numbing ourselves to the plight
of our ocean fisheries, oxygen-producing rainforests, coral
reefs, waterways, aquifers, cropland, air quality, and climatic
conditions a not a beautiful way to live.

Al Gore has vividly reminded us in his documentary *An
Inconvenient Truth* that global warming is not a fiction told by a
few paranoid fanatics. It is a catastrophe already in the making,
a catastrophe that has been and continues being caused by the
human species. Arctic and Antarctic ice is already melting at a
distressing rate. Stress is being applied to plants, animals, and
humans living at every latitude of the planet. These planet-
wide climatic changes will not be pleasant. We need to learn
to connect the above alterations to their consequences, such
as hotter Gulf waters spawning ever more violent hurricanes
crashing into Gulf coast cities and coastlines. We need to take
into our consciousness the full tragedy of submerged coastal
cities, good farm land becoming desert, temperate European

---

5 This is a bioregional spin by Gene Marshall (2000).

summers replaced by death-dealing heat waves, floods where floods have always been rare—the list goes on and on. Many of these consequences have already been set in motion. It is too late to stop them. We can, however, moderate them. We can still prevent more serious catastrophes and further devastation in the lives of our grandchildren.

Global warming is only one of many ecological crises. Our coal-fired power plants dump tons of mercury into waterways where fish become toxic. With a regular intake of mercury, infants and children may become brain damaged and adults may experience a loss of cognitive power and early death. And mercury is only one of many pollutants that lead to health maladies. How we can power our societies without polluting our planet or causing climatic catastrophes will be further examined in later chapters.

The ecological crisis is also about shortages of water, food, minerals, land for agriculture and forests, and habitats for wildlife.

The stark truth surrounding the severity of our ecological crisis is being brought home in volumes and volumes of frightening facts. Here are a few facts assembled by the Earth Policy Institute under the direction of president Lester R. Brown.[6]

- ❖ **Shrinking Forests:** "After having lost 97 percent of its Atlantic rainforest, Brazil is now destroying the Amazon rainforest. This huge forest, roughly the size of Europe, was largely intact until 1970. Since then, 20 percent has been lost." Such rapidly expanding loss of forests is a disastrous trend (p. 82).
- ❖ **Losing Soil:** A vast dust cloud larger than the United States was recorded by satellite on January 9, 2005, moving west out of central Africa. Such storms are slowly reducing the fertility of Africa. Soil loss is another huge crisis (p. 85).

---

[6] Lester R. Brown, *Plan B 2.0* (New York and London: W. W. Norton & Company, 2006)

❖ **Coral Reef Damage:** African dust storms deposit so much dust in the Caribbean that the water becomes cloudy and damages the coral reefs. Dust, pollutants, temperature changes, and other factors threaten coral reefs worldwide. Coral reefs are foundational to key ocean ecosystems. They have been called "the rainforests of the sea" (p. 86).

❖ **Advancing Deserts:** Overgrazing of rangelands reduces livestock productivity, destroys vegetation, leads to erosion, and eventually creates wasteland and desert. Desertification is concentrated in Asia and Africa where nearly 4.8 billion of the world's 6.5 billion people live. Through desertification in China, some twenty-four thousand villages have been entirely or partly abandoned over the last half-century (p. 90).

❖ **Collapsing Fisheries:** Many fisheries are in decline and 75 percent are being fished at or beyond their sustainable levels. In 1997 human population growth and fishing technologies combined to reach an all-time high catch of ninety-three million tons. Since then wild seafood intake per person is falling off (pp. 91–92).

❖ **Disappearing Plants and Animals** (*the following data was supplied in 2004 by the Species Survival Commission of the World Conservation Union*): "The share of birds, mammals, and fish that are vulnerable [to] or in immediate danger of extinction is now measured in double digits: twelve percent of the world's nearly 10,000 bird species, 23 percent of the world's 4,776 mammal species, and 46 percent of the fish species analyzed." Additionally, from Earth Policy Institute: "Among mammals, the 240 known species of primates other than humans are most at risk" (p. 9).

The above list of dire facts could be greatly expanded and elaborated, as Lester Brown and others have done. Minor repairs on these matters are welcome, but minor repairs are not good enough. The human species faces a possible ecological apocalypse that it may not survive. This ecological crisis must be given first priority. Unless other social crises are treated as secondary to the ecological crisis, important aspects of our other social needs will be lost. We believe it is possible to think our way through to an overall vision of a viable, realistic, appropriate social transformation, but we cannot do this unless we are fully awake to *"The Primacy of the Ecological Crisis."*

* * * * * * * *

For further reading on this topic we recommend the following, from among the hundreds of books on this topic, for their accessibility and pertinence:

Thomas Berry, *The Great Work: Our Way into the Future* (New York: Bell Tower, 1999)

Theodore Roszak, *Person/Planet: The Creative Disintegration of Industrial Civilization* (New York: Anchor Press/Doubleday, 1978)

Lester R. Brown. *Plan B 2.0, Plan B 3.0, and Plan B 4.0* (New York and London: W. W. Norton & Company, 2006, 2008, and 2009)

Mike Carr, *Bioregionalism and Civil Society: Democratic Challenges to Corporate Globalism*, (Vancouver BC, Canada: The University of British Columbia Press, 2004)

Richard Leakey & Roger Lewin, *The Sixth Extinction: Patterns of Life and the Future of Humankind* (New York: Doubleday, 1995)

Chapter 2

The Undermining of Democracy

A second awakening US citizens are experiencing is the cruel fact that democracy is being undermined by "big" money, whether from excessively wealthy individuals or from the managers of huge corporations that are using money that rightly belongs to the shareholders to shape public policy. Winning a national political campaign requires an enormous sum of money. Those with the money to finance these campaigns own the winner. In the United States we no longer have true democracy, we have government of the money, by the money, and for the money. And those with the money are willing to spend their money to stay in the money and increase their money and power. We have a "moneyocracy."

We sometimes call it a "corporatocracy" because the management of large corporations focus investors' money (other people's money) toward controlling governments in order to control the flow of money to keep in power those with the money. Five members of the US Supreme Court—Roberts, Alito, Kennedy, Scalia, and Thomas—recently ruled unconstitutional those aspects of the McCain/Feingold bill and other laws that put limits on the amount of investors' money corporation managers can use to finance candidates of their choice. This ruling opened an even wider floodgate for corporation money to enter the electoral process. Unlike labor unions, issue organizations, and political parties, corporations control trillions of dollars. Spending even one percent of this money in support of or in opposition to candidates can overwhelm the entire electoral system. This is not only wrong for the quality of our elections but contrary to the Constitution as laid down by our founding fathers. We citizens who wish to be citizens, rather than couch potatoes who knuckle under to such violations of our citizenship, must respond strongly to this situation. Sooner or later we must amend the US Constitution to make clear to every lawmaker and every future Supreme Court justice that corporations are not persons and have no legal role in the making of public policy.

The majority of US Supreme Court justices currently misinterpret the right to free speech in the US Constitution in a manner that protects the spending of corporation money to control government. A series of much-discussed Supreme Court rulings give the moneyed few huge megaphones and the rest of the population modest whispers.

Treating corporations as persons was not what the original authors of "freedom of speech" had in mind. The Bill of Rights grants freedom of speech to persons. The contemporary legal decision to call corporations "legal persons" with first amendment protections makes a travesty of the democratic principle of free speech. This decision began through a misinterpretation of the Fourteenth Amendment, which was written to give legal personhood to former slaves, not corporations. This current legal policy will continue to destroy our democracy until it is corrected.

Corporation-funded megaphones speak loudly and repeatedly with messages phrased by the best "experts" money can buy. This is not honest research; it is pseudo-science in support of economic dogma. Over the course of time a measure of credibility tends to be given to whatever the aristocracy chooses to promote as truth.

If, for example, the hired megaphones say that global warming is not caused by the human production of carbon dioxide and that we can go on expanding a fossil-fuel[7] burning

---

7 Fossil fuel includes coal, petroleum, natural gas, oil or gas from shale, and oil from tar sands.

economy, the commentators in a money-sponsored media tend to afford this "speech" the honor of being a valid position. The news commentators do not simply explain that the megaphones lie. They allow the megaphones credence beyond the worth of their proclamations. News organizations join the insidious game of giving these loud voices honor merely because they are loud, made loud by big money. Balanced reporting does not mean giving equal time to every viewpoint, however unfounded. For example, the views of a contemporary Geological Society and a Flat-Earth Society are not of equal worth. "Baloney" must be named for what it is.

A free press is not a privilege but an organic necessity for a democratic society. It is a tragedy for democracy that we no longer have a fully free press. Most news media are now owned and controlled by massive conglomerates created to squelch free competition among the media. Most news media today are owned by industrial mega-corporations, whose interest in that ownership is not to publish news but to promote an ideology. Fox News is the most blatant example. Rather than "news," we have propaganda used to shape public opinion and policy in ways that suit the purposes of the "news" outlet. We have almost lost the crucial roles of investigative reporting and incisive editorializing, unencumbered by ownership constraints. If we don't regain a free press by breaking up these deadly conglomerates, our democracy will end up a complete sham.

Investigative reporting needs to take positions on such questions as: Is global warming real? Were there any weapons of mass destruction in Iraq? Were Iraq and al Qaeda "in cahoots"? Investigative reporting is especially difficult when: (1) big money owns the media, and (2) big money has eliminated competition among reporting entities.

In the current US money-driven discourse, whatever the aristocracy wants to proclaim as true becomes a respected position. As an example of how a money-driven news affects us all, we only need to recall how the controllers of the media dealt with the topic of "victory in Iraq." The core supporters of this "victory" knew that victory meant controlling the oil wealth of the Middle East. But they feared saying that out loud, so something else *the war promoters* decided had to be the "truth," something like, "We are liberating the people of Iraq," or "We are protecting our homeland from terrorist attack." Some "devised truth" is constructed and propagated to the extent that it is believed by most people. This is not democracy. This is moneyocracy with a democratic façade.

The excessive power currently being given to big money is not unavoidable, as some seem to claim. There are simple changes that can be made. We can construct new modes of sharing the truth. We can construct effective and democratic means of choosing representatives. We can change the election laws. We can require television companies to provide free coverage to all accredited candidates as a part of their rent for using the publicly owned airwaves. We can, and we must, change the basic pattern of choosing our political leadership.

Public Financing of Political Campaigns

We can limit the power of big money over political campaigns with mandatory public financing of campaigns. Public financing is not a radical restructuring of government; it is a simple legal measure that has already been implemented to some extent in Maine and Arizona, and is being strongly pushed in California. The opponents of public financing of candidates keep asking a confused citizenry, "Do you want your tax dollars going into political campaigns?" Voters can learn to say, "Yes, we prefer that to being overwhelmed by billions of dollars from corporation treasuries." "Yes, we prefer public financing to using tax dollars to make the rich richer, the poor poorer, and the Earth devastated." Many politicians in every party prefer public financing on the grounds that they detest spending more time raising money than governing.

But at the present time the moneyed aristocracy is winning on this issue. They are willing to spend any amount of money to remain in control. And a great deal of this big-money corruption is being accomplished with other people's money.

Small stockholders are currently powerless to prevent this misuse of their invested money.

Also, the entire lobbying process needs to be reformed; strict laws need to be passed that curtail the amount of money being spent by corporations on lobbying. That money belongs to stockholders, employees, and customers. Corporations could be outlawed from using investors' money to influence public policy. The individual investor can then direct his or her investment earnings into public policy making as he or she wishes. We destroy democracy when we allow corporation money to be used as a plaything of executives and their handpicked boards of directors.

In order to make this change, the citizenry will need to be awakened to the difficulty of this fight. Voters will have to be awakened from their propaganda-induced sleep. We need a vital, populist revolt by ordinary citizens in every local place. We need to win back our democracy with careful thought, protests, demonstrations, voting, and whatever else it takes. Most of all, we need to insist and keep insisting upon effective, well-enforced campaign financing laws. We need to rule corporation money out of the political process. Otherwise, big money will continue to undermine democracy.

At this time, big-money control is the core policy of the Republican Party. The lack of integrity in the Democratic Party is more subtle but also devastating. The "centrists" of the Democratic Party test which way the opinion winds are blowing in order to raise enough money to compete with the Republicans. Then they shape their politics not in terms of what they believe is true but in terms of what their money sponsors are willing to support. This is assumed to be shrewd political strategy. Most members of the Democratic Party who have managed to combine a measure of integrity with an awakened constituency have been marginalized. Straight talk about "inconvenient truths" tends to be a threat to fund-raising.

Disgust with both major parties has spawned independents and third parties. These parties have the advantage of being able to say whatever they believe to be true, but they tend not to have the money required to make their speech widely heard. If they are as rich as Ross Perot and willing to spend their fortune to make a point, they can make some difference. The charismatic truth-teller Ralph Nader was able to raise enough money to enter the dialogue. But given the entrenched US two-party system, many voters consider voting for third parties to be a wasted vote—yes, even worse than wasted. Many third party votes result in support for the worst of two bad choices.

Instant Runoff Voting

The US two-party system is not authorized by our Constitution. It is a circumstance that we could change for the better with a relatively small tweak in our election laws: instant runoff voting. In this electoral design, voters would vote for their first and second choices for each office. If neither of the two leading candidates has a majority, then the computers would immediately recount using each voter's second choice if his or her first choice was not for one of the two leaders. The winner would then be the one of the two leading candidates with the most votes. This rather small but powerful innovation would widen the debate and tend to make third parties more effective. When there is no need to drift to the middle, candidates can more easily say what they actually believe. This change would tend to make truth rather than money a more deciding factor.

If progressive Democrats clearly understood their self-interest (as well as the good of the nation and the future of democracy), they would be pushing hard for both public financing and instant runoff voting. But achieving these innovations will remain an uphill fight because both Democrat and Republican turf protectors oppose them. And the turf they are protecting is their ties with big money. This will change only when an awakening population withdraws support from any candidate who opposes public financing and instant runoff voting.

Preventing Voter Fraud

Finally, money can undermines democracy in another insidious way: rigging elections. Unfair voter registration laws and flawed supervision of voting practices are another way that big money can buy elections. Computerized voting machines without paper trails can be rigged by the companies that manufacture the machines. Even the threat of this is disquieting. Those with money enough can influence governments into buying voting machines from companies that will favor the moneyed few with this hard-to-prove mode of cheating. Correcting voter fraud will be another uphill climb. People who are working for this change are working against forces who can outspend them many-fold.

* * * * * * * *

The possibility for having true democracy in the United States still exists, but to realize this possibility, the population will need to be awakened and organized to insist upon having true democracy. The popular response to big money rule needs to become, "I am mad as hell, and I am not going to take it any more."

The importance of winning back our democracy is well stated by journalist Chris Hedges:

> We must embrace, and embrace rapidly, a radical new ethic of simplicity and rigorous protection of our ecosystem—especially the climate—or we will all be holding on to life by our fingertips. We must rebuild radical socialist movements that demand that the resources of the state and the nation provide for the welfare of all citizens and the heavy hand of state power be employed to prohibit the plunder by the corporate power elite. We must view the corporate capitalists who have seized control of our money, our food, our energy, our education, our press, our

health-care system, and our governance as mortal enemies to be vanquished.[8]

The illustrations in this chapter have been taken from life in the United States, but similar dynamics exist in many places. Strong resistance to a full and workable democracy is planet-wide and rooted in thousands of years of aristocratic heritage. Nevertheless, we can still hope, as Leonard Cohen says in his song "Democracy": "Democracy is coming to the USA."

* * * * * * * *

For further reading we recommend the following, from among the hundreds of books on this topic, for their accessibility and pertinence:

David C. Korten, *When Corporations Rule the World* (San Francisco: CA: Berrett-Koehler Publishers & Kumarian Press,1995)

Naomi Klein, *The Shock Doctrine: The Rise of Disaster Capitalism* (New York: Picador, 2007)

Douglas Rushkoff, *Life Inc.: How the World became a Corporation and How to Take It Back* (New York: Random House, 2009)

Barry C. Lynn, *Cornered: The New Monopoly Capitalism and the Economics of Destruction* (Hoboken, New Jersey: John Wiley & Sons, 2010)

Robert B. Reich, *Supercapitalism: The Transformation of Business, Democracy and Everyday Life* (New York: Alfred A Knopf, 2007)

Cornel West, *Democracy Matters: Winning the Fight against Imperialism* (New York: The Penguin Press, 2004)

---

[8] Chris Hedges, "The Collapse of Globalization" TruthDig.com, March 27, 2011.

Chapter 3

The End of the Fossil-Fuel Economy

The ecological crisis and the loss of democracy increase in importance when we face the end of the fossil-fuel era. Misinformation on these issues is vigorously propagated by the current energy establishment. The energy transition from fossil fuels to alternatives is so important and complicated we have chosen to spend additional pages on this topic.

In its beginning industrial development was powered by coal. Now petroleum[9] is the ruling energy source for industrial civilization. The rapid rise of industrialization in China, India, and other places is being powered by petroleum. Coal and natural gas play their role, but petroleum is king. Many of our most common products, from gasoline to fertilizers to plastics, are made from petroleum. The ink on your daily newspaper is likely mostly petroleum. The suburban sprawl of our cities has been made possible by the availability of relatively cheap petroleum products.

To speak of a post-fossil-fuel society is to speak of an extremely huge transformation. Why must this change take place? Two developments, either of which is sufficient unto itself, are forcing us to change our energy patterns: (1) global warming and (2) fossil-fuel depletion.

---

[9] We will use the words "petroleum" and "oil" interchangeably.

(1) Global Warming

The popular moniker "global warming" sounds friendly enough, especially for those of us who hate cold weather. Perhaps "climate crisis" is the more appropriate name for this challenge. Most citizens of the United States know that the burning of petroleum products, coal, and natural gas is contributing huge amounts of carbon dioxide to the atmosphere and that carbon dioxide is one of the gases that creates a greenhouse effect, raising the average temperature on the surface of the planet. But too few citizens grasp the full extent of this crisis.

Millions of years were required for ancient microbes and plants to reduce the carbon dioxide content of the atmosphere from about 98 percent to about 0.3 percent. Humanity is now returning carbon dioxide to the atmosphere at a rate that far exceeds the rate at which natural processes can take it out. This is heating the planet. This rise in temperature is having vast consequences: the melting of polar ice and permafrost; rising ocean levels; flooding coastlines; shifting ocean currents; increased freezing in some areas; increased scorching in others; excess rainfall; desertification; stronger hurricanes; agricultural damage; disruption of entire ecosystems; and more, much more than we know.

It is understandable that people do not want to believe this, but the evidence is now overwhelming. Nevertheless, politicians as prominent as Senator James Inholf claim global warming is a hoax, and pseudo-scientists are hired by oil companies to subvert the truth. Many forces in the US business world are willing to "shape the truth" in favor of status quo approaches to energy policy. The Greenpeace website www.exxonsecrets.org documents 124 groups that Exxon-Mobil alone funds to confuse or deny the results of climate change science that are inconvenient for them. Often, these propagandists blame global warming on "natural causes" or a recurring cycle. Their theme is to cast doubt on any need to make large changes in energy use.

Who can we trust? Let's begin with Vice President and Nobel Peace Prize winner Al Gore and the scientists he draws upon in his Academy Award-winning documentary *An*

Inconvenient Truth. Gore shares his Nobel Peace Prize with the Intergovernmental Panel on Climate Change, a UN network of scientists. The conclusions of these experts should be enough to put global warming at the top of our agenda.

We also have the collection of first-rate researchers that Leonardo DiCaprio draws upon in his impressive documentary *The 11th Hour.*

National Geographic, Newsweek, and many others have published impressive reports. Also, we have those thousands of polar bears that are starving because the Arctic ice is breaking up. We have huge ice shifts taking place in Greenland and Antarctica, hotter Gulf water spawning harsher hurricanes, dying coral reefs, erratic weather, and more.

Global warming is not something coming someday— it is already happening. And we are experiencing only the beginning of a planet-wide disruption that may already be irreversible. Disastrous irreversible tipping points can occur. Eventually, we may face the loss of the lower third of Florida and half of Bangladesh to ocean waters. Climate changes will affect environments at every latitude in far-reaching ways. The issue is no longer whether there will be consequences from our extensive release of greenhouse gases, but how to act promptly to moderate those consequences.

Environmentalist Bill McKibbin named his recent book *eaarth* to symbolize that the planet we lived on four decades ago no longer exists. We live on a different planet, different from what has been the case for more than ten thousand years.

> I knew we'd never again inhabit the planet I'd been born on, or anything close to it. Because we're already past 350—way past it. The planet has nearly 390 parts per million carbon dioxide in the atmosphere. We're too high. Forget the grandkids; it turns out this was a problem for our *parents.*[10]

---

[10] Bill McKibben, *eaarth*: <u>Making a Life on a Tough New Planet</u> (New York: Times Books, Henry Holt and Company, 2010), pp. 15–16.

Many nations, including some large European users of fossil-fuel energy, have asserted their willingness to cap carbon dioxide output and roll back their fossil-fuel use, but the US government, China, and others have made very small efforts. Without strong, clear, and determined US leadership, the global efforts that are necessary to deal effectively with this global problem are likely to fail.

The horrendous consequences already underway can be moderated by phasing out fossil fuels and phasing in alternatives. Powering down our advanced societies with imaginative conservation measures will also be needed. When coastal cities are underwater and whole ecosystems decimated, it will be no comfort to hear the sad-faced hypocritical foot-draggers say, "Mistakes were made."

(2) Fossil-Fuel Depletion

Burning fossil fuels at the current rate is not only destructive of climate stability, soils, lakes, and life on Earth, but, it also rapidly depletes these fuels, which are finite resources. Much of the earth's oil resources have already been used, and the resources yet to be used will undoubtedly be harder to find and produce, and therefore be more costly. Further, the billions of people in China and India are joining the United States and others in oil guzzling. As demand continues to rise and available resources continue to shrink, we are seeing and will further see the end of the era in which oil can be cheaply priced. As natural gas becomes more expensive, the electric power companies that are now using the cleaner-burning natural gas are opting for the cheaper and more plentiful coal. But coal is dangerous and dirty to mine, as well as dirty to burn. Air can become unbreathable, and waterways can be poisoned with mercury. The replacement of oil and natural gas with coal is not a pretty prospect. Furthermore, coal produces more carbon dioxide per unit of energy output than natural gas or oil. As we will explain shortly, coal needs to be the first fossil fuel not the last to be phased out. And the tar pits of the world should not even be thought of as possible energy sources. The same can be said of oil and gas from shale. These sources are extremely dirty, costly, and environmentally destructive.

So what will it mean to power our societies without petroleum, coal, and natural gas? What does it mean for us to enter a post-fossil-fuel period in human affairs?

The rapidity of industrial development and our hopes for its benefits have resulted in a vast and large pattern of energy wastefulness. Though we have already seen price increases in gasoline and other oil products, oil is still a cheap fuel. As long as oil is cheap, we will continue building air-conditioned glass buildings, thin-walled houses, and gas-guzzling vehicles. Eight-lane highways filled with mostly single-passenger vehicles will keep growing. More and more airplanes will crowd the airways and continue to discourage the development of an infrastructure of fast and efficient trains. Our wasteful patterns are everywhere. Our societies use many times more energy than is actually needed for a viable style of relatively affluent living.

This wastefulness will not change as long as oil is relatively cheap and oil-related industries have the political clout to insist on policy that encourages growing fossil fuel consumption. The population is still awakening (much too slowly) to the horrors of the energy status quo. People frequently complain about paying half a dollar more for gasoline, but they do not complain enough about using trillions of tax dollars in military expenditures to shore up our oil imports. Indeed, most people in the United States still listen to and believe politicians who claim that the Iraq war was not about oil.

In his recently published memoirs, Alan Greenspan stated, "I am saddened that it is politically inconvenient to acknowledge what everyone knows: the Iraq war is largely about oil."[11] Henry Kissinger, another man of strong conservative leanings,

---

11 Alan Greenspan, *The Age of Turbulence* (New York: Penguin Press, 2007), p. 463.

has made similar statements. These men openly believe that we should wage war for oil. Many others are less honest. Condoleezza Rice, Donald Rumsfeld, Colin Powell, Dick Cheney, George W. Bush, and a long list of others have stated emphatically that the Iraq war was not about oil. They found it politically inconvenient to raise the question: "How much blood are we willing to expend for our cheap oil supply?"

Here are similar questions for citizens to consider: Is ten dollars a gallon for gasoline too much to spend in order to save tens of thousands of lives and injuries to youth whom we consider priceless? Is irreparable damage to our priceless planet a cost we are willing to pay for our fossil fuels?

We must face the grim truth that US oil companies and oil-related industries have enormous influence on our current government. We must admit that they are willing to lie to us and ask our youth to fight oil wars indefinitely rather than endure a reduction in their profits.

(3) So How Is This Huge Change Possible?

For the United States, the appropriate response to global warming, fossil-fuel depletion, and US dependence on Middle Eastern oil is to launch a huge energy conservation program and to foster a massive shift to wind, solar, geothermal, and other alternative energy sources. These changes are new and pose unique challenges, but this is no excuse for evasion or further delay. Profound economic policy changes can be made quickly when leaders find the necessary political will.

Franklin Roosevelt's program of retooling US industry to defeat the Nazis is an example of what sufficient political will can accomplish. Though our current challenge is different and much more difficult, it is encouraging to note that in a single year Roosevelt's USA stopped manufacturing cars and turned a whole nation's output to war machinery. Through his competent aides and the bully pulpit, Roosevelt used the power of his office to make these massive changes.

Unfortunately, the political will necessary to launch an adequate program for moderating global warming and creating a sane energy transition is not evident in the United States today. In a market economy, most of us will buy the cheapest products without even trying to understand the skullduggery, violence, and hidden costs that go into making them cheap. Strange as it may seem to financially stretched citizens, we need to insist upon carbon taxes that increase the price of gasoline and all other fossil fuels. Indeed, this carbon tax should escalate to the point that a transition to sustainable energy sources is economically viable and driven by market forces. If government bodies are responsive to the people and their long-range needs rather than to energy company interests, the carbon-tax revenue can be used to smooth the path of energy transition and to alleviate the inequities caused by the rapid expansion of alternative energy sources and the launch of huge conservation programs. This is plain common sense, a new aspect of the common sense we need.

We also need to insist upon a whole new transportation system. We need to increase the number of those who work and shop within walking distance or bicycling distance of where they live. We need to become accustomed to traveling by fast cross-country trains and urban rail or other energy-efficient inter-urban and intra-urban systems. We need to become accustomed to living and working in new styles of architecture. We need to get used to efficient lighting and appliances. These changes are enormous but not impossible. We can create a workable post-fossil-fuel future.

But instead of beginning now to accomplish the massive transitions required, we seem to be waiting for some still-larger disaster to befall us. We have already waited fifty years too long. Many disasters are already unavoidable. Perhaps our possibilities have already been reduced to simply moderating the disasters and preparing our grandchildren with the tools they will need to endure them.

Also, the impending disasters can come more quickly than many past-oriented optimists are predicting. The remaining relatively cheap oil will be depleted quickly unless big changes are made. Rather than leveling off, the demand for oil is rapidly increasing. Eventually, such factors will greatly increase the cost of oil and therefore increase the cost of everything in our societies that depends on oil. Continuing the current energy patterns can lead surprisingly quickly to untenable planet-wide disasters. Economies can collapse. Suburban communities can become slums. Governments can become incapable of responding to the effects of climatic instabilities. Violence and war can break out almost everywhere between the have-nothings and the still-have-somethings. Oil-powered industrial civilizations can simply "drive off the cliff" and take billions of passengers with them.

In spite of the possibility of these horrific scenarios, we will be insisting throughout this book that although our situation is not entirely hopeless, we must move boldly, massively, and soon. This will entail big shifts in our imagination about the ways we use energy and the ways we hope to supply energy for our use.

(4) Some Details to Think Through

The overall nature of the energy awakening outlined above is becoming clearer to the general population, but many details remain confusing. We need to examine these details because they are being denied, minimized, or misconstrued by the forces that oppose huge and necessary changes. Also, many pat answers to the energy transition twist our perspectives out to shape. So, we need to discuss the energy transition in greater detail than we will do for the other nine awakenings.

1. Oil

Accurately estimating our remaining petroleum resources is difficult, perhaps impossible. Nevertheless, it is obvious that our increasing demand for oil is becoming increasingly difficult to meet. This means that the cost of petroleum products, over the long haul, will surely increase. If our massive use of oil continues, we will experience a huge increase in the price of using oil.

The 2008–11 recession has caused some moderation in oil demand, but the overall global demand for oil will escalate unless strong measures are taken. Industrializing regions such as China and India are expanding oil use at a furious rate. The United States, the largest oil user, is also expanding its oil use. Though the United States is the third largest producer of oil, exceeded only slightly by Saudi Arabia and Russia, this nation uses all of the oil it produces and approximately that much more. A pressure to pump more oil is being placed on the largest oil exporters, many of which are in the Middle East, where severe and seemingly endless conflicts rage. This will tend to become an even uglier picture as competition for petroleum continues to heat up among China, India, Europe, the United States, and other highly developed and developing oil guzzlers. We face the prospect of endless oil wars unless we find a way to restrain oil use.

It is no longer the case that an increasing demand for oil can be easily met by simply investing in more drilling. OPEC nations typically exaggerate their reserves in order to be allotted a greater market share by OPEC rules. Oil companies publish exaggerated estimates to keep their stock prices up. Offshore drilling is very expensive and only becomes viable as the price of oil increases. Also, deep-water drilling has proved very risky.

The British Petroleum (BP) disaster in 2010 in the Gulf of Mexico has brought that point home. Oil has become a product that can no longer be treated as if it were boundless. From now on, oil availability for modern industrial civilization will remain an issue, and over the long haul its price will rise as the scarcity of it increases and the demand for it continues to climb. The era of even relatively cheap oil is over. There may be ups and downs as various world events and seasonal shifts affect this market, but the long-range price trend is for it to go up and up and up unless an extensive reduction in demand can be achieved.

In passing, it is important to note that offshore oil drilling and drilling in places like the Arctic National Wildlife Refuge (ANWR) threaten sensitive habitats, beaches, and fisheries. Such drilling is expensive, and its impact is far too small to affect world oil prices. The pressure to drill in difficult places comes only from companies and individuals who stand to profit from these actions.

Within an unregulated market system, oil-related corporations can be expected to seek increased production and increased sales of their products and will do this in ways that increase their profits. The very nature of a corporation's structure requires such behavior. Therefore, our recommendations on oil policy must not rely upon volunteer efforts from the oil, coal, and natural gas industries but upon overarching plans, laws, and enforcements by democratic governments.

2. Natural Gas

Natural gas has been a relatively clean burning fossil fuel, convenient to use for home heating and power generation. It can also be a transition fuel for free-roaming transportation; this is already happening. But natural gas is a serious offender relative to expelling carbon dioxide (although less serious per unit of energy than oil or coal). Also, natural gas mining that uses hydraulic fracturing chemicals (hydraulic fracturing is also called "fracking") to release the gas are destroying water tables and streams and surprising water-well-using residents with flammable gas coming out with the water from their water faucets. Strict rules that restrain the practice of fracking are missing.

In the long term, natural gas prices tend to track oil prices. As natural gas becomes increasingly expensive, home-heating costs will rise and electric power companies will seek to shift to the cheaper and more plentiful coal. This is already happening. In order to prevent a return to coal, we need to find ways to make coal more expensive through taxation.

For electric power production, we recommend a slow phasing out of natural gas, but not replacing it with coal. We need to move promptly toward wind, solar, geothermal, and other alternative technologies.

3. Coal
Coal has huge disadvantages. It is a dirty product to mine, transport, and burn. Its mercury content alone makes it problematic. Lester Brown summarizes this problem well in the following quote:

> In 2004, 48 of the 50 states in the United States (all but Alaska and Wyoming) issued a total of 3,221 fish advisories warning against eating fish from local lakes and streams because of their mercury content. EPA research indicates that one out of every six women of childbearing age in the United States has enough mercury in her blood to harm a developing fetus. This means that 360,000 of the 4 million babies born in the country each year may face neurological damage from mercury exposure before birth.[12]

Even a tiny bit of mercury taken into the human body on a regular basis is profoundly injurious to human health. More and more dentists recommend removing our silver/mercury fillings. Some health authorities have warned us about the miniscule amount of mercury present in long-lasting florescent light bulbs. If we are going to avoid breaking these bulbs in our houses and not put them in our landfills, surely we must be even more concerned about coal-burning power plants. Furthermore, mercury is only one of the contaminants that coal-burning power plants emit. Acid rain is formed from some of these contaminants. This acidity is a serious issue for forests and other plant and animal life, including humans. Burning coal results in widespread contamination of the air, water, and soil, and thereby results in serious health

---

12 Lester R. Brown, *Plan B 2.0* (New York and London: W.W. Norton and Company, 2006), p. 107

hazards for humans and other animals. These factors provide insurmountable limitations on the massive use of coal.

Coal-fired power plants could reduce contaminants by gasifying the coal and burning only these gases, but this is costly and requires a use of energy to do this. And these "cleaner" coal-fired plants still emit carbon dioxide: they produce even more carbon dioxide per net BTU than would be produced by the direct burning of the coal itself. Some coal proponents are proposing carbon dioxide capture, but this entails another significant expense as well as insurmountable technological and practical barriers. Capturing carbon dioxide in the quantities needed to be an effective solution approaches the absurd. Furthermore, serious obstacles appear when we consider storing vast amounts of "captured carbon" in a permanent manner. If a vast pool of "stored" carbon dioxide were released quickly, catastrophic climatic results would be probable. We would be bequeathing horrendous risks to future generations. We believe that the very best way to permanently store the carbon that is in coal is to leave the coal in the ground. Don't use it at all. Of course there must be a period of transition, and solutions must be found for such things as the metallurgical use of coal in the making of steel. But coal use on a large scale is clearly a bad choice.

Coal profiteers can be expected to vigorously oppose this no-coal policy, so we will have to work community by community on a coal moratorium. In the final stage of this transition, we will need national governments to essentially outlaw the mining and importing of coal.

In summary, here is our overall fossil-fuel policy: in this order, put coal, petroleum, and natural gas on a steep downslope, phasing out their use in a measured but rapid fashion. Our present dependence upon fossil fuels is neither sustainable nor desirable.

4. Nuclear Energy

Nuclear energy power plants have the advantage of adding negligible carbon to the atmosphere compared with fossil-fuel-fired plants. It is not true, however, that nuclear plants add no carbon to the atmosphere. The processes of mining uranium, transporting nuclear fuels and wastes, and managing plants and waste facilities do add carbon to the atmosphere. When we cease to use carbon fuels for these tasks, these processes will be an energy cost that further limits the competitiveness of nuclear fuel.

Most important, nuclear power plants have major drawbacks that do not disappear no matter how refined their technologies become. Safety issues and waste disposal issues persist as unsolved problems with no realistic solutions in sight. No one knows the real costs of nuclear energy, which needs to include nuclear waste disposal, insurance against accidents, and decommissioning of plants, not to mention actual damage due to accidents. Lester Brown suggests that ". . . with international terrorism on the rise, the vulnerability of nuclear power plants to attack combined with their use by countries as a stepping-stone to the acquisition of nuclear weapons virtually eliminates nuclear fission as a future energy source."[13] The primary lesson from the recent Fukushima disaster is this: nuclear energy is not a viable alternative.

James Lovelock has claimed that we cannot moderate global warming without using nuclear energy.[14] At the other extreme, Arjun Makhijani put together a detailed book of charts and statistics that show we can power a scaled-down modern society without resorting to either fossil fuels or nuclear power plants.[15]

The fact that nuclear technologies have been improved and can be further improved is being used as an argument for a vast nuclear expansion. But even in Canada and France, where improved technologies are already in use, the fundamental drawback of handling long-term waste storage is not solved

13 Ibid, pp. 39–40
14 James Lovelock, *The Revenge of Gaia: Why the Earth Is Fighting Back—and How We Can Still Save* Humanity (New York: Basic Books, 2006)
15 Argun Makhijani, *Carbon-Free and Nuclear Free: A Roadmap for US Energy Policy* (Muskegon, MI: RDR Books & Takoma Park, MD: IEER Press 2007)

and may never be. Furthermore, safety issues will continue to be a crucial consideration. The nuclear option requires strict governmental regulation, large investments, and highly skilled management to make plants safe. There have been more than fifty unsafe nuclear plant occurrences that have happened beneath the radar of widespread public attention.

The 2011 Japanese experience due to the earthquake and tsunami have freshened our awareness of the potential dangers of this technology. Jonathan Schell suggests that "the Japanese are as orderly and efficient a country as exists on Earth." He further suggests that we humans are "stumbling, imperfect, probably imperfectable creatures ... unfit to wield the stellar fire released by the split or fused atom."[16] He suggests that we pause and study the matter before proceeding further. How long? It takes 24,000 years for half of the mass of a chunk of plutonium to become harmless. Schell suggests that we study the matter for half of that time—12,000 years. During that time, we may be able to become "wise enough to make good use of the split atom."

Other hidden costs of the nuclear option are exposed in this six-point summary by Ralph Nader:[17]

1. Wall Street will not finance new nuclear plants without a 100 % taxpayer loan guarantee. Too risky. That's a lot of guarantee given that new nukes cost 12 billion dollars each, assuming no mishaps. Obama and the Congress are OK okay with that arrangement.
2. Nuclear power is uninsurable in the private insurance market—too risky. Under the Price-Anderson Act, taxpayers pay the greatest cost of a meltdown's devastation.
3. Nuclear power plants and transports of radioactive wastes are a national security nightmare for the Department of Homeland Security. Imagine the target that thousands of vulnerable spent fuel rods present for sabotage.

---

[16] Jonathan Shell, "Hiroshima to Fukushima," *Nation* magazine, April 4, 2011, P. 8.

[17] Ralph Nader, "Nuclear Nightmare," *Reader Supported News,* March 19, 2011.

4. Guess who pays for whatever final waste repositories are licensed? You the taxpayer and your descendants as far as your gene line persists. Huge decommissioning costs, at the end of a nuclear plant's existence, come from the taxpayers' pockets.

5. Nuclear plant disasters present impossible evacuation burdens for those living anywhere near a plant, especially if time is short. Imagine evacuating the long-troubled Indian Point plants 26 miles north of New York City. Workers in that region have a hard enough time evacuating their places of employment during 5 p.m. rush hour. That's one reason Secretary of State Clinton (in her time as Senator of New York) and Governor Andrew Cuomo called for the shutdown of Indian Point.

6. Nuclear power is both uneconomical and unnecessary. It can't compete against energy conservation, including cogeneration, wind-power, and ever more efficient, quicker, and safer renewable forms of providing electricity.

We cannot justify governmental subsidies to care for nuclear wastes, decommission plants, and insure communities against nuclear accidents or sabotage. Wind and solar power will prove safer, cheaper, and simpler, and their use can be expanded rapidly if we choose to do so.

Nuclear fission might be useful for a few highly restricted and carefully monitored uses, but a massive use of nuclear fission to boil water to produce electricity is a highly questionable option for both economic and safety reasons. Governments should give no support to this energy option. And citizen groups would be wise to oppose the licensing of new plants in their neighborhoods.

5. Fusion Energy

The conclusions stated in the previous section apply only to nuclear fission, the energy derived from the splitting of very large atoms. Energy can also be derived from fusing very small atoms. Fusion energy production works well within the huge gravitational field of the sun that crushes small atoms together;

however, it is problematic here on Earth to apply the forces required for the fusion of atoms. This has been achieved in the hydrogen bomb, but it has not been achieved in a controlled fashion. The hope of doing so may be many decades away or never. Fusion research deserves continued support, but hope for a fusion solution in the short term must be counted as highly unlikely. We must not let such hope become an excuse for avoiding the hard choices that need to be made now. For the time being we must be content with the sun, a nuclear fusion plant conveniently located ninety-three million miles away

6. Biofuels

The actions that Brazil has taken toward replacing oil imports with biofuels made from sugar cane are impressive. We see a place for biofuels, especially in the transition period of phasing out fossil fuels, but biofuels also have serious drawbacks. As their use increases, they enter into long-range competition with food production and fresh water usage. Shortages of fresh water and arable land are already serious issues. Simply raising the cost of food can create planet-wide food distribution crises. Food and water trump all other economic values. This is a serious drawback that places an unavoidable limit on the extent of using the biofuel option.

Also, biofuels are carbon fuels. Some argue that they are different from fossil fuels in that they take their carbon from the air and then return that carbon to the air when these fuels are burned—thus adding no additional carbon to the atmosphere. But this is not entirely accurate. The land that is being used to grow biofuels was previously growing trees or grasses that were removing carbon from the atmosphere; therefore, when we burn the carbon in biofuels, that carbon is no longer being taken from the atmosphere. Also, current biofuel production entails using fuels (currently fossil fuels) in the growing of the plants and in the processing of the plants into biofuels. Moreover, if biofuels themselves are consumed for this growing and processing, there is a deep cut into the usefulness of the biofuel option.

So here are two key tests for the viability of a biofuel: (1) Does it actually reduce carbon dioxide? (2) Does it compete with food production? These tests render corn ethanol an extremely questionable option. It may benefit corn growers, but it is not a solution to the overall energy problem. Switch grass grown on nonagricultural ground meets these criteria better. The processing of waste cooking oils can add some help. The use of animal manure to produce methane gas to make electricity is already a successful practice on many dairy farms.

The combustion of methane results in carbon dioxide, but this practice has two benefits: (1) Carbon dioxide is not as bad as methane when it comes to exacerbating global warming, and (2) Some energy that is now wasted can be recovered.

The use of algae to produce fuel oils may also hold some promise. But each of these biofuel innovations makes a very small contribution to the overall energy needs.

In conclusion, biofuels may provide limited help in some applications and temporary help during the transitional period. But long-term biofuel use provides only a small part of the solution to our long-range energy supply. We must look elsewhere for our core solutions.

7. Solar

The amount of solar energy striking the planet every day is many orders of magnitude greater than humanity needs to collect in order to fully energize a modern society. Extensive progress has already been made toward effective solar devices. Solar energy is probably the key source for the long-range energy future of humanity on this planet.

Solar energy has a number of meanings. It can mean using the sun's heat to warm buildings and energize water heaters. It can mean using solar cells to directly produce electricity. It can mean using mirrors to focus the sun's rays to boil water, drive turbines, and produce electricity in that way. It is already being proposed that huge mirrors be built in the sunny deserts of North Africa to focus sun heat to produce a large portion of the electrical needs of Europe and North Africa.[18] Although the total amount of solar energy striking the planet every day is enormous, tapping it for human use is the challenge. Green plants are good at it; humans can get better.

Solar cells are currently rather expensive, but like any technology these costs can be reduced as their use increases and new technologies are developed. Another drawback is that the sun is not always shining on the solar devises, and the storage of the huge amounts of electrical energy remains a largely unsolved problem. We will examine the prospects for electrical storage in Section 11.

The rising costs of fossil fuels will make solar technologies more competitive and release more funding for the research to improve them. With sufficient political and social will and some effective education, we could create a society in which almost every roof is partly made of solar cells. Private homes can generate much of their own energy and even sell any excess back to the grid. Again, the barrier here is not viability but lack of public imagination and a lack of political and social will to meet the strong opposition arising from fossil-fuel suppliers and fossil-fuel-dependent businesses.

8. Wind

Wind is a close second in importance to solar power. Highly effective wind turbines have already been developed. Only the absence of political will prevents us from financing a massive effort to build large wind farms and the infrastructures that can deliver wind energy to where it is needed.

As a source of electrical energy, wind generation has huge advantages. Wind is free and abundant. The technology is simple, but accessing this vast energy source does have drawbacks. Wind farms take space and need to be strategically placed in order to honor other values such as food production, transportation needs, and the flight patterns of migratory birds.

---

[18] For a full-page article on this topic see *The CCPA Monitor*, Volume 13, No. 10, April 2007, p. 31.

Adaptations, however, can be made. A wind farm can also graze animals or raise crops. Wind turbines placed over water can still leave room for fishing and transportation. Measures can be taken to limit bird impact.

The fact that the wind does not always blow is a significant issue, but wind can be combined with other energy sources to generate a constant flow of energy. The electricity-storage issues mentioned in our discussion of solar also apply to wind-generated electricity (see Section 11). Nevertheless, the arguments against rapidly moving ahead with wind generation are extremely shortsighted. Once money and public will shift in that direction, solutions will be found. It would have been hard to imagine in advance the improvements that have been made in automobiles and computers.

Another advantage of both wind and solar energies is their potential for decentralizing the energy grids. Wind and solar generation can take place close to home. The brownouts and blackouts caused by far away foul ups in the grid can be fewer in a more decentralized system. Decentralized systems can still sell energy to one another as needed. A more decentralized grid is opposed by some current energy producers, for they view centralization as one of their ways of corralling bigger profits.

Does moving to wind and solar power mean phasing out gasoline stations? If all those stations can no longer sell gasoline or even biofuels, they can sell hydrogen or provide sockets for charging the batteries of electric vehicles. Some are recommending electric vehicles and stations that allow for an exchange of uncharged batteries for charged ones.

Hybrid or fully electric cars and trains could keep a lot of carbon out of the air if the electric power grids are powered by wind and solar. But strong economic interests will continue to resist these options. The fuel-service industries have fought electric forms of transportation for decades. Electric private cars and electric streetcars have been intentionally destroyed as options by powerful oil and automotive interests. (See the documentary film *Who Killed the Electric Car?*) We also confront the momentum of current practices and the hesitation of many citizens, governments, and investors to phase out current practices and try new options.

Human societies can learn to live on the energies produced by the sun, the wind, and the flow of water, plus some help from geothermal, ocean movements, and perhaps biofuel production from manure, waste oils, and other unused sources of biomass. These power sources are safe, clean, and immense, and some are virtually endless.

9. Hydropower, Geothermal, and the Use of Ocean Currents

River flow and geothermal sources are already adding safe and inexpensive energy. Ocean-wave movement may also hold promise. All three of these sources may be small compared to the need, but they can be a meaningful part of the mix.

Hydropower from damming rivers has already been largely exploited. Some further possibilities exist, but many dams have serious environmental drawbacks. Nevertheless, in combination with wind and solar, hydropower can continue to make an important contribution. Wind has the disadvantage of producing energy only when the wind is blowing the turbines. And solar only produces energy when the sun is shining on the solar devices. But a hydropower dam can produce energy at any time of day or night. An electric power grid powered by wind and solar can partially fill those downtimes of wind and solar with hydropower. This will not be enough; we will still need effective means of storing the power generated by wind and solar means. Still, wind, sunshine, and gravity-water-flow are generously provided by the natural world and will continue as long as the sun and Earth exist.

Geothermal has to do with using the temperature differences between the deep earth and the surface as a source of heating or cooling. In Iceland this can be the main source of energy. In general this source is quite limited, but like hydropower it can make a contribution to smoothing a wind and solar grid.

Ocean currents as an energy source has to do with using the motion of waves and tides to produce electricity. This is a vast energy source, but the technologies for accessing this widely scattered source of power do not promise huge gains in the foreseeable future.

Over the long haul, all three of these energy sources may hold significant promise. But for now their contribution is relatively small, so our main focus must be elsewhere.

10. Powering Down

Energy conservation will play a big role in the energy transition. It will also foster the habits we need in the new societies being built. A large portion of our energy crisis can be solved by powering down our grossly wasteful systems.

Human society will always need energy, but the US society is so extremely wasteful of energy that even with existing technologies we can substantially reduce our energy use. Some of these changes may seem inconvenient to many and painful to some interests, but the conservation of energy is the easiest and most cost effective part of the transition. Already in existence are large buildings that are cooled and heated with a quarter of the energy that is typically used in comparable structures.

A few thousand dollars of easily available technologies can halve the energy use of many private dwellings. Electrically propelled public transportation options can transport one person with an efficiency equivalent to about a thousand miles per gallon of gasoline compared with the 15 to 35 miles per gallon used by our current single-occupant automobiles. Such savings could provide the resources necessary to make public transportation safe and convenient. Compared with the hassle of single-passenger vehicles driving in aggravating six-lane traffic jams on roads that are constantly under repair, a great public transportation system can also relieve strain. Great public transportation does not mean spending money we do not have; it means rearranging how we spend our money. In the end we will save money, energy, and CO_2 emissions.

Our society can thrive with far fewer private vehicles. And each vehicle can be driven less and be much more energy efficient. Existing hybrid cars can already average 46 or more miles per gallon. Hybrids that plug into the grid can reduce carbon production even further if that grid is powered by non-fossil sources. Such change in the transportation system are huge, but they can be accomplished in years rather than decades if the decisions are made by "the people" rather than by growth-addicted automotive, tire, and fossil-fuel companies.

Finally, energy conservation must be driven by more than volunteering individuals and businesses. Governments can launch and fund bold conservation programs. Governments can establish laws that force compliance with conservation needs. Such laws will need to be firmly enforced by adequately funded regulatory agencies. Energy conservation can cease to be a novelty for social pioneers and become mainstream common sense.

11. Hydrogen, Batteries, and other Energy Storage Means

Hydrogen, like electricity, is not an energy source; hydrogen must be understood as a means of energy transfer and storage. Hydrogen is plentiful on the earth's surface, but it is chemically combined with other elements, mostly with oxygen to make water. It has already been burned, so to speak. It takes energy from some other source to free the hydrogen in order for it to be used as a fuel.

Hydrogen and batteries serve a similar function in the energy world. Just as we must free hydrogen with some other energy source, so batteries must be continually charged and recharged from some other energy source. Each has its advantages and disadvantages. For example, it's hard to conceive of a hydrogen-powered flashlight, but hydrogen is the fuel of choice for space travel.

Both hydrogen and batteries are potential drivers for transportation vehicles. Railroads are currently almost entirely powered by electricity, either directly by trolleys or indirectly by diesel-powered electric generators located on the train itself. The technology of hydrogen-powered electric generation located on the train is surely feasible. The easy of storage and low cost of diesel fuel provides a big advantage at this time, but that can change. Hybrid automobiles are essentially electric cars with an onboard gasoline-powered generator. It is a small step toward an onboard hydrogen-powered generator. We are also seeing drive batteries that can be recharged at night or replaced frequently at a battery charging station. Post-fossil-fuel air travel cannot stand the weight of heavy batteries; the use of hydrogen fuel is the likely option.

Besides hydrogen and batteries, we may develop a few other significant means for storing and transporting energy. Clearly, we are facing a complicated energy storage revolution to take the place of fossil fuels, which can be easily stored and transported. But we must not let the difficulties with this problem discourage us. It has to be done. Fossil fuels have to be phased out.

Nevertheless, one of the questions that comes to the fore when we seriously take on designing a post-fossil-fuel economy is the question of feasibility. Is there actually a technological replacement for fossil fuels? This problem is most pressing in the transportation arena. Solar- and wind-powered power plants can produce electricity, but electricity needs to be used now or stored in relatively heavy and expensive batteries. Battery-stored electricity for air travel is impossible, and heavy truck work is also difficult and expensive.

David Sanborn Scott in his book *Smelling Land: The Hydrogen Defense Against Climate Catastrophe* spells out for us how liquefied hydrogen is better, less expensive, and safer for air travel than jet fuel.[19] You may have to read his book to be convinced. Also, he shows us how the problem of post-fossil-fuel land transportation can be beautifully solved with hydrogen-powered fuel cells rather than internal combustion engines. The technological details of this are not familiar to most people.

Again, we need to remember that hydrogen is not a fuel source; it is what Scott calls a "fuel currency." Like electricity

---

[19] David Sanborn Scott, *Smelling Land: The Hydrogen Defense against Climate Catastrophe, Enhanced Edition* (Trois-Rivières, Quebec: Canadian Hydrogen Association, 2008). See Chapter 40 for details on hydrogen-fueled air travel.

it carries energy from a source to a use. And like electricity, hydrogen can be produced from any energy source. Scott claims that the flexibility of electricity and hydrogen make them the fuel currencies of tomorrow. He claims that we should begin building our hydrogen infrastructure immediately. Hydrogen and electricity can be the core energy currencies that dominate the ordinary lives of people and propel almost all the technologies we use in our daily lives. Scott's book goes a long way toward visualizing how a post-fossil-fuel era in human affairs is feasible.

12: The Role of Government in Energy Policy
Some say government should not meddle with choosing which energy sources are best—"Let the market decide the winners." But the market is not free when huge oil, coal, and natural gas businesses control it. The market is not a dependable decision tool when total costing is not in effect, and therefore, ecological values are not factored into the decision making. We see no possibility for a successful transition from fossil fuels unless governments (democratically controlled and ecologically wise governments) stop supporting oil, natural gas, coal, and nuclear and instead do everything governments can appropriately do to encourage wind, solar, conservation, a hydrogen infrastructure, plus the other innovations we have mentioned.

If democratic governments do not participate in establishing the master energy trends, those trends will continue to be set by the largest economic players who use their economic self interest as their only criterion. These huge players currently include businesses that emphasize fossil fuels, nuclear power, automotive transportation, tires, and military equipment. It is either *we,* the citizens of democratic governments, or *they,* the old energy establishment, who will set the major trends of energy production and use and thus of the future of our societies. Governments need to forge an energy policy that serves the citizenry and is agreed upon by the citizenry. Such a policy can then guide every decision that the government or the private sector makes that has energy consequences. Governments need to be prevented from coddling individual companies. At the same time, governments need to be empowered to set the policies that serve the whole society and the planet. We citizens must insist upon this. Only then can we allow market dynamics to determine the details concerning which specific alternative energy technologies work best.

Also, we must face the fact that in an unregulated market economy, cheap fossil fuels will be used extensively as long as they are cheap. Governments need to abandon their efforts to keep fossil fuels cheap, and the population needs to be enlightened to welcome increased fossil-fuel prices.

Here is a well-established principle: any social practice we wish to reduce or phase out needs to be heavily taxed. We have done this with tobacco. A hefty tax on all fossil fuels is the simplest way to reduce their use. In spite of the protests of fossil-fuel industries, automotive companies, truck drivers, and private car owners, taxation of fossil fuels remains the most effective policy for promoting an energy transition that benefits us all. Substantial fossil-fuel taxation is already the practice in most European nations and has been so for decades.

A hefty carbon tax will profoundly and effectively reshape market forces toward conservation and alternative energy production. It is a direct attack on the problem of the disastrous consequences of cheap fossil fuels and, therefore, their widespread use. Such taxation needs to be an excise tax on the product, not a tax on the profits of energy companies. It is the use of the product we need to reduce. Excess profit is another issue.

If such taxation is increased too quickly, this could be excessively disruptive. Nevertheless, a phased-in disruption of the established pattern is the smoothest way to promote creative change that is driven by market forces. Such a scenario is greatly preferable to our current continuing expansion of fossil-fuel use, which will lead to a society even more addicted to fossil fuels at a time when these fuels become ever more severely limited. This is a catastrophic scenario.

A hefty tax on fossil fuels will, for a time, be politically difficult. Public support for higher fossil-fuel prices will be difficult to sustain unless remedies are included for those whose increased heating and transportation costs push them into poverty. People who spend most of their money for food, transportation, and housing have little tolerance for increased costs in these areas. How is this difficulty to be handled? Here is one answer: use the income tax system to give a credit or stipend to the most threatened parts of the population. This is an easily doable means of accommodation. To enhance political support, we will need to scorn the frequent accusations of "government take-over" and "socialism." These are just lies used to support the insanity of an unregulated market.

However we resolve the transition and injustice issues, it remains true that large carbon taxes will force the whole economy to shift in favor of its ordinary citizens. Such taxation will enable wind, solar, and other sustainable energy industries to rapidly take over the energy provision field. It will encourage food to be grown more organically. It will encourage a shortening of transportation distances. It will moderate the consequences of global warming. Carbon taxes will also discourage power companies from poisoning us with coal-burning power plants and join the wind- and solar-power revolution. Nothing but good, long-range consequences derive from taxing carbon more and more each year until fossil-fuel burning is minimized. Fossil-fuel companies that now advertise the need for expanding "all energy sources" need to be outed as the lying scam artists they are.

Allowing huge fossil-fuel taxes to go to governments is something the carbon industries will view as unthinkable. Leaving unburned coal in the ground? Unthinkable! Leaving unprocessed tar pits alone? Unthinkable! And what about automobile companies phasing out energy guzzlers and instead competing with one another for the most energy-efficient vehicles? This is already thinkable but nevertheless opposed by some of the old heads of these industries who bet billions on big-car popularity and ever-increasing coast-to-coast trucking.

Truck drivers may also find a large carbon tax difficult to accept. Independent truckers tend to believe that paying many more thousands of dollars at the diesel pumps will be a barrier to earning a living. Clearly, some of these truckers will have to become wind-turbine mechanics or public-transportation electric-train repairmen, or other post-carbon workers. Indeed, there may be more and better jobs in the post-carbon economy. Also, we need to ask if truckers are going to be all that unhappy with giving up driving trucks bumper-to-bumper, coast-to-coast on highways that never cease to be under repair. Will truck drivers always insist that it is unthinkable to alter these existing trends? Maybe they will also accept the needed changes when they actually stop to think about it.

And what about continuing the following trends: Doubling the cars? Doubling the trucks? (At a modest 3 percent growth rate, anything doubles every twenty-three years!) Doubling the highway lanes? Doubling the time it takes to drive to work? These are the truly unthinkable outcomes.

What about doubling the smog, doubling the force of hurricanes and tornadoes, doubling the weird weather patterns, doubling the height of coastal levies? Are any of these outcomes thinkable?

Strange as it may seem at first, the truly "thinkable" (i.e., feasible) alternative is to have our governments tax carbon and do it now before the truly "unthinkable" consequences actually happen to us. A stiff carbon tax is the best way to use market dynamics to smooth the transition, and it can move the transition with deliberate speed. A voluntary approach to energy use by citizens and businesses will never work. It is simply an excuse for failure.

If we include cutting the costs of conducting military operations to assure our oil provision, we will be saving a substantial amount of public money that can be redirected. Over the long haul we are shooting ourselves in the foot by keeping fossil fuel cheap. We are wrecking our energy system as well as storing up disasters for our children and grandchildren.

Using taxation as the means for increasing fossil-fuel prices is preferable to allowing the increased prices to result from scarcity and demand factors. If we do not tax fossil fuels, the increasing margins per unit of energy will go to the fossil-fuel industries and mineral owners. If we tax fossil-fuel use, these increases will go to governments that, if democratic, have the possibility to direct that income toward developing an energy transition that will serve us better. So the options boil down to a choice between favoring the people of the planet or favoring growth-hungry, profit-addicted fossil-fuel corporations and mineral owners.

* * * * * * * *

Progressive and intelligent energy policy, based on sustainability and environmental wisdom and firmly enforced by democratic governments, is an essential part of any viable transition to a sustainable human presence on this planet. Unless we are awake to these factors, learn the details, and take strong positions on this topic, we will ride our social vehicle off the cliff into a sea of chaos. Some say that this destiny has already been set. Do not believe them. They are simply lacking in imagination and courage to advocate for and do what has to be done. A post-fossil-fuel energy system is a huge change in our lives fraught with huge difficulties, but it is feasible. And more important, it is necessary.

From the thousands of books on the energy topic, we recommend the following for their accessibility and pertinence:

Mark Hertsgaard, *Hot: Living through the Next Fifty Years on Earth* (Boston & New York: Houghton Mifflin Harcourt, 2011)

Bill McKibben, *eaarth: Making a Life on a Tough New Planet* (New York: Times Books, 2010)

David Sanborn Scott, *Smelling Land: The Hydrogen Defense Against Climate Catastrophe, Enhanced Edition* (Trois-Rivières, Quebec: Canadian Hydrogen Association, 2008)

Arjun Makhijani, *Carbon-Free and Nuclear-Free: A Roadmap for US Energy Policy* (Muskegon, MI: RDR Books & Takoma Park, MD: IEER Press, 2007)

The Post-Carbon Reader: Managing the Twenty-First Century's Sustainability Crisis, edited by Richard Heinberg & Daniel Lerch, (Healdsburg, CA: Watershed Media, 2010)

Chapter 4
The Population Plight

We have all heard of overpopulation and of the need to control the expansion of the human population, but we may not have fully considered the extent of the problem. This limited planet now contains seven billion people, a billion more than when the following chart was drawn. These numbers compare with the one billion humans that Earth housed as recently as the middle of the nineteenth century. This is a very steep curve that if unchanged will reach twelve billion by 2050.

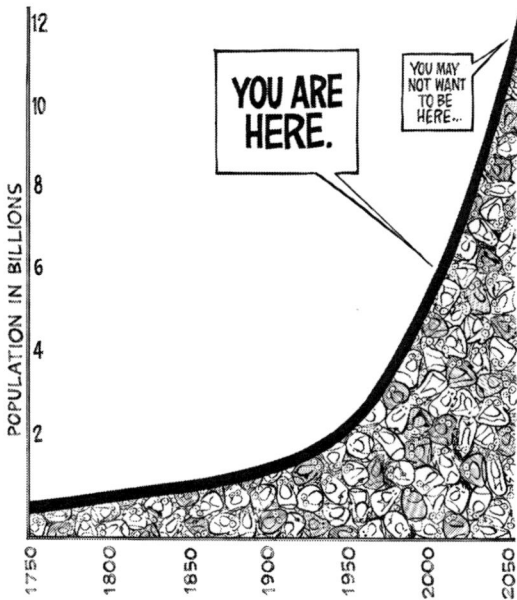

In the so-called Middle Ages, having more babies was an actual need in every civilization. Large families were encouraged. More peasants were needed to farm the land. More soldiers were needed to defend and expand the empire. More children were needed to carry on the family tradition and its properties, or perhaps simply to care for elderly parents, uncles, and aunts. Indeed, more babies were needed to offset high infant mortality rates and short life expectancies. Until modern times there were good reasons to keep birth rates high enough to make the family, the tribe, the nation, or the empire viable. But in modern times our population problem has become the exact opposite.

From this point forward an expanding human population is a liability, not a need. The human population has already reached or is surely reaching a planetary limit. There are those who say that there are still unoccupied spaces and that several more billion can be sustained on this planet, but that is untrue. We need to face up to some grim facts: if we have food in a refrigerator, clothes in a closet, a bed to sleep in, and a roof over our head, we are in the most prosperous 25 percent of the human population.[20] If everyone on the planet were afforded the prosperity everyone reading this book insists upon, we would need another planet or two to accommodate these wishes. Such highly generalized statistics only vaguely sketch the scope of the problem: the person-by-person cost of overpopulation is far more grueling. When squalor, disease, illiteracy, sheer hopelessness, and warfare are figured into our vision, "too many people" is not a pretty sight. And on top of that we need to consider the trees, the frogs, the birds, the wolves, the caribou, the polar bears, the penguins, and more. Indeed, entire ecosystems of living beings are threatened by too many humans.

Each group of people tends to have an impetus to increase their number. We need to shift our vision about population to a global perspective. Do we really need more Catholics,

---

[20] See www.miniature-earth.com.

more Baptists, more Mormons, more Jews, more Muslims, more members of "your" or "my" family? Do we need more customers, more workers, more drivers of cars and trucks on ever more crowded highways? Do we need more people? Even if we are able to employ the appropriate ecological magic to reduce many-fold the ecological footprint of each human being, how many billion humans is still too many? Is six billion too many? Is four billion? Surely such questions cannot be answered in terms of the preferences of an individual family or nation or religious body. What would it mean to address these questions in the same broad ecological perspective with which we would address the question of how many bears is too many bears? If half the bears are starving to death, we surely have too many bears. If bears are overturning garbage cans in almost every village street, we surely have too many bears. We need to reflect on the human species in a similar way. How many is too many for the well-being of humans and the other species among whom humans dwell?

And how are we to curtail population expansion or reduce the population? Awakening to the need to do this includes awakening to the ways that population trends are related to everything else. We are not likely to reduce the population unless we are able to assure old people that they do not need children to provide for their old age security. If the general society, rather than each extended family, provides a safety net for the elderly, the impetus for breeding children is reduced. This is one of the values of the US Social Security system as it was originally intended and as it has functioned well for most of a century. Every nation needs something like it.

We will also need the full education and empowerment of women if they are to take full control of their reproductive lives. It has been clearly shown that an educated and empowered population of women controls the population explosion. Poverty also aggravates the population explosion. We need a full-scale dedication by all human societies to launch effective programs of economic equity. And we need to dissolve the medieval mindsets that make big families an accomplishment of social loyalty. Also, we need communities of interpersonal richness that enable single people, childless couples, small families, and their children to live in closer association with one another, thus replacing the family and the extended family as the primary source of close relations.

Finally, we must include the controversial topic that every person should have full access to education and the means for both controlling conception and opting for abortion. The stigma against birth control needs to end; the encouragement of birth control needs to be a matter of public policy as pervasive as paying taxes. An unconstrained option for birth control will most certainly reduce the need for abortions. And we need to notice the hypocrisy of a blanket moralism against abortion combined with a failure to think through how each new baby can be cared for in a manner that yields a viable human life and viable planetary ecosystems.

Finally, it is important to note that the extensive human population growth has been enabled by fossil-fuel energy. As fossil fuel is phased out and as energy conservation becomes urgent at every point, the control of population becomes increasingly imperative.

Like the other basic awakenings on this list, awakening to the population plight includes awakening to the vast changes that are needed in the entire fabric of every human society. Solving the population problem entails moving from empire to Eco-Democracy.

* * * * * * * *

Population is most commonly discussed in books that are concerned about the whole range of topics that overpopulation intensifies. The following books have helpful chapters on the population issue:

Donella Meadows, Jorgen Randers, & Dennis Meadows, *Limits to Growth: The 30-Year Update* (White River Junction, Vermont: Chelsea Green, 2004)

Lester R. Brown, *Plan B 4.0* (New York: W. W. Norton & Company, 2009)

Richard Heinberg, *Peak Everything: Waking Up to the Century of Decline,* (Gabriola Island, BC, Canada: New Society Publishers, 2007)

Also visit *Population Connection* at www.popconnect.org

Chapter 5
The Continuing Drag of Patriarchy

The resurgence of women's sensibilities about their oppression presents us with a huge challenge: to root out thousands of years of bad habits that have been named with this often-misunderstood word "patriarchy," "the rule of the fathers." Whatever else overcoming patriarchy means, it means accessing a deeper grasp on what is real in the lives of both women and men.

Although many men and some women talk as if gender equality were already achieved (or as if this achievement were a matter of tying up a few loose ends), men are still oppressing women religiously, sociologically, institutionally, and physically throughout the world. Worldwide, women contribute half the world's population, perform two-thirds the work hours, receive one-tenth the income, and own less than one one-hundredth of the world's property (UN Report, 1980). We live in a world where women can be bought and men can rape and even kill their wives under the protection of the law. In the United States women are being abused, raped, and killed by still dreadfully unawakened men. In this country some two thousand to four thousand women are beaten to death annually, one out of four women is severely beaten during the course of her marriage, every nine seconds a woman is battered, and there are three thousand animal shelters but only seven hundred shelters for battered women. The recent US Congress indicated a disinterest in women's health. The craze to criminalize abortion is at its root an insistence that male-dominated governments should have control over women's bodies.

In the twentieth and twenty-first centuries women in the United States and other parts of the world have made big steps toward liberation from patriarchal entanglements. But in some places in the world, the ancient patriarchal oppressions are almost unchanged. Girls are not educated. Women are still vulnerable to the worst forms of abuse, including the selective abortion of female fetuses. Women are still stoned to death by the Taliban, and not too long ago widows in parts of India were expected to immolate themselves on their husband's pyre (and sometimes were drugged and forcefully thrown on the pyre). Women are not only overtly mistreated and neglected, they are the first to starve and the last to receive the health care they need and deserve.

To the extent that a society is shackled with patriarchal laws and customs, it is not benefiting from half its talent pool. Slowed progress is quite obvious in Islamic societies where women are not allowed to work or only allowed to work in very narrow range of work. In many parts of the world when aid money is given to the male heads of household, it often goes for alcohol and prostitutes. In contrast, when seed money is given to women, it almost always goes for improvement projects. Our more developed societies also suffer needlessly from restrictions on the participation of women.

Patriarchy and Ecology

Activists in ecology and feminist movements have discovered that the same social attitudes that debase nature also debase women. A movement called "ecofeminism" has illuminated this tie between the ecological crisis and the oppression of women.[21] This awareness is quite deep but still largely unknown to many. Nevertheless, humanity is slowly coming to see how the gang rape of Muslim women by Serbian soldiers trained for genocidal warfare is of one tapestry with the gang rape of ecosystems

21 *Healing the Wounds: The Promise of Ecofeminism,* edited by Judith Plant (Gabriola Island, BC, Canada: New Society Publishers, 1989)

by human economies trained for ecocidal treatment of planet Earth. Deepening our understanding of "the continuing drag of patriarchy" deepens our understanding of "the primacy of the ecological crisis." The combination of these two flaws spells out a survival problem for the human species. If we are not fully awake to both of these imperatives, we do not have the insight or motivation we need to replace patriarchal/ hierarchical society with something better. These statements will be further elaborated throughout this entire book, but at this juncture let us simply note that overcoming patriarchy is not dabbling in some cultural inessentials that do not measure up to the importance of the hard-headed stuff of those first four awakenings already described. Overcoming patriarchy is at the heart of the massive many-faceted shift that we must navigate.

How did Patriarchy Come About?

Let us continue our unmasking of patriarchy with a brief story about how we got into this women-demeaning, nature-demeaning mess. Primitive tribal societies were seldom if ever patriarchal. Women and men had different roles, but they were not hierarchically ordered. In the earliest forms of settled societies, respect for nature and women predominated in religious practices, in family relations, and in society in general. There may have been wandering and settled tribes that leaned toward the patriarchal styles, but for the most part tribal society was well grounded in a wholehearted obedience to the mysteries of nature and the mysteries of the womb that brought forth males and females through the mediation of women. It is plausible that in early matrilineal societies, humans did not yet understand the relationship between sex and reproduction.[22] The women manifested a powerful magic from which both men and women arose. In these early

22 Merlin Stone, "The Great Goddess: Who Was She," *The Politics of Women's Spirituality*, edited by Charlene Spretnak (New York: Anchor Books Doubleday, 1982), pp. 8–9

times, womanly "magic" seemed the appropriate symbol for the "final mysterious reality" that births us, sustains us, and becomes our grave. Evidence of the veneration of the Great Goddess reaches back at least 25,000 years. Comparatively, patriarchy is a recent development. Even though we find varying assertions concerning the nature of human society in this dim, prerecorded past, we have learned this truth: *human nature did not dictate the origin of patriarchy and does not support the continuance of patriarchy today.* It was a human choice, not an imperative of male nature or female nature. Patriarchy came into being as a humanly initiated shift in human devotion from the mysteries of nature, birth, nurture, aliveness, death, and women to the grandeurs of civilizations and their military kings, emperors, pharaohs, and other semi-divine male royalty. The dawn of the hierarchical social order we call "civilization" preceded patriarchy in some places such as Minoan Crete, but in most places the hierarchical pattern of civilization was soon applied to men over women. Once this shift toward the veneration of civilization and its male royalty began, it reshaped the whole of those human cultures and spread across the world, conquering the still enduring nature-affirming and woman-affirming civilized and pre-civilized cultures. In whatever manner we tell the story of this ancient shift (and there are many versions of the story), we are left with the solid truth that patriarchy was not always here and need not always be here.

An important element in this ancient story is that the patterns of *patriarchy* are thoroughly mingled with what we have called "empire" or "civilization." The latter two of these three terms are still coated with colorations of near holiness. "Patriarchy" is the one of these three terms that plainly notes that human society has been on a huge detour for a very long time. The undoing and redoing of our patriarchal sensibilities will not be accomplished in an afternoon.

Patriarchal civilizations gave priority to the "virtues" designed for male kingship in a top-down or "hierarchical" social order. A civilization required a large military establishment to maintain order within and protect itself from neighboring civilizations. Military duty became a big part of being male. A large part of being male included a "patriotism" that encouraged willingness to die, if need be, for the "fatherland." These "virtues" of the male meant demeaning or neglecting intimate relations, emotional life, right-brain intelligence, sensitivity to beauty and mystery, childcare, and women. These patriarchal attitudes were not dominant in tribal societies, where the adoration of nature and nature's Mysterious Source still shaped social life and the roles of men and women.

Both Women and Men Suffer under Patriarchy

Both women and men suffer when loyalty to one's civilization or nation is put above loyalty to the wider reality of nature, including human nature and including the mysterious ground of nature that is also the mysterious ground of human nature. In civilization/patriarchy the aristocratic royalty, though coddled, also suffer loss, a loss of their contact with reality. But women suffer most. The cultural, political, economic, and overtly physical abuse of women simply because they are women is grim, sometimes subtle, and insufficiently noticed. Our language systems—the very words we have for talking about ending patriarchy—are polluted with patriarchal overtones.

While women have had to be subservient and obedient, men have had to suppress their emotions. While women have not been allowed to fully develop their power in the world, men have been expected to be more than they are and lie about it, super warriors ready to die for their country when called upon. Though women bear the brunt of patriarchal oppression and have the core experience needed for threading the way out of this box of illusions, men are estranged from their nature by the patriarchal patterns of living. As Caucasian people learned in the US civil rights movements of the sixties, an oppressor is inwardly harmed by the act of oppressing others. Charlene Spretnak describes in her book *States of Grace* how males have been warped by their standard acculturation within hierarchical/patriarchal civilizations.[23]

The male within hierarchical civilization has been acculturated to aspire to the following so-called "virtues": (1) being a firm ruler in some contexts, (2) being a subservient servant in other contexts, and (3) seeking to control nature through new techniques and social organizations in all contexts. These "virtues" seemed necessary to make civilization functional. The hierarchy of a civilization was engaged in a continuing conquest of its interior peasant forces and slaves, which required a formidable military organization to defend it from within as well as from adjacent civilizations. The male was assigned to these tasks of defense and acculturated in the "virtues" these tasks required.

But these "virtues" of the "civilized" male were in tension with the emotional and sexual ebbs and flows of the human body. In order to maintain these "civilized virtues" of the male ego, the male's inward nature had to be controlled. So the male feared being undone by being lost in the "swamp" of a sensitive relationship with a down-to-Earth woman. Therefore, women were in various ways kept at arms-length, sometimes by degrading them, sometimes by idealizing them and then requiring them to live up to these male ideals. While women could be allowed to be emotional with one another if they wished, males (that is, the fragile male ego of civilizational "virtue") had to be protected from the emotional power of women. Women had to be subservient, obedient, and careful not to undo these "virtues" of the males. These ancient patterns exist to this day. This interior acculturation of men and women continues as a deep and abiding part of our "patriarchal lives."

This patriarchal obsession with masculine "virtues" also lies behind the common aversion toward same-sex intimacies among men. The male fear of all intimacy, and especially intimacy with other males, is tangled with the fear of being

---

23 Charlene Spretnak, *States of Grace* (San Francisco: Harper Collins, 1991), pp. 114 –55

thought "womanly." The labels used for gay men have included words that mean weaklings or cowards, as well as woman-like. Through violence, ridicule, and exclusion administered by parents and teachers and then by their peers, men are taught to be frightened of tenderness, vulnerability, and trust, especially among men, or at least being the passive male in a same-sex arrangement. This fear of being "put down" motivates men to aggressively enforce the old "rules" of masculinity to avoid being suspected of "softness." Same-sex relations among women have also been opposed by the patriarchy as unnatural. These insidious patterns of patriarchy have formed a complex entanglement for both sexes.

For patriarchy to be overthrown, both men and women must make changes. Here are some examples of the subtle and not so subtle aspects of patriarchy we need to exit:

Men face the shift of learning to respect and value women's thinking and intellect, listen to women without interrupting, and give women credit for their ideas and not reproduce them as their own. Men face a shift from ordering women about and not patronizing them or condescending to them or speaking for them. Men are faced with learning to not touch women unawarely or touch them sexually without permission. Men are faced with learning to share their feelings with women, to ask women how they feel and what they think, and then listen to women talk about their lives. Men are called to become unequivocal in challenging anyone who demeans women directly or in jokes, as well as opposing the male battering of women.

Women face the shift of learning to value their own work and not compete with or criticize one another. Women are called to "toot their own horn" and hold up high expectations for each other, challenging one another to greatness. Women are called to stop looking to men as the standard for what it is to be a genuine human being. Women face the imperative to refrain from sinking into resignation. Women face a shift toward speaking up and not assuming they have nothing to say.

Both women and men are called to read women's history and learn about women's achievements and issues. And women are also called to become unequivocal in challenging anyone who demeans women directly or in jokes, as well as opposing the male battering of women.

* * * * * * * *

In summary, civilized/patriarchal society has valorized the cold application of reason and violence and dismissed as naïve emotional communication, deep personal connection, empathy, and mercy. The greater presence of these gifts among women has been used as an excuse for excluding them from public life. The presence of these gifts among men has been viewed as reason for demeaning these men and thus served to rob men of their deeper and truer masculine gifts.

The continuation of patriarchal patterns is a drag on the overall transformation of society. As long as patriarchy reigns in homes, religious bodies, and cultural associations, the hierarchal domination of males over females will be reflected in our political and economic institutions and in our care of the Earth. This is a huge and unnecessary hardship for women, and too often an excuse for overt violence. Men as well as women are hurt by the patriarchal patterns that require men to take an unnatural attitude toward women and toward one another. The lives of children are impaired. The creativity of the entire society suffers. Important changes have already been made, but much more personal and social change remains to be worked through and socially established.

* * * * * * * *

For further reading on this topic we recommend for their accessibility and pertinence the following books, from among the vast libraries on this topic:

Charlene Spretnak, *States of Grace: The Recovery of Meaning in the Postmodern Age* (San Francisco, CA: Harper, 1991), pp. 114–55. This book is about great wisdom teachings, not just patriarchy, but pages 114-155 "Embracing the Body" is a remarkable summary on the core topic of overcoming patriarchy.

Healing the Wounds: The Promise of Ecofeminism, edited by Judith Plant (Gabriola Island, BC, Canada: New Society Publishers, 1989)

Rita M. Gross, *Feminism and Religion* (Boston, MA: Beacon Press, 1996),

Mary Daly, *Amazon Grace: Re-Calling the Courage to Sin Big* (Hampshire, UK: Palgrave Macmillan, 2006)

The Politics of Women's Spirituality: Essays on the Rise of Spiritual Power within the Feminist Movement, edited by Charlene Spretnak (New York, NY: Anchor Books Doubleday, 1982)

Chapter 6

The Enduring Curse of Racism

It can seem almost inevitable that people will twist differences in physical appearance and cultural inheritance into differences in status, worth, and perceived potential. Tribal societies often viewed their own tribe as "the humans," thus implying that other tribes were deviant. Civilizations have typically highly valued "uniformity" and created deeply violent forms of behavior toward groups of people who did not fit into that uniformity.

Our experiences of cultural shock in our relations with other social groups are perhaps not quite racism, but experiences of culture shock often potentiate into a vicious demeaning of others. Racism, as the demeaning of another group for strictly biological characteristics, is a special and perhaps more insidious version of the general demeaning of different cultures, subcultures, and other "oddly" behaving or "odd-looking" people. The Irish, the Polish, the Jewish, and other European groups faced ethnic oppression as they migrated to the United States. We will use the term "racism" as our general category, even though "ethnic oppression" might be the more inclusive term for the overall enduring curse we are dealing with in this chapter.

In spite of its intensity, racism is based on nothing more than a story that civilized human beings have told themselves. We have never even been clear about what a race is. The genetic diversity among black Africans is greater than the genetic differences between Africans and the rest of the planet. And how strange it is that even a small percentage of African blood has made one an alien race in the classical US attitude.

The differences between human races are almost negligible when compared with the sameness of being human. Racism is nothing more than an idea in the heads of those humans in whom it exists. Giving up racism means giving up the illusion that our "in group" is the "be all" of what it means to be human. It means admitting that we don't know what it means to be human, that being human is more, much more, than what our own "in group" has emphasized. We can learn some of that "more" from every other race and culture of humans on Earth.

Though each new group arriving from Europe typically had to struggle against the contempt of the earlier European arrivals, these intra-European conflicts were mild compared with these two forms of racism: (1) the inhumanity of European descendents toward the Native American cultures; and (2) the inhumanity of European descendents toward African American slaves, ex-slaves, and their descendents.

Racism toward Native Americans

In the annals of infamy, the viciousness, displacement, and slaughter of Native American cultures ranks with the Nazi holocaust. Indeed, Adolph Hitler said that he was inspired for his grim work by the American "accomplishment" with native cultures. Native American racism was manifest not only in the slaughter and displacement of Native American cultures, but also in the boarding schools for Indian youth run by "concerned Christians." These schools were overt modes of oppression and destruction of Native American cultures. Here on the North American continent the ancient prejudice of civilizations toward tribal peoples took on the outright form of genocide. This historical curse still requires understanding, repentance, and healing.

Racism toward African Americans

African American slavery and the struggle to abolish it has also been a wrenching experience for this nation. To this day, the aftermath of slavery in our cultural attitudes and superstitions remains an enduring curse. Great progress has been made. The end of slavery and the civil rights revolution stand as stunning achievements in our common life. But even with our first President being 50 percent African descent, we are far from free of the curse of racism toward African American descendants. Much of the irrational opposition to President Obama is rooted in hidden (and not so hidden) feelings that Caucasian identity is somehow demeaned by the very existence of such a "racially incorrect" primary leader.

Many US citizens have learned a great deal about the depth of the scars this oppression has left on the psyches of both whites and blacks. We have come to see that the oppressor injures himself with his oppression of others. We have come to see that a commitment to uniformity (with being "like us") depletes "us" as well as "them." Diversity, however disquieting at first, results in enrichments that uniformity prevents. When the mysterious strangeness of others is held in fear or contempt, our potential for humanness is depleted. US citizens are still learning to be open to the full potential of our humanity rather than drawing back into the perceived safety and rightness of the way of life of "my" inherited in-group.

Racism toward Hispanic Americans

The current Hispanic immigration issue has brought to the surface another dimension of US racism. Those who want to restrain "south-of-the-border" immigration with inappropriate laws and increased law enforcement are engaging in a repeat performance of the old drama of Jim Crow laws in the Deep South.

People from many political backgrounds are expressing opposition to "rewarding" Hispanic workers who have broken US immigration laws with anything that resembles amnesty. Their assumption is that this lawbreaking should be punished, not overlooked or forgiven. The appropriateness or inappropriateness of these laws is hidden from view in this narrow perspective. The breakers of these laws are not only south-of-the-border workers but those who hire them as well. All sorts of employers are glad to have immigrant workers who are dedicated to a better life for their families and are willing to go the second mile to get it. Many families, including prominent politicians, hire "illegal" Hispanics to clean their houses and care for their children. The lawbreaking, if that is what we must call it, is pandemic. And it has been going on for so long that these so-called laws are engulfed within a vast need to start over with a whole new set of laws. We are facing the usual consequence of a deliberate failure to enforce or revise immigration laws. We are challenged to face our failure and seek justice, not revenge.

We need to provide a widespread forgiveness for everyone involved. And this "everyone" includes every US citizen. All of us have tolerated this situation for decades. It is too late for us to be pious and righteous about lawbreaking. Most US citizens have been passive, thoughtless, irresponsible people who have tolerated these bad laws. So let us allow the past to be past and the future to be open to something fresh. The notion that we should more strongly enforce inappropriate laws before we repent for having enacted these laws in the first place is surely unethical thinking.

Many are mistakenly worried about threats to the jobs currently held by African-American and Euro-American workers. The truth is that the threat to these jobs comes from a different direction—it comes from the typical attitudes of current employers toward all workers. Rather than support the rise of wages and respect for hardworking people throughout the Americas, these employers find the most destitute people to work for them and thereby drive down wages for everyone at home while also outsourcing jobs to the cheapest places. This is the enemy, not Hispanic families that are so desperate that they send family members away from home through dangerous passages to foreign lands to put bread on their tables.

We need to confess that along with self-righteous piety about lawbreaking, there exists an admixture of racial intolerance.

Too many US citizens are too worried about seeing our English-speaking and rather coolly rational culture invaded by a Spanish-speaking and more hotly emotional culture. These invaders might challenge our status-quo styles of living.

If we want to actually resolve all these so-called immigration problems rather than massage our legalistic piety and hide our unacknowledged prejudices, we have to open ourselves to make new laws and forge new attitudes. This would include a general forgiveness toward all the "stupidity" that has been operating for so many decades. And let's not call these changes "amnesty," let's call them "compassion."

So let's stop kidding ourselves. It is racism to enforce obsolete laws rather than create new laws that handle actual realities. It is hypocrisy to condemn "illegal" workers and yet tolerate the US employers who hire cheap Hispanic laborers and oppress them with horrific living conditions. It is both racist and stupid not to recognize that these workers and immigrating families are an economic and cultural enrichment of this nation as well as a multibillion-dollar enrichment of South-of-the-border economies.

Any appropriate solution to this immigration dilemma will include creating laws that reward rather than discourage the participation of immigrants in the US common life. Also, more effort needs to be made in assisting South-of-the-border economies to provide good jobs at home. This is a continental justice problem, and action to address it is being blocked by US fear of diversity, US idolization of uniformity, and US refusal to be open to the full potential of our humanity. We are suffering from a severe case of mass xenophobia, which we must overcome in order to face reality. The increasing number of Hispanic peoples in our midst provides US citizens with another opportunity to overcome the enduring curse of racism.

Such further liberation of the human psyche from racial oppression is a necessary awakening needed to build the sort of planet-wide solutions that make for a viable presence of the human species on planet Earth.

For further study of these topics, consider these books:

Native American Testimony: A Chronicle of Indian-White Relations from Prophecy to the Present, 1492–1992 edited by Peter Nabokov (New York, NY: Penguin Books, 1991)

Henry Louis Gates Jr. and Cornel West, *The Future of the Race* (New York, NY: Alford A. Knopf, 1996)

James H. Cone, *Risks of Faith: the Emergence of a Black Theology of Liberation* (Boston, MA: Beacon Press, 1999)

Justine Akers Chacon and Mike Davis, *No One is Illegal: Fighting Racism and State Violence on the US–Mexican Border* (Chicago, IL: Haymarket Books, 2006)

Chapter 7

The Death Throes of Theocracy

It is easy for US citizens to view the theocracy of the Taliban in Afghanistan as a violation of humanity. We can also see the tragedy of a Sunni Muslim theocracy or a Shia Muslim theocracy. It is easy for us to view the continuing civil war between Sunnis and Shiites in Iraq as ridiculous. Most of us are glad that open warfare between Protestants and Catholics is largely over (though still seething somewhat in Ireland).

In a country like Turkey, where the majority of the population is Muslim, US citizens prefer to see a secular government (rather than a Muslim government). Why then are US citizens and politicians claiming that the United States is (or should be) a Christian nation?

The plain truth is that the United States is not now and has never been a Christian nation. Thomas Jefferson, Benjamin Franklin, and George Washington were "free thinkers," certainly not traditional Christians. Those who were traditional Christians, such as John Adams and James Madison, were avid readers of secular books and supporters of the separation of church and state. None of these founders were supporters of the sort of theocracy being advocated in 2011 by so many US conservative Christians.

The First Amendment to the US Constitution explicitly prohibits a governmental establishment of religion. "Congress shall make no law respecting an establishment of religion, or prohibiting the free exercise thereof." Additionally, Article 6 declares, "No religious test shall ever be required as a qualification to any office or public trust under the United States." It is true that the Constitution does not contain the phrase "separation of church and state." This term first appears in a letter by Thomas Jefferson to the Danbury Baptists Association in 1802 in which he says: "I contemplate with sovereign reverence that act of the whole American people which declared that their legislature should 'make no law respecting an establishment of religion, or prohibiting the free exercise thereof,' thus building a wall of separation between church and state."

The intent of our nation's founders was to create one nation. Several of the thirteen colonies were or tended to be theocracies. Some wanted their citizens to be Episcopalians; some wanted their citizens to be Congregationalists; and so on. Catholics, Jews, Muslims, Buddhists, and others had not yet immigrated in significant numbers to create a theocratic push. The Anabaptists at that time supported diversity. Roger Williams created the colony of Rhode Island to protect "liberty of conscience" from the Puritan religious disciplines of the Massachusetts Bay Colony.

Today, this nation is a melting pot of significant minorities of almost every religion in existence. This diversity includes many people who reject every religion they have so far experienced. This vital interreligious culture is not going away. Theocracy is dying worldwide. Theocracy needs to die. It is a form of oppression. It cannot be reinstituted in the United States, and it need not be sustained anywhere else. In earlier civilizations, including the European Middle Ages, theocracy was simply part of the overall top-down way of organizing social life. During the European Middle Ages the question was not whether there was going to be a theocracy but only which religion was to be the state religion.

Relative to a viable future for humanity, theocracy is a reactionary position that creates nothing but injustice. Perhaps the US founding fathers and mothers understood that theocracy needed to die when they wisely favored the principle of the separation of church and state. The separation of church and state never meant that religion was not to be a vital part of US culture. It meant that state power was not to collude with any one religion in the suppression of other religions. It meant that religions were to make their own way as part of a free exchange of vision, ideas, and passions. The imposition of a sectarian doctrine or a sectarian morality upon all citizens was seen to be what it is: a nemesis that undercuts true democracy.

For US citizens to claim our constitutional heritage concerning the separation of state power and religion means being clear that any morality deserving legal structure must be supported by a broad consensus of the entire population and directed toward the common good. Our laws against murder and theft are examples of commonly supported legal restraints. But the US voters are deeply divided over the criminalization of abortion. We are also seeing the cultural consensus widening on honoring legal family covenants between gay and lesbian individuals and granting those families taxation and other legal privileges. Within certain bounds, a religious group can define "marriage" for its members, but no religious definition of marriage needs to be supported by the state. Insisting on state support for a given form of marriage is theocracy.

Christian theocrats are as destructive of democracy as Taliban theocrats. Rejecting theocracy is not an extreme position; it conserves one of the most important pieces of founding wisdom expressed in the US Constitution. Perhaps the early supporters of democracy understood that if power was to flow upward from the people, then the separation of church and state was mandatory, that theocracy and democracy are inherently mutually exclusive.

If the United States were uncompromising in its rejection of theocracy, it would be a good example for other nations. One of the root problems beneath the Israeli-Palestinian conflict is a commitment to theocracy by many Jews and many Muslims. It is not appropriate for any nation to be Jewish or Muslim, just as it is not appropriate for any nation to be Christian. For a government to have any hope of being democratic, it must be secular in form. The Israeli government could reflect basic Jewish values without the Israeli government being a Jewish State. Jews, like Christians, need to become accustomed to the death of theocracy. It may have been appropriate for King David to support a theocracy in 1000 BCE; but it is not appropriate for his "spirit" descendants to support theocracy today. Every attempt to do so will lead to injustice, hypocrisy, and unending slaughter. When in this high-tech era opposing theocrats are willing to use violent means, an advantage goes to the suicide bombers.

The violence being spawned by theocratic passions cannot be justified. Theocratic movements are futile attempts to recover a lost past. These passions and their violence are reactions to the inevitable death of the theocratic ideal. It behooves us to assist theocracy to finish dying, and to get on with our lives. Public school committees that want to rewrite history from a theocratic perspective must be scorned or laughed into extinction. Awakening to the need for a deep and complete interior dying to theocracy is another awakening that is necessary for the building of a viable human society for the ensuing centuries.

The Positive Value of Religious Diversity

Affirming the separation of state power and religious practice need not be understood as a demeaning of religion. Rather, a proper understanding of this separation provides a chance for all vital religious practices to flourish. The religious impulse can be described as essential to human life and a function within every fully healthy social order.

Here is poem by Gene Marshall (2011) about this religious impulse that may resonate for a wide scope of awakening humans.

> We live in a Land of Mystery.
> We know nothing about it.
> We don't know where we have come from.
> We don't know where we are going.

We don't know where we are.
We are newborn babes.
We have never been here before.
We have never seen this before.
We will never see it again.
This moment is fresh,
Unexpected,
Surprising.
As this moment moves into the past,
It cannot be fully remembered.
All memory is a creation of our minds.
And our minds cannot fathom the Land of
Mystery,
much less remember it.
We experience Mystery Now
And only Now.
Any previous Now is gone forever.
Any yet-to-be Now is not yet born.
We live Now,
only Now,
in a Land of Mystery.

Rather than living consciously in this land of mystery, we project our views of the natural and social worlds onto this background of mystery. We thereby rob reality of its mystery and substitute our view of reality as an oppressive dogma. In the best-case scenario, our views of the natural world have been constructed with our scientific knowledge, our personal experience of nature, and our love of nature and its benefits to us. Similarly, in the best-case scenario, our views of the social world have been constructed with our scientific knowledge, our personal experience of being human, and our common experience of what it takes to have a workable social order. But even these best views are limited pictures created by our finite minds. More limiting still are our pictures of nature and society that are created by our revolts against scientific knowledge, our estrangement from ourselves, and our sheer superstitions. Some of our views of nature and society may not be totally out of sync with mysterious reality, but they are definitely incomplete. We live in a land of mystery that perpetually upsets our views of nature and society.

If our various religious communities and practices assist people to take up residence in this land of mystery, they are promoting clearer vision on social matters and an openness to new aspects of social critique and social improvement. In such openness we can find a huge affirmation of religion as a feature of our society without spawning any need for any of us to impose our particular practice of religion on everyone else.

Following are some helpful books for further exploring this controversial topic and its far-reaching implications:

Joe Bageant, *Deer Hunting with Jesus: Dispatches from America's Class War* (New York: Three Rivers Press-Random House, 2007)

Brian Swimme & Thomas Berry, *The Universe Story: From the Primordial Flaring Forth to the Ecozoic Era* (New York: Harper Collins, 1992)

Steven Runciman, *The Byzantine Theocracy* (Cambridge, England: Cambridge University Press, 2004)

Charlene Spretnak, *The Resurgence of the Real: Body, Nature, and Place in a Hypermodern World* (New York: Routledge, 1999)

Jerry Mander, *In the Absence of the Sacred: The Failure of Technology & the Survival of the Indian Nations* (San Francisco: Siera Club Books, 1991)

Chapter 8

The Obsolescence of War

If war means an all-out military conflict between nations, is there a place for war any more? What is the role of military power? What is the role of violent coercion? What is the proper means of governmental restraint of human corruption? A deeper understanding of the values that underlie these questions can begin with a brief history of warfare.

A Brief History of Warfare

The animal species evolved horns, tusks, teeth, and claws that function as means of defense. These tools of violence are also used to capture food and establish sexual rights. Like all species, the human species has from the beginning participated in the use of violence. For example, when the ancient Clovis people moved onto the North American continent, they used a hollowed stone spear point to dominate and feed upon the large animal species, driving many of them to extinction. The massive herds of short-horned buffalo evolved to deal with this conflict with humanity.[24] Early American humanity formed a sort of negotiation with these herds, feeding upon them but allowing them to persist. This negotiation was broken when civilized humanity arrived from Europe. With more powerful

---

[24] Tim Flannery, *The Eternal Frontier: An Ecological History of North American and its Peoples* (New York: Atlantic Monthly Press, 2001), Chapter 17, "The Making of the Buffalo."

weapons and disrespect for this life-form, these newcomers decimated the massive buffalo herds.

Violence-Assisted Negotiation

Pre-civilization societies also used violent means toward neighboring human groups, but these actions were limited in scope. They were part of a process of establishing hunting and gathering territories. Before hierarchical civilizations were constructed the means of conflict resolution might be called "violence-assisted negotiation." These early societies were usually mobile and, in any case, preferred migration to all-out war.

All-Out War

All-out war is the invention of "civilized" people. Both internally and externally an all-out use of armed force has been a primary characteristic of civilized societies. Early civilizations were composed of previously independent peoples; their now peasants and slaves were held in place with threats of violence. It has been said that civilization was born at the point of a sword, and later at the barrel of a gun. This is an important part of the truth. Even in times of relative peace, civilizations were prepared to defend their ground from external and internal enemies. All-out war meant the mobilization of the resources and humanity of an entire civilization for defense and internal order as well as conquest and expansion.

Civilizations' massive and effective military organizations were made possible by the captivation of large populations through impressive economic, architectural, and artistic achievements as well as the almost unlimited power and quasi-divine status afforded those who came to be called "royalty." Admired or hated, royalty is part of the militarization commonly present in the social organization we call "civilization."

Even in our semi-democratic United States, the militarization of our society remains a taken-for-granted component in the mindset of most citizens. Patriotic support for our military personnel constitutes a major cultural and political force. A

US presidential candidate who cannot show toughness as commander-in-chief has little hope of being elected.

The End of All-Out War

During the last century the common psyche of humanity has begun to reject the fifty-four-hundred-year-old acceptance of all-out war. This departure began with the horrors of the machine gun in World War I. Armies stalemated in opposing trenches made a lasting impression on the human psyche. Following World War I additional energy was given to resolving conflicts through negotiated settlements, such as through the creation of the League of Nations.

Tanks and airplanes allowed military tactics to move beyond the trench stalemate. Hitler and his Nazi Party believed that an industrialized nation that was fully mobilized for "total" war was invincible. Winston Churchill and Franklin D. Roosevelt believed Hitler could only be stopped by mobilizing Britain and the United States for an all-out war to defeat him. The horror of World War II in both Europe and the Pacific soured humanity still further on the conduct of all-out war.

The development of the nuclear bomb and the nuclear arms race further established the feeling that all-out war is now obsolete. The horror of living in the shadow of a potential nuclear winter launched an era of conflict resolution we called the "Cold War." The United Nations has made a much stronger contribution than did the League of Nations in fostering international negotiation and conflict resolution. Though still weak in many ways, the UN remains a statement of our growing awareness that all-out war is obsolete.

Nevertheless, the ancient commitment to all-out war is far from dead. The United States has remained strongly committed to a huge military outlay and to a readiness to use that power to resolve its conflicts. Also, many groups of people have been willing to use localized forms of all-out war to "liberate" local places. Vietnam is a revelatory example. For twelve years the French were unable to defeat a North Vietnamese people who were dedicated to all-out war against their assumed "oppressors." In the years following, the United States, with even stronger military means, was also unable to impose its will. The conclusion that humanity might have drawn from this experience is this: a local population fully dedicated to all-out war cannot be defeated by a nation who wishes to impress its will with something less than all-out war. The United States backed out of that war because the North Vietnamese forced upon the US leadership the choice to either withdraw or continue a costly genocide of an entire Vietnamese society.

Gandhi accomplished a similar result in India with nonviolent means: he forced the British to decide between genocide and withdrawal. Whenever a huge majority of a population is willing to persist in its noncooperation, there is nothing to be done except give in to or slaughter them. And if such slaughter costs too much or violates too deeply the conscience of the oppressing nation, withdrawal is the only alternative. The British withdrew from India.

Many US citizens are still learning this lesson. As long as a significant portion of the Vietnamese population did not wish to be westernized or to be a US "client state," the United States was powerless to win that war. Nevertheless, some US citizens still believe that a stronger war effort in Vietnam would have prevailed.

In Iraq and Afghanistan the US citizenry have once again experienced the plain truth that no amount of military effort can prevail without strong majority support from the local population. If the local population does not support the aims of the US military (or rather if the US military does not support the aims of the local population), then a foreign "war" is not winnable. The US faces the choice between withdrawal and an unending or genocidal outcome. US observers keep hoping that Iraqi and Afghan forces will take up the task of imposing the US "aims" so that US forces can withdraw in "victory." But any long-lasting and meaningful victory will be designed and accomplished by the most persistent component of the local population, not by an invading imperial power.

The ancient ideas about military victory are obsolete. An occupying force can no longer call the shots. In the end the most powerful portion of the local population will call the shots. In Iraq, for example, the United States had to either "surrender" (oh shameful horror!) to the impossibility of imposing our will or stay on indefinitely in an irresolvable war of occupation. In the Afghanistan/Pakistan theater, if the populations do not want to halt (i.e., kill off) the Taliban mode of governing, then the Taliban form of governance cannot be defeated unless a complete genocide is the United States' choice.

In previous centuries, a "great power" did not experience such limits we have just described: the mightiest army was usually able to "pacify" a conquered situation and impose its will on the conquered population. Why is this no longer so? The combination of cheap bomb making, effective weaponry, Internet communication, and suicidal dedication have a resilience that can only be quelled by non-military means of conflict resolution. Bare violence, especially when attended by disrespect and refusal to negotiate with enemies, is a futile means of conflict resolution. The fifty-four hundred-year-old practice of all-out warfare has been called into question by "facts on the ground."

But the long-operative militaristic mindset of civilized people does not die quickly. The total-war mindset still has a strong hold on many minds. Such minds do not grasp the truth that their supposed "truth" is no longer valid.

Is There a Future for Military Forces?

Does this changed situation mean that military force has become obsolete? No, a role for military force continues. While we must move beyond the illusions of an imperialistic militarism and its "all-out-war" attitude, a thoroughgoing pacifism is based upon another set of illusions. At times pacifism may be a useful strategy, but thoroughgoing, idealistic pacifism is a wish dream; it is a denial of the never-absent potentialities of the human species for dangerous perversions. Violence and threats of violence will always exist. What the US Constitution calls "domestic tranquility" and "common defense" will always be needed. In order to enjoy "domestic tranquility," human waywardness will always need to be policed with violent enforcement when necessary. And each organized region of humanity will always need to be prepared to defend itself from other organized regions of humanity.

Nevertheless, the old pattern of all-out warfare is obsolete. A new means of conflict resolution has appeared, and it needs to become the norm if we wish to avoid species suicide. Following are four proposals for planet-wide conflict resolution.

Conflict Resolution Policies for a Post-All-Out-War Era

We will discuss four aspects of a workable conflict-resolutions policy for humanity:

1) Violent forms of conflict resolution are a last resort and must no longer be viewed as "war" but as "international restraint."
2) We are entering a new age in which negotiation is primary.
3) Actions of international restraint initiated by planet-wide "enforcement agencies" presuppose the development of an international law to which all organized subparts of humanity are equally subject.
4) The quality of standing military forces needs to be transformed to serve three purposes: self defense; catastrophe relief; and handling crises like genocide, crimes against humanity, and imperial overreaching.

1. International Restraint

Since both the ideology of "all-out war" and of complete pacifism are illusory, we need to devise realistic policies of restraint that fall somewhere between these two extremes. Such policies include assembling a planet-wide consensus among the vast majority of humanity on how to responsibly restrain humanity's worst impulses. This will require careful definition of the "crimes" that are appropriate for international restraint, such as genocide, ecocide, crimes against humanity, obvious imperial overreaching, and so on.

Until effective, democratic, global institutions come into being, the problem of restraining global corruption is extremely complex. World stability will have to be maintained with the military forces of various nations, coordinating through the currently weak international associations.

An interesting case study is the recent assistance by NATO and the United States of the citizen movement in Libya that overthrew the oppressive dictatorship of Muammar Gaddafi. Progressives will need to work out guidelines for their nations to participate in only those coercive restraining actions that are international in purpose. The singular interest of the home nation (or a business organization resident in the home nation) must not be the motive for military action. Only globally objectionable issues can be an adequate motive for violent coercive actions of an international sort. And such actions are always a last resort.

The occupation of any nation by the military forces of another nation will always create a political nightmare for both the occupying and occupied countries. In most cases, such an occupation needs to be judged as a crime against humanity. A functioning world court would condemn and restrain such an operation. Such a court would also disallow all "small wars" launched by powerful (imperial-minded) nations to protect their business interests; promote their ideological biases; or prevent some supposed, predicted, or possible violence from occurring.

The above considerations imply a rejection of national sovereignty as the overriding context for the deployment of coercive forces. Progressives need to abandon "ultra-patriotic" notions of national "super-sovereignty" and work toward the establishment of global institutions that have effective clout against a carefully defined set of destructive behaviors by renegade social bodies. These considerations further imply that criminal actions by national and sub-national groups need to be treated as criminal actions, not as a "call to war." War is something that civilizations do. In the post-civilization era, coercive restraint takes on a different form than war, and especially all-out-war. However confusing and difficult it may be to think this through, progressives need to open their thinking to all these challenges.

2. True Negotiation

We propose a type of negotiation that includes full and open dialogue among opposing positions without preconceived outcomes. In addition to practicing openness, clarity, and firmness, nations need respect for their enemies and a willingness to talk through issues toward as much common ground as can be found. For at least the next hundred years, there will be serious international conflicts.

We hear the word "negotiation" a lot, but we need to clarify its meaning. We need an understanding of negotiation that is "outside the empire mentality." Imperialistic thinkers view negotiation as a means of getting their way. But in this new age of negotiation, negotiation becomes a means of discovering what "the way" needs to be. National leaders need to learn to enter into negotiations without presupposing the outcome they currently think is necessary.

For example, let us suppose that all the Muslim-majority nations of the Middle East and West Asia met together not to get what they wanted or to protect what they have, but simply to explore what consensus they actually hold in common. They might discover, for example, that they do not want to waste their resources and manpower fighting a region-wide war in defense of Sunni or Shia culture. They might discover that they do not want a return to some idealized medieval Islam that never existed. They might discover that they do not want refugees pouring into places that cannot handle them. They might discover that they do not want Europe, the United States, China, or India having a military presence in their lands or having a tyrannical influence over what they do with their resources. They might decide that getting rid of these outside influences is more important than having a uniform mode of religious law. They might decide that (in their own way and in their own good time) they will take steps toward more democratic ways of operating, if for no other reason than to slow the violence that is threatening rich and poor alike. They might decide to live in peace with an independent Israel and an independent Palestine. This is negotiation. To say that these nations do not know how to handle this sort of negotiation is probably true, but they are as likely to learn it as many current US leaders. George W. Bush openly and explicitly opposed the above style of negotiation. Bush approached domestic and world affairs with a "my-way-or-the-highway" attitude. He even refused to talk with key enemies unless he was assured in advance of getting his way on his key items.

The style of negotiating that we are advocating here is new enough that almost no one knows how to do it well. At the same time, such negotiation is obviously needed for human survival. Such a threat surely provides some motivation to learn open-ended negotiation in all but the most rigid members of our species. Of course, our species has many rigid members whose rigidities seem justified to them because they have not yet noticed that civilization (which includes all-out warfare) is a pattern of social order that is now obsolete.

3. International Law

The style of negotiating discussed above needs to be supported by further development of international law. Steps toward a workable practice of international law have already taken place through the organization of the United Nations, the Geneva Conventions, and other treaties. Small steps have been made toward a World Court. If it is true that organizations such as the World Bank and the International Monetary Fund can be revamped and run appropriately, they might also count as steps toward international law. (We will continue using the word "international," for we will continue to have nations for at least a century. In future centuries other modes of organized humanity may prevail.)

At least three weaknesses exist in the current state of international law: (1) The current international organizations tend to be used by the more wealthy and powerful nations to force their way upon the weaker nations; (2) Wealthy transnational corporations tend to have more influence in the key international organizations than national governments and their citizens; and (3) The strongest nations tend to consider themselves exempt from any serious enforcement of international law against them.

Let us suppose we had an enforceable international law against any nation that was unilaterally using military force to impose regime change upon another nation. If that had been the case during the last sixty years, the United States would have been in court for causing or attempting to cause regime changes in Cuba, Haiti, Ecuador, Venezuela, Chile, Argentina, Panama, Nicaragua, San Salvador, Granada, Iran, Iraq, and other places. Afghanistan might be viewed as a multilateral operation. In none of the above instances was there an actual threat to the US homeland. US politicians have rationalized their unilateral actions as self-defense (e.g., containing communism, defeating terrorism, and so on). For the most part, the actual motive for these military actions was maintaining or extending US imperial rule, usually on behalf of a set of corporations. There are still US leaders who say that the United States is exempt from international law. Indeed, some Pentagon strategists still have plans for effecting regime change in Iran and Venezuela on their drawing boards. And many of those who hatch these schemes are averse to any limitations or restraints upon US action from an international body. The invasion of Iraq by the United States is an example of blatant disregard of UN mandates and massive international opposition.

On the other hand, let us explore a few cases in which effecting regime change might be a valid action on the part of the whole international community operating together. For example, it is hard to deny that international interference is appropriate when a national government is conducting genocide. Perhaps genocide was stopped through actions by the United States and others in Kosovo. Genocide was certainly stopped in Pol Pot's Cambodia by the Vietnamese. It was stopped in Idi Amin's Uganda by the action of neighboring African nations.

To its shame the world community has allowed genocide to proceed unimpeded in other places. Such inaction characterized the world's response to Rwanda when genocide took the lives of at least half a million of its ten million citizens. A similar inaction has characterized the international response to the killing in Darfur region of Sudan. The existence of an effective and impartially enforced international law and policing system would bring Sudanese leaders to court. If they were convicted, the international community would use some combination of military and economic force to stop this wholesale slaughter. However messy and ambiguous such legal enforcements might be, the international community needs to establish such a resource and become able to operate it swiftly and effectively. The very existence of such a capability would curtail many tragedies.

An out-of-date concept of national sovereignty is one of the factors that prevents an adequate development of international law. In our globalized world, the nation state is no longer entirely sovereign. As long as the United States and other large nations are unwilling to subject themselves to international law, they will impede the development of a world court with enforcement capabilities. We cannot have a true form of justice when some nations are exempt from laws that are imposed on other nations. Equality before the law must be applied to the international scene if we are to develop workable international enforcements.

So what role do military forces play in a world where international law and an upgraded form of negotiation are taking place? Nations may still need military capabilities for their own defense. Planetary associations of some sort will still need to be able to assemble military enforcement for the most persistent international law violations. No law is law unless it is enforceable. Without enforceability all concepts of justice collapse, including the notion that no one, great or small, is above the law.

The key to enabling a viable international pattern of military enforcement is the development of democratic processes that all the stakeholders trust. The United Nations is a start, and an important start. We may never know how many horrors the existence of the UN has avoided. We can build upon this experience and this trust, but there is much more building to do.

4. The Transformation of Military Forces

Finally, the shape, style, and extent of military forces need to be profoundly altered. For example, the vast storehouse of nuclear capability can certainly be scaled down to a small, very safe, very competent form of deterrent. Eventually, we need to find a way to eliminate nuclear weapons completely, along with poison gas and biological weapons. Global bodies need to universally disallow any threats to use such weapons in a first strike action. Also, these bodies need to disallow the militarization of outer space. Such militarization can have no other purpose than expanding the rule of some imperial nation.

We also need to develop military outlays that are different from the ones we now have. We do not need to prepare for the type of warfare that characterized WW II; huge outlays for conventional war are no longer needed. The astonishingly excessive current expenditures on military research, development, and production can be scaled back by many orders of magnitude. In the United States numerous items in the current military outlay can be entirely eliminated. Others might be cut in half. Some military capabilities need to be increased; for example, we need more forces especially trained in the cultures of the world and in working delicately and appropriately in various and dangerous relief and genocidal situations. These newer capabilities are needed to meet the "threats" that will most likely call for military action in the future. Knowledgeable persons with military experience are already articulating such a direction. Completing this change will require more research, a revised style of military professionalism, and populations educated to support it.

* * * * * * * *

In conclusion, our policies for planet-wide conflict resolution must reject both imperialistic militarism and thoroughgoing pacifism. Both are obsolete idealisms, having no basis in current reality. Instead, we need to move toward careful multinational restraints, a new style of negotiation, a strengthening and enforcing of international law, and a transformation of our military capabilities to fit these contexts. This is an economic problem, a political problem, and a cultural problem. And it is an urgently needed transition. Indeed, it is a change that is absolutely necessary for the survival of our species. And unless we resolve it soon, we will continue to see needless quagmires of death and destruction. Also, resources will be needlessly sapped from every other aspect of carrying out the massive transition from civilization to the next form of social order.

Here is a selection of books for further study of this topic:

Arundhati Roy, *An Ordinary Person's Guide to Empire* (Cambridge, Massachusetts: South End Press, 2004)

Mark Hertsgaard, *The Eagle's Shadow: Why America Fascinates and Infuriates the World* (New York: Farrar, Straus, and Girox, 2002)

Andrew J. Bacevich, *The Limits of Power: The End of American Exceptionalism* (New York: Metropolitan Books, Henry Holt, 2008)

Naomi Klein, *The Shock Doctrine: The Rise of Disaster Capitalism* (New York: Picador, 2007)

Noam Chomsky, *Hegemony or Survival: America's Quest for Global Dominance* (New York: Metropolitan Books, Henry Holt, 2003)

Chapter 9
The Tyranny of the Banking Oligarchy

We are still reeling from the shock of the 2008–10 banking crisis. Trillions of dollars of supposed "wealth" evaporated into thin air. The entire world economy was and still is threatened by this event. Many people who thought they had equity in a home found that their property was now valued at less than their mortgage. Citizens who normally paid little or no attention to matters of high finance were moved to ask, "Why do things like this happen? How can supposed wealth be so fragile? How can the reckless behavior of some big US banks threaten the functioning of planet-wide money systems? And why does the US government have so little leverage to do something about this?"

The Truth beneath the Recent Banking Crisis

The recent crisis occurred because poorly regulated banking institutions made bets that were outlandish. They took risks that at one time had been illegal. Deregulation measures had opened these doors. They made assumptions that were both self-serving and untrue. Government officials felt they had to bail out these institutions or risk seeing the entire economy sink into a sea of chaos.

In their book *13 Bankers,* Simon Johnson and James Kwak tell this grim story in detail. They begin their tale with a meeting that President Obama had with the CEOs of thirteen of the biggest US banks in March 2009. Here is part of Johnson and Kwak's telling of this story:

Any modern economy needs a financial system, not only to process payment but also to transform savings in one part of the economy into productive investment in another part of the economy. However, the Obama administration had decided, like the George W. Bush and Bill Clinton administrations before it, that it needed *this* financial system—a system dominated by the thirteen bankers who came to the White House in March. Their banks used huge balance sheets to place bets in brand-new financial markets, stirring together complex derivatives with exotic mortgages in a toxic brew that ultimately poisoned the global economy. In the process, they grew so large that their potential failure threatened the stability of the entire system, giving them a unique degree of leverage over the government. Despite the central role of these banks in causing the financial crisis and the recession, Barack Obama and his advisors decided that these were the banks the country's economic prosperity depended on. And so they dug in to defend Wall Street against the popular anger that was sweeping the country—the "pitchforks" that Obama referred to in the March 17th meeting.[25]

At the meeting referred to by Johnson and Kwak, Obama is reported to have said to these bankers, "My administration is the only thing between you and the pitchforks."[26] While it was true that the banks at this juncture needed the government, it was also true the banks had the upper hand. Here is what Johnson and Kwak wrote on that point:

The political influence of Wall Street helped create the laissez-faire environment in which the big banks

---

25 Simon Johnson & James Kwak, *13 Bankers: The Wall Street Takeover and the Next Financial Meltdown* (New York: Pantheon Books, 2010), p. 4.
26 Eamon Javers, "Inside Oblama's Bank CEOs Meeting" *Politico* April 1, 2009.

became bigger and riskier, until by 2008 the threat of their failure could hold the rest of the economy hostage. That political influence also meant that when the government did rescue the financial system, it did so on terms that were favorable to the banks. What "we're all in this together" really meant was that the major banks were already entrenched at the heart of the political system, and the government had decided it needed the banks at least as much as the banks needed the government. ...

The Wall Street banks are the new American oligarchy—a group that gains political power because of its economic power and then uses that political power for its own benefit. Runaway profits and bonuses in the financial sector were transmuted into political power through campaign contributions and the attraction of the revolving door.[27]

To still further aggravate our sense of fairness, these failing banks took bailout money from the US government and did not invest that money in our struggling economy but used it to buy other banks, make some more complex gambles, increase dividend payments to raise stock prices, and pay bigger executive salaries and bonuses. At some point in this story, we the citizens and taxpayers are justified in being very angry. We might call what happened "an unregulated rampage of greed." Here is a colorful paragraph on the topic of greed from the pen of David Korten:

Individual greed will surely be with us so long as there are humans, but if we are to survive and prosper, we must recognize that greed is a sin, not a virtue—a form of addiction and a sign of psychological dysfunction. Any public subsidy for

---

[27] Simon Johnson & James Kwak *op. cit.* p. 6.

persons so encumbered should be limited to payment for rehabilitation service as part of a national health-care program.[28]

Almost two years after the banking crisis very little has been done to effectively regulate the banking institutions and thus prevent the greed of bankers from causing another meltdown. Why has action on this been so slow? Part of the reason is that bankers and their political supporters have spent millions of dollars opposing effective regulation. Indeed, in order to avoid being regulated the huge banks have used their "too big to fail" status as a threat, effectively blackmailing the US government with their power to collapse the economy. This is intentional greed at the expense of everyone else. If a less politically powerful group of persons behaved in this manner, we would have passed laws and enforced laws that would have assigned the perpetrators to jail terms.

Further, if banks are so big and so essential to our economy that their huge mistakes have to be bailed out by government because they are "too big to fail," we are operating a bad system of money services. "Too big to fail" needs to be translated as "too big to exist." Clear-headed economists, such as those we mention in this chapter, recommend that the largest US banking institutions be broken up into institutions that are not too big to fail and therefore cannot take the economy down with them or need to be bailed out. The supporters of these huge banks claim that the global economy requires their hugeness, but Simon Johnson and James Kwak make a strong case that the needed global activities could be and should be accomplished with smaller institutions.[29]

The violation of our lives by huge banks tells us something about our whole economy. David Korten's observations expose the magnitude of the problem:

---

[28] David C. Korten, *Agenda for a New Economy: From Phantom Wealth to Real Wealth—2nd Edition* (San Francisco: Berrett-Koehler, 2010), p. 114.
[29] Simon Johnson & James Kwak, *op. cit.*

[The banking managers] justified their innovation in part by the argument that such innovations reduced risk. In fact, they were simply passing the risk to the credulous. In the end, the managers who made the losing bets walked away with impressive fees collected in the good times and left to others the messy work of sorting things out when Wall Street's sophisticated version of a Ponzi scheme collapsed. In 2007 alone, the fifty highest-paid private investment fund managers walked away with an average of $588 million each in annual compensation—19,000 times as much as an average worker earns. The top five each took home more than 1.5 billion.[30]

In our view no human is worth 19,000 times as much as an average worker. Only two forces have the power to do something about this: (1) informed citizens who insist on major changes, and (2) government institutions with the coercive clout to force different behaviors from our financial institutions. We the citizens, through our governmental agencies, have to take charge of our system of money services.

Regulating Wall Street

In the United States, what kind of government regulation needs to be implemented to keep another Wall Street meltdown from happening? Citizens have already advanced many good proposals. We will list some of them in following paragraphs. Government must set strict boundaries on many activities that are now considered legal. The financial sector cannot be trusted to regulate itself. Nor can these matters be "regulated" by the invisible hand of market forces. Ideologues who rant that governments should let market forces work "freely" in the financial markets are colluding with a serious scam.

---

30 David C. Korten, *op. cit.* p. 75 Also see Korten's footnote: Sarah Anderson et. al., "Executive Excess 2008: How Average Taxpayers Subsidize Runaway Pay."

An obvious place to begin effective regulation is to require banks to make only sound loans (loans that have a high probability of being repaid). Legal improvement number two could be outlawing derivatives that obscure risks and hide outlandish betting.

We have already mentioned breaking up banks and other financial institutions that are "too big to fail." This was formerly called "anti-trust legislation." Such laws have been intentionally eliminated, eroded, or skirted in recent years.

Before the "deregulation craze," interstate branch banking in the United States was illegal. The McFadden Act of 1927 specifically prohibited interstate banking. Some states even outlawed branch banking within the state. A simple reinstatement of the prohibition against branch banking, both interstate and intrastate, would go a long way toward reaching many improvements in the banking industry, especially toward preventing banks from becoming "too big to fail." This regulation would most certainly encourage thousands of new local small "Main Street" banks to exist, compete, and flourish. Ending branch banking would be simple, direct, easily understood, and very effective.

Finally, accounting practices need to be rebuilt. The accounting profession has become morally and intellectually bankrupt. Our worst jokes about accountants have come true. What are now "Generally Accepted Accounting Practices" conceal rather than inform, distort rather than reveal. What is perfectly legal and "generally accepted" fails miserably to serve accounting's primary function: to inform management, investors, government, and the public of the *facts*, and especially to highlight existing or potential problems. In theory, outside auditors are accountants elected by shareholders to be their watchdogs over management. But in practice they are handpicked by management to be their household pets. This invites corruption that is difficult to locate and correct. We must remove this self-serving power from management.

Can we imagine creating the political will to get adequate financial laws passed? This is a serious question, illustrated by recent events in which US government reform efforts have been watered down to almost nothing by expensive lobbying and huge campaign contributions to political figures from the financial institutions. Clearly the public is not now sufficiently awake to these complex issues to marshal the forces necessary to tip the political balance toward solutions on this topic. Greed rules and will continue to rule until citizens demand its firm regulation.

Is Regulating Wall Street Enough?

Even if political will could be assembled for a strict governmental regulation of Wall Street, can federal government action ever be enough to control the greed of our fiscal institutions? "No," is David Korten's conclusion. He makes a convincing case that our entire monetary system needs an overhaul. He says that the goal is to "Redesign the money system to direct the flow of money to productive Main Street businesses rather than to Wall Street speculators. Real resources follow the money, so design the financial system to put the money where it will produce the greatest living-wealth benefit."[31]

Part of this redesign has to do with shifting who benefits from the massive interest being paid to someone in our debt-driven society. When we consider how much of the typical housing or car payment consists of interest, and multiply that by all the people making those interest payments, we are looking at trillions of dollars. Furthermore, almost every business is built with borrowed money and is paying interest on those loans. A large portion of the cost of almost any item we purchase is the result of someone paying interest to someone. In general, those interest payments flow from those who have need of money to those who have more money than they need.

Also, when banks issue loans, this has the effect of increasing the amount of money in the system. The bank owns the loan that is being repaid, and the loaned money is out there in the

---

31 Ibid., p. 170.

world being used by those to whom it was loaned. Perhaps the loaned money is deposited in a bank and then that bank makes loans based on that deposit. The rationale for giving such authority to the banks is to keep the amount of money in circulation balanced with the size of the economy. Too little money in the system can mean deflation. Too much money in the system can mean inflation. We trust the Federal Reserve (the Fed) to use its powers to keep inflation and deflation in check, but the Fed almost always leans toward inflation. Consider, for example, how much cheaper everything was fifty years ago.

The people who administer our money system have been following the policy of regularly inflating the economy—apparently doing so slowly enough that those of us on fixed incomes or slowly increasing wages do not revolt. These policies have worked reasonably well as long as we were living in a continually expanding economy. But perpetual overall economic growth is not viable on a finite planet. We are entering a period in the world economy in which the control of the amount of money in the system will become a serious matter of justice. We citizens will need to learn enough about these complex money matters to vote for policies that end the current tyranny (a monetary system favoring the wealthy elite) and put in its place a stable system of exchange on which ordinary people and honest businesses can count. This is a huge demand upon those of us whose money-matter mastery reaches no further than balancing a checkbook and making it to the next payday. We will need to work together on these changes using the expertise of those economists whom we can trust.

New Money Systems

Experiments with local money systems are already taking place, but simply creating these new money systems will not usher in the new economy. It will be the other way around: creating the new economy will open the need for these new money systems—systems that support a fair exchange of living values among all the citizens. Over the long haul, we will need to thoroughly revise not only local monetary systems but also national, continental, and planetary monetary systems. Most of the current money management on this planet favors the wealthy at the expense of the rest of us. The current money management also assumes a global economy in perpetual overall growth. As we are forced to give up perpetual overall growth, we will need systems of money management that supports this new global economy.

On the topic of new money systems, we recommend the overview spelled out by Charles Eisenstein in *The Ascent of Humanity* (Harrisburg, PA: Panenthea Press, 2007), pp. 256–75 and 442–54, as well as in his recent book *Sacred Economics* (see list below).

* * * * * * * *

For those who want to study further on the overall topic of the banking oligarchy, we strongly recommend three recently written books, already mentioned above. They can help ordinary citizens take responsibility for their money systems and thereby restrain the addiction to greed that characterizes our current situation. We have chosen to emphasize David Korten's book because it is a thorough examination of how the current system is failing us and what we can do to replace this system. The book by Simon Johnson and James Kwak provides us with a careful telling of the recent banking crisis and some illuminating history on this topic. And just off the presses, Charles Eisenstein's book *Sacred Economics* is a roundly provocative look at an innovative economic future.

David C. Korten, *Agenda for a New Economy: From Phantom Wealth to Real Wealth, 2nd Edition (A Declaration of Independence from Wall Street)*, (San Francisco: Berrett-Koehler, 2010)

Simon Johnson & James Kwak, *13 Bankers: The Wall Street Takeover and the Next Financial Meltdown* (New York: Pantheon Books, 2010)

Charles Eisenstein, *Sacred Economics: Money, Gift & Society in the Age of Transition* (Berkeley, CA: Evolver Editions, 2011)

Also useful are the following older sources:

Hazel Henderson, *Creating Alternative Futures* (West Hartford, CT: Kumarian Press, 1996)

Margrit Kennedy, *Interest and Inflation Free Money* (Gabriola Island, BC, Canada: New Society Publishers, 1995)

Chapter 10
The Horror of Poverty

If a group of human beings are turned loose in some fertile place and left alone, they will find food and water, create shelter, and commence their pursuit of happiness. Grueling human poverty is a social malfunction. It is a failure of civilization. It is a sign that civilization has failed as a workable form of human organization. The absolute needlessness of poverty is our tenth core awakening.

We have been studying poverty, fixing poverty, moderating poverty, weeping over poverty, taking up alms for the poor, and creating relief organizations for centuries. These efforts express our compassion and our awareness that something is wrong. But they do not deal with the cause of poverty. Civilization itself is the cause of poverty. If we want to end poverty we have to end civilization. And this means ending every form of civilization.

The dawn of civilization initiated social classes. Civilizations stored food in a central location and put an aristocracy in charge of the food and wealth distribution. These aristocracies took more than their share of the wealth and gave the "lower" classes just enough to avoid their revolt. In the best-case scenarios, the aristocracy entered into a grand and taken-for-granted bargain with the peasants and other lower classes to provide protection from enemies and an adequate living in exchange for their hard work and minimum status. As part of this bargain, many classes of citizens were recruited to be frontline troops in gaining the protections that were promised.

Too often, civilization's aristocracies reneged on their promises. They allowed grueling poverty to exist. They failed to provide protection. They pulled away into their separated havens of wealth and leisure and pretended not to see the grueling conditions that they were creating. Still worse, they rationalized the presence of poverty as the fault of the poor themselves. Civilization became a creation of the "takers" and the "taken." It also created patterns of unconsciousness about the horror of poverty. Some of us are now awakening to this horror, to its needlessness, and to our responsibility for ending it.

As democracy expanded to include the lower classes, it enabled laws, unions, and other organizations that to a significant extent have moderated the horror of poverty. But moderation is not enough. And even the moderations achieved by labor unions and other organizations are currently being undone. We need a complete democracy, one that does away with poverty and aristocracy. This has not yet happened.

The following comments from US Senator Bernie Sanders (I-VT) express well the horror of the current US pampering of the wealthy and the accompanying neglect of the poor:

> The billionaires are on the warpath. They want more, more, more.
>
> In 2007, the top 1 percent of all income earners in the United States made 23.5 percent of all income—more than the bottom 50 percent. Not enough! The percentage of income going to the top 1 percent nearly tripled since the mid-1970s. Not enough! Eighty percent of all new income earned from 1980 to 2005 has gone to the top 1 percent. Not enough! The top 1 percent now owns more wealth than the bottom 90 percent. Not enough! The Wall Street executives with their obscene compensation packages now earn more than they did before we bailed them out. Not enough! With the middle class collapsing and the rich getting much richer, the United States

now has, by far, the most unequal distribution of income and wealth of any major country on Earth. Not enough!

The very rich want more, more, and more, and they are prepared to dismantle the existing political and social order to get it. During the last campaign, as a result of the (Republican) Supreme Court's Citizens United decision, billionaires were able to pour hundreds of millions of dollars of secret money into the campaign—helping to elect dozens of members of Congress. Now, having made their investment, they want their congressional employees to produce.

… despite all their loud rhetoric about the "deficit crisis," the Republicans want to add $700 billion to the national debt over the next ten years by extending Bush's tax breaks for the top 2 percent. Families who earn $1 million a year or more would receive, on average, a tax break of $100,000 a year. The Republicans also want to eliminate or significantly reduce the estate tax, which has existed since 1916. Its elimination would add, over 10 years, about $1 trillion to our national debt and all of the benefits would go to the top 0.3 percent. Over 99.7 percent of American families would not gain a nickel. The Walton family of WalMart would receive an estimated tax break of more than $30 billion by repealing the estate tax.

That's just the start. The billionaires and their supporters in Congress are hell-bent on taking us back to the 1920s and eliminating all traces of social legislation designed to protect working families, the elderly, children and the disabled. No "social contract" for them. They want it all.

They want to privatize or dismantle Social Security, Medicare, and Medicaid and let the elderly, the sick, and the poor fend for themselves.

They want to expand our disastrous trade policies so that corporations can continue throwing American workers out on the street as they outsource jobs to China and other low-wage countries. Some also want to eliminate the minimum wage so that American workers can have the "freedom" to work for $3.00 an hour.

They want to eliminate or cut severely the US Department of Education, making it harder for working-class kids to get a decent education, childcare, or the help they need to go to college. They want to rescind the very modest financial reform bill passed last year so that the crooks on Wall Street can continue to engage in all of the reckless behavior that has been so devastating to our economy.

They want to curtail the powers of the Environmental Protection Agency and the Department of Energy so that Exxon-Mobil can remain the most profitable corporation in world history, while oil and coal companies continue to pollute our air and water.

They want to make sure that billionaire hedge fund managers pay a lower federal tax rate than middle-class teachers, nurses, firefighters, and police officers by maintaining a loophole in the tax code known as "carried interest."

We know what the billionaires and their Republican supporters want. They've been up front about that. … The time is late. The stakes are extraordinary. While it is true that the billionaires and their supporters are "fired up and ready to go," there is another more important truth. And that is that there are a lot more of us than there are of them. Now is the time for us to stand together, educate, and organize. Now is the time to roll back this orgy of greed.[32]

This obsession for more and more and still more, which Sanders outlines, is at the root an unrealistic desire to be infinitely wealthy. It is an inhuman attitude toward self and others. In the United States and elsewhere a greedy aristocracy is still firmly in place, despite whatever veneer of democracy is also present. A fully operative democracy need not mean a complete equality of wealth, but it would mean ending boundless wealth and grueling poverty. It would mean allowing everyone to enjoy some sort of "middle-class" standing in which the protection of life, the provision of liberty, and the pursuit of happiness are actual possibilities.

The **horror of poverty** is intensified by each of the other nine failings of civilization to which we who count ourselves progressives must awaken.

(1) **The primacy of the ecological crisis** points our attention to the final limits of this finite planet. If we do not reorder our lives in order to live within the planetary limits, poverty becomes ever more extreme, ending in a total collapse of social order in many places.

(2) **The undermining of democracy** destroys the only hope that we have of building societies that manifest a viable degree of economic equity.

(3) **The end of the fossil-fuel economy** must be fully embraced and a new energy system built or our current trajectory will reduce most of the middle class to poverty.

(4) **The population plight** is another serious cause of poverty. If we are not able to feed, clothe, shelter, and care for seven

---

[32] From Senator Bernie Sanders's blog published in *Readers Supported News*, November 2010.

billion people, what will our situation be with nine or twelve billion? Total social collapse for rich and poor alike is our prospect.

(5) **The continuing drag of patriarchy** is also a cause of poverty. Until women are released from their shackles, women and children will suffer most. The end of patriarchy also means fewer children per couple.

(6) **The enduring curse of racism** divides the poor into warring groups and dissipates their power to throw off the shackles of their poverty. Racism also grants the aristocracy another excuse for blinding themselves to the plight of the poor.

(7) **The death throes of theocracy** indicates another grim pattern that results in poverty. Theocracy is a top-down attitude that supports a cultural aristocracy who imagine that they are closer to human than everyone else. This justifies and extends the horror of poverty.

(8) **The obsolescence of war** means awakening to yet another cause of poverty. War not only saps wealth from a whole society, it destroys Earth environments and social systems that economically support people.

(9) **The tyranny of the banking oligarchy** means that our current banking and currency-issuing process is another blatant means of protecting and expanding the wealth of the wealthy at the expense of the poor and powerless.

The **horror of poverty** is the straw that breaks the back of the camel we call "civilization." As the aristocracy's "promises" to the lower classes become broken in thoroughgoing and obvious ways, civilization will come unglued. Humanity as a whole will be swept into chaos.

For a relatively rich nation such as the United States, Martin Luther King Jr. suggested that there is no excuse for abject poverty. Poverty could be entirely eliminated, he said, by a simple act of Congress—the provision of a minimum income to every adult citizen. This could be accomplished easily through the income tax system. We could simply give every citizen a rebate equal to this anti-starvation minimum, whether that citizen had other income or not. Tax rates on earned income would then be raised to handle that cost. King maintained that this would save money for the whole society, turning the impoverished into customers rather than wards of the state, occupants of expensive public housing projects, and inmates in even more expensive prisons. Obviously we have a failure of imagination where poverty is concerned. Our minds are filled with silly notions about who deserves prosperity and who does not. Why don't we simply proclaim to one another that birth is a sufficient qualification for a deliverance from poverty?

Ending poverty in the poorer nations will be more difficult than in a rich nation such as the United States. We will need to curtail the oppressive neocolonialism of multinational corporations that drain away natural and human wealth from these poorer places. Further, we will need to insert fiscal and intellectual energy into the poorer communities to enable their local resources to be utilized in bettering the lives of the people who live in those places. Micro-loans to disempowered women have proved to be a shining example of the sort of programs that work. In spite of the huge challenges involved, there is no excuse for poverty to exist anywhere on the planet. Let us never tire of saying that wherever poverty exists, it is a sign that our current mode of human society (i.e., civilization) is failing.

For additional reading, here are two books that focus directly on the topic of poverty:

Martin Luther King Jr., *Where Do We Go from Here: Chaos or Community* (Boston, Massachusetts: Beacon Press, 1968)

Jeffry D. Sachs, *The End of Poverty: Economic Possibilities for our Time* (New York: Penguin Books, 2006)

* * * * * * * *

The ten awakenings outlined in the ten chapters of Part One of this book might be named differently. More could be said about each of them. Other awakenings might be mentioned. Nevertheless, addressing these ten challenges is crucial for human survival and flourishing. Unless we are awake to all ten, we will not discover effective actions that can lead to a viable future for humanity. Further, it is crucial to recognize that these ten awakenings are inexorably intertwined. None can be solved until all ten are addressed.

In Part Four we will describe how we can move from where we are to a future in which these challenges are effectively handled. But first, in Part Two we will describe how the ten challenges of Part One are part of an inclusive shift in the planetary history of humanity. Then in Part Three we will describe how we must see human society in a holistic fashion in order to resolve any one of these challenges. As already indicated these challenges do not exist in isolation from one another; they cannot be resolved separately. The awakening portion of humanity needs to visualize an inclusive, comprehensive, integrated grasp of the entire social transition that we are all called to navigate.

Part Two:

Taking the Long View

A severe flaw in much current social thought is its overemphasis on short-range thinking and action. Without a long view, we confine ourselves to minor repairs on a social system that is barreling at increasing speed toward ecological doom. In Part Two, we will paint a portrait of the long view of our planet-wide social history. We will look back before civilization and before agriculture to those many centuries of hunter-gatherer life, and we will look forward to what can be a viable alternative for the centuries ahead. We will take an especially close look at the last five hundred years in order to clarify the amount of momentum we have already built for making the vast changes required of us.

We do not see a return to tribal ways, but we do see the thousand centuries of tribal living as a resource of wisdom. We also see the fifty-four centuries of civilization as a resource of wisdom. At the same time, neither the tribal mode of social organization nor the civilizational mode of social organization is an adequate pattern for our future. We face an unprecedented turning in the story of humanity. This turning is at least as vast as the transition from tribal societies to civilizations. We are taking this long view in order to illuminate the nature of a turning that must be turned in order to have a viable and flourishing humanity compatible with planet Earth.

Chapter 11

The Dawn and Demise of Civilization

For the last fifty-four hundred years, increasing numbers of people have lived in a form of social organization we call "civilization." For most of them civilization has been like water to a fish; no other form of society was known to them. In recent centuries more members of civilized societies have become aware of current tribal societies and pre-civilization tribal societies, but these societies are typically seen through the screen of civilized values. To many civilized people tribal organizations have seemed remote and almost pre-human.

As more people awaken to the antiquity and wonder of pre-civilization societies and their remnants today, we are coming to know that this older mode of social organization housed and enabled the survival of our species for perhaps a hundred thousand years. The 5400[33]-year-old mode of social organization we call "civilization" appears to be in its end time. Increasing numbers of writers and thinkers use the terms "pre-civilization" and "post-civilization." What would it mean to have a social vision that is not about "saving civilization" or "creating a better civilization"? What would it mean to have a social vision that is about dismantling civilization and creating a third basic mode of human social organization?

---

[33] We will count the appearance of monumental temples in the city of Uruk in what is now Iraq as the dawn of civilization, crediting Sumer as the first civilization. Settled agricultural villages existed much earlier, but we will define "civilization" as the advent of hierarchical structure.

So in this context, what do we mean by the term "civilization"? This question is not about what is written in our dictionaries, but about how we compare the essence of our current mode of social organization with what came before and what might come after.

Large shifts in our understanding often include fundamentally new mental pictures. For example, Einstein's theory of relativity includes new pictures for understanding the natural cosmos. A new set of mental designs replaced those of Newton for understanding space and time, mass and energy, gravity, and other aspects of physical reality. Similarly, we might view the dawn of civilization as rooted in a shift in the basic mental design applied to social organization. We can name that design "hierarchy" or the "social pyramid."

The social pyramid does not characterize tribal societies. And by "tribal societies" we mean all pre-civilization organizations and their various surviving forms. In most tribal societies kinship relations provided the basic imagery for organizing society. Most tribes took pains to delineate the various types of kinship relations and what was appropriate for each type. Tribes sometimes expanded the kinship imagery to include various animal species—brother bear, sister deer, for example. Even the cosmos could be seen in kinship terms—sister moon, brother sun. "All my relations" was a phrase that could include humans, animals, and natural structures. If not all, perhaps most tribal societies have been organized with these kinship relations as the basic organizational design.

In stark contrast, the dawn of civilization can be correlated with the use of the pyramid as the basic design for organizing human society.

The Basic Design of Civilization

Imagine yourself a peasant in an ancient civilization viewing a rather large pyramid (a.k.a. a ziggurat) with a flat top, perhaps containing a small building. Think of this monument as an educational poster that is teaching the population a new design that is being applied to the whole society. Picture royalty symbolically occupying the top of this pyramid. Let the upper layers of rocks represents the aristocracy including the generals and other top military officers. The next layers of rocks represent other classes: artisans, musicians, merchants, etc. The rocks at the base of the pyramid represent the foot soldiers, the peasants who work the land, and the slaves who do whatever is asked of them by some higher ordered class of "masters." This is the basic design of civilization. We have stopped building pyramids, unless we count skyscrapers, but the image of pyramid in our mind organizes how we civilized people view people as upper, middle, and lower classes.

The democratic revolutions of the eighteenth century modified this basic design, but these revolutions did not do away with the social pyramid. They abolished or sidelined the king and other royalty. In the place of the king they elevated a somewhat kingly leader elected by at least some of the elite social classes. They limited this kingly executive with assemblies of representatives, a written constitution, a limited term of office, and basic notions of law that were in some measure derived from the consent of the governed and were applied to everyone (including the chief executive).

After these changes the social pyramid remained, but with the abolition of slavery and giving women voting rights and leadership opportunities the pyramidal image was further reduced in the minds and practices of large numbers of people. All forms of "second-class citizenship" are now being opposed by many people; nevertheless, the social pyramid remains, and the eroding of the pyramid continues. What would it mean to end completely the pyramidal structures of civilization and construct social life with an alternative basic design—a viable, functional design that eliminates hierarchical order entirely?

Let us assume that the eighteenth- and nineteenth-century democratic revolutions were an attack on pyramidal society—that is, an attack on a basic characteristic of civilization. That is, let us assume that these democratic movements carried something revolutionary with regard to what civilization has always been. Even though these democratic revolutions made deep compromises with hierarchy, the very idea of democracy gives us hints about what a post-civilization form of social organization might look like. These democratic revolutions can be viewed as the beginning of the end for the pyramid of civilization. The rather recent realization that humans are responsible for the care of the ecology of the planet is another attack on pyramidal design. Deep ecology movements claim that human society must no longer be viewed as "above" nature, as ruling "over" nature. This view is an attack on the pyramidal mind. Society and nature can be viewed as horizontal partners in providing a viable home not only for humanity but also for whole ecosystems of living species.

Thomas Berry claims that humans taking responsibility for the ecology of the whole planet is the dawn of a new era in Earth history. He calls it "the Ecozoic Era."[34] He contrasts this new era with the Cenozoic Era, an era that Berry claims humanity is currently bringing to an end. (The Cenozoic Era began sixty million years ago with the dying out of the dinosaurs.)

Following Berry's lead, we have chosen the term "Eco-Democracy" to refer to our vision of a future society that is capable of sustaining a viable human presence on this planet. Eco-Democracy is not a better civilization; it is a new mode of social organization. Eco-Democracy is a mode of social organization that is as different from civilization as civilization is different from tribal society. Furthermore, Eco-Democracy is not a high-tech version of the tribal mode of social organization. "Eco-Democracy" is our name for a fundamentally new design in social organization. We are still filling in the detailed meaning of this term. "Eco-Democracy" points to a consensus being built by the awake and awakening portion of humanity.

---

34 Thomas Berry, *The Great Work: Our Way into the Future* (New York: Broadway, 1999), (reprint edition), p. 8.

The Basic Design of Eco-Democracy

One way to clarify the shift to Eco-Democracy is to sketch an abstract picture of this new basic design. It will be something different from a pyramid—with royalty on top (or a skyscraper with CEO offices on the top floors). Instead, let us imagine a horizontal design, a design that nets together a large number of diverse roles into a functional social operation.

Picture a dozen ping-pong balls all the same size strung together through a network of connecting strings. One of those balls is colored red. That red ball does not represent a kingly role but a leadership role among other equally significant roles. The red ball has been assigned by the others to play a coordinating role for the other eleven balls. This coordinating role is no more important than all the other roles; it is just one more role alongside the others. There is no hierarchy here, no pyramid. Nevertheless, this twelfth role is important for holding together the other roles into a functional whole. Each of the other balls in this model would have its own significant role—alongside rather than below the coordinating role.

The signal calling or managerial roles of an organization need not be thought of as an upper class—a higher layer of a hierarchy. The need for such roles does not necessitate a hierarchical or pyramidal design. In particular, wealth and power and political control need not gravitate upward in some pecking order. Differences in talent, leadership power, and consciousness will always be a factor in social groups, but these differences need not be structured hierarchically.

The array of horizontal ping-pong balls mentioned above can represent governmental bodies as well as individual persons. Eleven of those balls might represent state or regional governments. The twelfth ball, the red ball, might represent a national or continental coordinating role that webs together the other eleven. This coordinating body does not rule over the regional governmental bodies; it serves them as their coordinator. This coordinating function is accountable to each local government, and each local government through the coordinating body is accountable to all the other local governments in that coordinated network of governing bodies. While these various bodies will surely contend with one another over real issues and choices, they do not need to war with one another for some sort of sovereign top-down control. Ruling-over becomes a hangover from an antiquated past—the pyramidal, hierarchical, civilizational design of human affairs. When we speak of "post civilization" or "Eco-Democracy," we mean a new, post-pyramidal basic design.

This new social design is already making its appearance in many places, but it is not yet widely understood and accepted. We will experience a period of time in which we are learning, thinking through, and teaching our way out of the old box of civilization (pyramidal hierarchy) into a wider imagination concerning viable social order. We are symbolizing that widening view with the term "Eco-Democracy."

The End of Empire

With remarkable imagination Mahatma Gandhi fostered an extensive movement of noncooperation with the British Empire, and thereby won independence for India. Strange and offensive as it may sound to our propaganda-inebriated ears, we who are citizens of the United States are also living under the tyranny of an empire - —not the British Empire or the Roman Empire, but the US Empire.

What is an empire? Empires have been around since the dawn of civilization. The usual definition of "empire" pictures a civilization that has expanded its jurisdiction over other lands. But a deeper definition of "empire" could include all civilizations, for all civilizations have extended their rule over an extensive area that was previously occupied by independent tribes or villages. Also, a civilization rules over its internal constituencies, which would fly apart if "imperial force" were not being applied.

Here is our summary of some of the main qualities of an empire: an empire is a society dominated by the top-down rule of a wealthy aristocracy that controls a large section of the planet with economic and military forces in order to protect and extend the wealth and power of that aristocracy. Caring for its own population is secondary to maintaining huge military forces that can be sent anywhere to protect the values of the aristocracy. Empires tend to be on a constant war footing. Empires tend to create, exaggerate, and demonize their perceived enemies; and patriotism is twisted to mean supporting the troops in whatever endeavors the aristocracy chooses for them.

Empires also tend to centralize power in the control of tight cabal. Democracy, if it exists at all in an empire, becomes a façade for pacifying the masses with the delusion that they have a meaningful say in the course of events.

Empires tend to put security before civil rights. This can include jailing presumed enemies without cause or due process. Empires use misinformation to pacify and motivate their own populations. They use torture to secure information from their presumed enemies. They justify predatory trade practices, secret political interference, assassinations, invasions, and anything that advances their over-glorified goals. And because empires make loyalty to the empire more important than efficiency or righteousness, boondoggles occur and corruption spreads. Empires can become so focused on serving their ruling aristocracies that they undermine their own economies and plunge themselves into collapse and ruin.

Most of our public media would have us believe that the United States manifests few of the qualities of empire, and that even those few are excusable. Whatever our flaws, so the story goes, we are not an occupying power, a neocolonial force, or any other kind of tyrant. US troops are present in many places in the world, but we are there only to help out, however we can, in the interest of justice, democracy, and free trade. Along the way, of course, we are watching out for our national self-interest, as all nations are obligated to do. Statements like these, even when somewhat true, avoid a larger truth. The United States, like all civilizations since the dawn of civilization, has critical imperial qualities.

For a while, it seemed that the unwarranted invasion of Iraq might awaken large segments of the US population to the reality that the United States was an empire. But those who hoped for such an awakening were disappointed. Some US citizens have joked that there would have been no conquest of Iraq if its main product were olive oil instead of crude oil, but these same people often fail to draw the conclusion that crude oil and the power it bestows have been the main reasons for our occupation of Iraq. Further, we hear that the United States must not allow the control of that oil to fall into *other hands,* such as China, the European Union, or (God forbid) the Muslim nations under whose land this precious resource lies. Is this not imperial prerogative? In spite of the fact that qualities of empire clearly apply to the United Sates, most citizens do not concede that our nation is imperial.

Even propagandists who have admitted we are in Iraq for the oil go on to claim that securing that oil from falling into the *wrong hands* is a key part of our national self-interest. They also justify US saber rattling against Iran and Venezuela on similar grounds. Such nations, so they say, are likely to fashion uses for that oil (meaning "our oil") that are not in our national interest.

These commentators seldom explain clearly what "national interest" means or exactly whose interest is intended. More citizens are beginning to think that sending more and more and still more of our sons and daughters to war may not be in our best self-interest, that spending more and more and still more trillions on military operations may not be in our self-interest, that provoking more and more and still more millions of people to hate us may not be in our self-interest.

Surely there is a fundamental point to be made here. What is in the self-interest of most members of the US society? What is the self-interest for this society as a whole? And even deeper, what is our responsibility as a compassionate and justice-loving people?

Still, many claim the United States is not an empire. Even if our presence in Iraq is rather imperial, Iraq has been a special case. But is it? Since World War II, the United States has sent military forces to scores of foreign places. We have clearly interfered with the political and economic affairs of several dozen nations, mostly to preserve the advantages of US corporations. For instance, in relation to almost every Latin American country, US administrations have demonstrated paranoia toward any form of government that is perceived to be not good for US businesses.

These actions indicate that the United States is some sort of empire. Can we deny that this nation has ruled or attempted to rule over large sections of the world? Do we citizens feel fully in charge of this supposed democracy? Do we in deny that big money forces, quite beyond citizen control, make the big policy decisions?

If we conclude that we, the citizens of the United States, are indeed ruled by the US Empire, then how do we win our independence from this empire? Our first step is to admit the seriousness of the problem. Perhaps Gandhi's job in India was simpler; at least a majority of the population of India knew that they were being ruled by an empire. We need to focus not on how to run a better empire, but on how to phase out empire as our mode of social order.

Our challenge is more inclusive than bringing to an end the US empire; that goal is not big enough. All civilizations tend to be empires. All civilizations are hierarchical organizations using military force to hold their diverse parts together and to protect their geography and/or to expand their geographical scope. Tribal societies were not (and are not) imperial social bodies. They have their own disadvantages, but empire is not one of them. Empire is a trait of the social mode we call "civilization."

Empire is a fatal flaw of civilization, a flaw not found in tribal societies, and a flaw that need not be found in the societies of the future. Civilization has fostered other fatal flaws: the alienation from nature, from the human body, and from the geographical places where we live. Undervaluing the solitary person and intimacy among persons is another flaw of civilizational designs. If we are going to imagine a viable future for humanity, we must imagine an alternative to the civilization mode; to hierarchy; to the social pyramid; and to the demeaning of the natural world, the human body, solitude, intimacy, and the richness of local democratic process within specific Earth places.

Nevertheless, civilizations have gifts to contribute to the future that are not contributed by tribal societies. Without the long history of the civilization mode of social organization and the gifts of thought and organization developed by civilizations, we would not be able to even imagine a planet-wide form of responsibility. Civilizations have widened our scope both geographically and temporally. For example, an awareness of "making history" was very weak in pre-civilization societies. These societies were extremely tradition-oriented. Their survival depended on adapting to nature and they treasured the wisdom for doing so, as held by the elders and tested for hundreds of years. Social change in the pre-civilization period occurred very slowly. This careful approach to social innovation worked well for thousands of years, but it is a tight box for the human imagination that we dare not reenter. A widened human consciousness is one of the gifts that civilizations have given to us. This gift and many others are important batons to be passed to the next runners in social construction.

A Historical Picture of the Dawn and Demise of Civilization

Chart 11.1 is a historical diagram that outlines the dawn and demise of civilization and the dawning of something better. This chart assumes that the hunter-gatherer tribal society was the only social mode used by humans until the dawn of agriculture. At the dawn of agriculture about 8000 BCE, the human population of the world is estimated to have been approximately 5 million.[35] At the beginning of

---

35 For this and following population data, see peopleandplanet.net.

the Common Era, the human population was an estimated 300 million. During that 8000-year interval, population grew very slowly by contemporary standards, but rapidly in comparison with the previous 90,000 years. Population growth accelerated with the spread of agriculture and the dawn of civilization.

Some equate the dawn of civilization with the dawn of agriculture and sedentary societies, but the earliest agricultural societies were tribal in organization, not hierarchical in structure. *We are defining the dawn of civilization as the dawn of pyramidal organization.* This is an important distinction, for when we speak of the demise of civilization, we do not imply the end of agriculture. Agriculture needs vast improvements for an ecological era, but we do not equate agriculture itself with the obsolete mode of social organization we are calling "civilization."

When did a full-blown, hierarchical civilization begin? By 3400 BCE in the river valleys of what is now Iraq, Sumer was flourishing as a hierarchical organization. This date might be adjusted earlier or later, but we will use this approximation to tell our story.

Chart 11.1 pictures the approximate relative percentages of the human population living in these three modes of social organization: pre-civilization (tribal societies), civilization, and post-civilization (Eco-Democracies). The precise percentages are not important here, and the somewhat vague data we have about early societies need not affect the basic point we are making. Let us assume that there were about 100 million humans living on Earth in 4000 BCE and that they lived in either hunter-gatherer tribal societies or sedentary-agricultural tribal societies. We will also assume that by 2000 BCE, 100 million people lived in civilizations, and another 100 million still lived in tribal societies. In other words, about 50 percent lived in each mode of social organization. Four thousand years later (in year one of the Common Era), it is likely that at least 200 million were living in civilizations. Another 100 million, let us assume, still lived in tribal arrangements. In other words, two-thirds of human beings lived in civilizations. Today, millions of people still live in tribal arrangements, but as a percentage of humanity tribal peoples are a small portion of the now seven billion humans occupying the planet.

Chart 11.1 also assumes that the civilization mode of social organization is already being replaced by the Eco-Democracy mode. We are anticipating that those living in the civilization mode of social organization will become a small percentage of the human population in a couple of centuries. This may seem a bold prediction, but if rapid changes of that magnitude do not occur, we will likely drive our civilization vehicles off the ecological cliff into human species extinction. Our chart expresses the optimism that humanity will wake up in time to act boldly in bringing to fruition the viable Eco-Democracies we are envisioning. In the least optimistic picture, humanity rides the vehicle of civilization into extinction.

Chart 11.1 also reflects the assumption that by the year 2100 civilizations and Eco-Democracies will each characterize about fifty percent of the population. That may also seem unduly optimistic, for that is only nine decades away. But when we look nine decades into the past, we can glimpse how quickly vast changes can take place. Also, in the next chapter we will show how we already have several centuries of momentum built up toward the possibility of Eco-Democracy. We are not starting from scratch. Amid the seemingly invincible civilizations of the current world, a subversive presence has been building for a long time. Millions, perhaps billions, of people are already dedicated in their hearts to something better than civilization. Our images about this future may be diverse and confused, but a longing for a new mode of society abounds. A fresh new social mode can grasp the consciousness of billions of people, and such clarity can break out in a burst of creative change that moves the civilization mode of social organization onto the sidelines of history. This is our hope. Chart 11.1 is a statement of that hope.

Chart 11.1

The Great Transitions from Tribal Societies to Civilizations and from Civilizations to Eco-Democracies

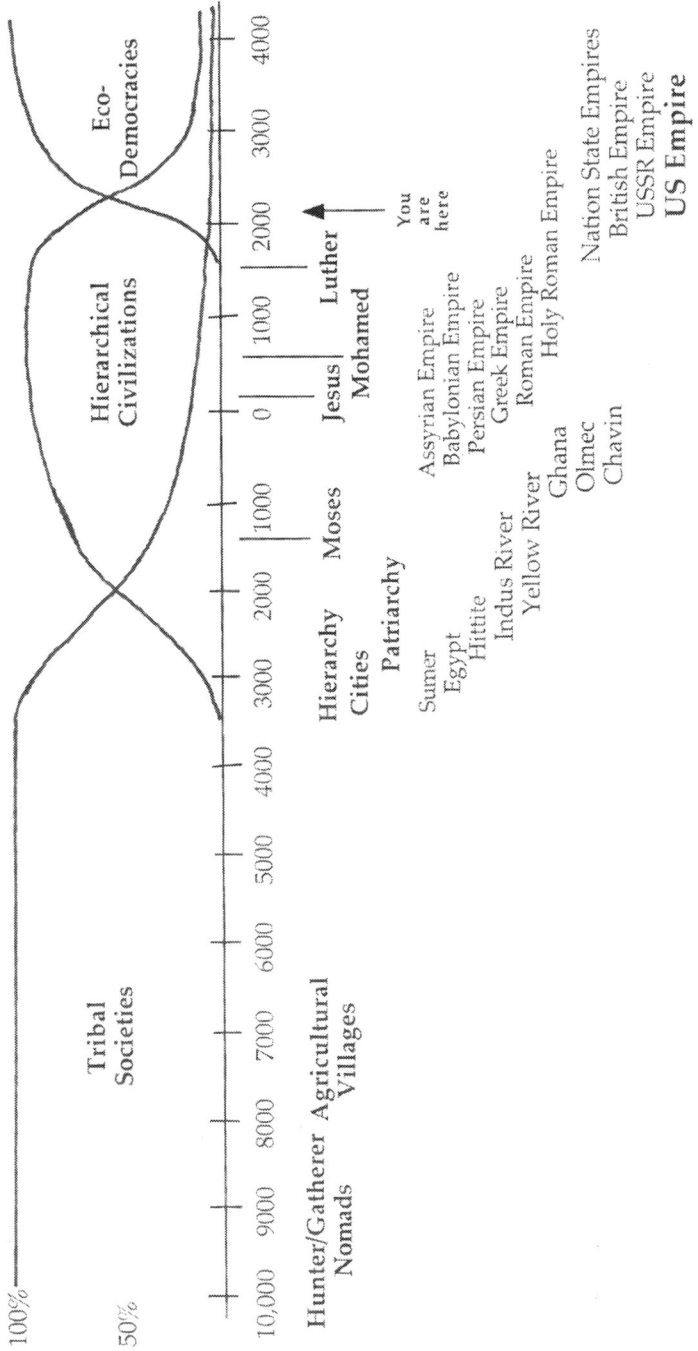

The rest of this chapter is further commentary regarding details of Chart 11.1. In 3200 BCE, a scant two centuries later than civilization appeared in Sumer, a full-blown civilization existed along the Nile River in ancient Egypt. By 2600 BCE a fully formed civilization was functioning in India along the Indus River, and a bit later in China along the Yellow River. Between 1400 or 1000 BCE the civilization mode of social organization appeared in Africa (Ghana) and in the Americas (Olmec and Chavin). By then civilizations had begun to characterize the lives of most human beings.

As late as 2000 BCE there were hierarchical civilizations that were not yet patriarchal civilizations. That is, males had not yet been hierarchically exalted over women. In the period between 3400 and 2000 BCE, there were still pre-patriarchal civilizations. The Minoan civilization on the island of Crete has been among the most studied. In these civilizations, the goddesses of nature and the influences of this religious practice had not yet been replaced by male deities that symbolized civilizations and their male military commanders-in-chief. Hierarchy preceded patriarchy in at least some places. Economic class oppression preceded the male oppression of women. The dawn of civilization and the dawn of patriarchy were not simultaneous events, at least not in every place. Just as human societies were not always patriarchal and need not be patriarchal in the future, so human societies were not always civilizations and need not be civilizations in the future.

Perhaps it would be helpful for Jewish, Christian, and Muslim readers to relate these huge social shifts with biblical history. Moses, the prophets, and Jesus lived in a world already dominated by civilizations and by patriarchy. Moses led slaves out of the Egyptian civilization about 1300 BCE. Two and a half centuries later, the twelve tribes of Israel living in Palestine faced the choice of having a king, which meant becoming a small civilization among the great empires. Saul, David, and Solomon were the realization of that option. After 850 BCE Amos, Hosea, and Isaiah wrangled with the kings of Israel and Judea in a period dominated by the rise of the Assyrian

Empire. Jeremiah and Ezekiel lived during the reign of the Babylonian Empire and its practice of deporting the leading members of stubborn little kingdoms like Judea. Then, with the rise of the Persian Empire and its more generous policies, Second Isaiah found it possible to call Israelites to return home to Palestine from their Babylonian captivity.

Chart 11.1 also contains some examples of European empires. Alexander the Great conquered the Persian Empire and created a Greek Macedonian empire. Then the Roman Empire took over from the Greeks. The Romans provided the stage on which Christianity was born, spread, and eventually created a state religion and a state structure that came to be called the "Holy Roman Empire."

Luther, Calvin, and others initiated a fundamental challenge to the Holy Roman Empire and by implication to the entire heritage of empire and theocracy. The Protestant Reformation split the Holy Roman Empire and set the stage for Nation States, which were still imperial civilizations but were somewhat less dominated by theocracy. The British Empire is the most important of these from the perspective of US history.

In recent decades we have not viewed the word "empire" in a favorable way. We have called the USSR and the United States "superpowers" rather than "empires." But in the long story of humanity, these two latecomers will also be remembered as empires. Indeed, all civilizations have imperial qualities even though all civilizations have not been superpowers or been inclined to extensive expansionist aspirations.

In addition to naming some of the more familiar empires, the above chart suggests to us that we are currently in a long period of transition. In the twenty-first century the tribal mode of society is completing its decline, and civilizations are also beginning their decline toward becoming a marginal mode of human social organization.

Finally, Chart 11.1 suggests that the next mode of social organization has been rising for centuries. New qualities of social order have been inserted into our common civilized life by the Reformation, the Enlightenment, the Romantic movements, the democratic revolutions, the abolition of slavery, the women's revolution, the anti-colonial revolutions, the civil rights revolution, the end of South African apartheid, and numerous ecological movements. All these movements and others challenge the core qualities that have characterized civilization.

After almost five centuries of anti-hierarchical movements, the civilization mode of social organization can seem as strong as ever. Nevertheless, the fresh qualities that the above movements have introduced are alien to the essence of civilization. These qualities undermine civilization or at least moderate some of its excesses.

Though the ecological movements are relatively recent, they are fundamental to our vision of Eco-Democracy. Other elements of this vast transition have roots that are several centuries deep. Unfortunately, most of the older movements have been co-opted by civilization and/or accrued modern perversions that minimize the power of their critique of civilization and thus cloud their contribution to the future. Our transition period (often called "the modern world") is extremely complicated. For a study of the lively complexities of modern history, we recommend Charlene Spretnak's book *The Resurgence of the Real*.[36]

Though this transition period is extremely difficult to sort out, these many movements of civilizational critique have the potential to combine their energies toward shaping our vision of another basic mode of social organization.

Seeing this vision and completing this vast transition is our hope for a viable future for the humans on this planet. We are not starting from scratch. We have centuries of preparation. The possibility of completing this vast transition is made more plausible when we notice how far we have come, how deeply we have articulated our critique of civilization, how extensively we have already created foundations for the next master mode

---

[36] Charlene Spretnak, *The Resurgence of the Real: Body, Nature, and Place in a Hypermodern World* (New York: Routledge, 1999)

of human social organization. Eco-Democracy is coming. It is rising out of the ruins of our collapsing US Empire. It is being assembled by the creativity of millions of people. Humanity may be running out of a lot of things, but we are not running out of imagination. Every ecological system is threatened, but the living planet is very resourceful, and our species is very resourceful. Life can continue on this planet, and human life can be part of that continuation. But in order to accomplish this, civilization as a mode of social organization must be dismantled and a fully alternative social mode must be constructed in place of civilization.

In the next chapter we examine this great transition in more detail. David Korten calls this transition "The Great Turning."[37]

---

[37] David Korten, *The Great Turning: From Empire to Earth Community* (San Francisco: Berrett-Koehler Publishers, 2006)

Chapter 12
Living in a Transitional Period

Chart 12.1 shows how human history can be divided into five periods, two of which are transitional periods between the other three.

Chart 12.1

Chart 12.1
Five Master Periods of Human History

TRIBAL SOCIETIES	TRANSITION PERIOD from Tribal Societies to Civilizations	CIVILIZATIONS Displace Tribal Societies	TRANSITION PERIOD from Civilizations to Eco-Democracies	ECO-DEMOCRACIES Replace Civilizations
	Hierarchy Uniformity Patriarchy Massive Warfare		Democracy Racial Diversity Gender Equity Negotiation & Restraint	

The first major transition period from about 3400 to 1000 BCE saw the dawn of civilizations, hierarchy, large cities, uniformity, patriarchy, and massive warfare. These structural developments entailed a departure from tribal life and its gifts of intimacy and connection with nature. It also meant a departure from tribal patterns and a widening of human consciousness. This widened consciousness was both a blessing and a curse. It led to scientific, contemplative, and organizational potentials that humanity will never consent to be without, but it also led to a number of horrific estrangements among humans and to a loss of connection with the natural Earth. These curses of civilizations did not plague tribal societies, and they need not dominate future societies. They are acquired habits, not human nature.

Today we are immersed in a second epic period of vast social transition. We are abandoning old patterns, recovering lost wisdom, and discovering wisdom and ways of living together that were never before explored. The Reformation, the Enlightenment, and the democratic revolutions of the eighteenth century initiated the rejection of hierarchy, theocracy, empire, and long established mode of social organization we are calling "civilization." The abolition of slavery, the women's rights movements, the labor movements, the anti-colonial movements, the civil rights movements, and the ecological movements have furthered the attack on hierarchy and patriarchy as well as on the uniformity that civilizations tend to impose.

The maturing of democracy has meant an increased emphasis on the value of diversity. As human life on Earth has become ever more connected, an appreciation of diversity has become ever more important. We are learning that the type of "globalization" we need is not the imposition of one human culture upon all locations, but a loosening of our attachment to any one culture and an openness to learning from all cultures. Our challenge is to renounce old uniformities and become more inclusively human.

All-out warfare, which has typified civilizations, is being challenged by horror over the futility of such weapons as nuclear bombs and biological agents. We see a fresh emphasis on negotiation and on measured police operations used only to restrain violence and aggression. Reliance on all-out warfare to resolve conflicts has become obsolete. A last resort using of coercive force will continue to be part of human life, but the style of all-out war that has characterized civilizations is now suicidal behavior.

The focus on sovereign nations and centralizing cities is also being challenged with a fresh emphasis on strong local communities and regions as well as planet-wide regulatory and service institutions. We can envision a mutually beneficial interdependence among regions being balanced with relative self-sufficiency in each region. We see an emphasis on producing food closer to where it is eaten. A new balance of the local and the global is arising in the vision of many people, though action to accomplish a better local-to-global pattern is only beginning.

Agriculture is also entering a period of transition. Rather than treating Earth as a mere mine for our food, we now see fresh emphasis upon the preservation and building of soils. Organic agriculture, permacultural design, an increased use of perennial plants, and other innovations promise to be part of realigning our relations with Earth.

All these well-known and not so well known movements combine to paint a picture of a vast transition that has and will extend over several centuries. This transition will affect every aspect of life from outward structures to the inner being of people. The inner transformation will include an increased capacity to see the history of civilization as a relatively small bump in the long story of human life and history of industrial civilization is a very tiny blip fueled by an nonrenewable resource called "fossil fuels."

We can learn wisdom for relating to Earth from a hundred millennia of tribal life. We can also learn wisdom from more than five millennia of civilizations. We can imagine creating a future that is very different from both tribal life and civilization. This imagination is new but powerful and capable of finding a way through the rubbish of the past into a viable future for the human species.

A more careful look at the progressive elements within the history of recent centuries may help us envision our hopeful prospects. Chart 12.2 highlights some of the progressive elements that are gaining momentum in European and North American societies during the modern transition period. The remainder of this chapter offers a brief discussion of the elements indicated on this chart.

Chart 12.2

Highlights of the Western World's Transition from Empire to Ecozoic Democracy

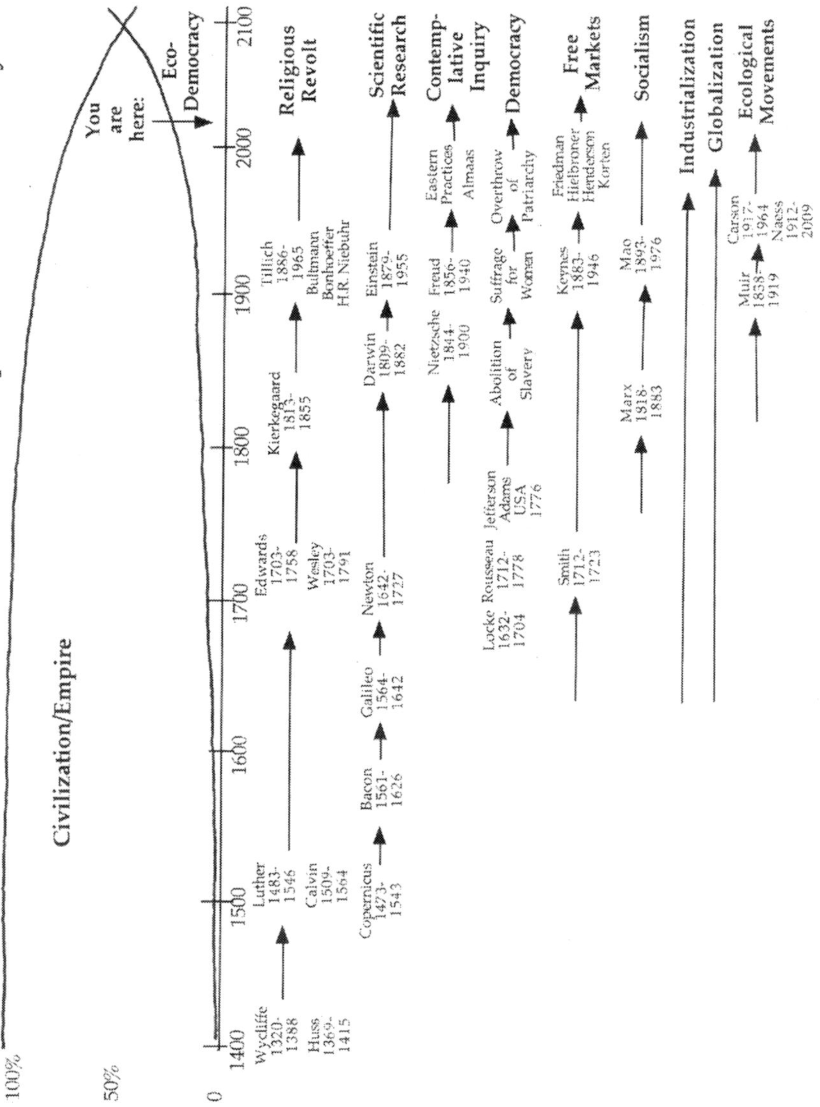

100%

50%

0

Civilization/Empire

You are here:

Eco-Democracy

1400   1500   1600   1700   1800   1900   2000   2100

Wycliffe 1320-1388

Huss 1369-1415

Luther 1483-1546

Calvin 1509-1564

Copernicus 1473-1543

Bacon 1561-1626

Galileo 1564-1642

Newton 1642-1727

Edwards 1703-1758

Wesley 1703-1791

Kierkegaard 1813-1855

Tillich 1886-1965

Bultmann Bonhoeffer H.R. Niebuhr

Religious Revolt

Darwin 1809-1882

Einstein 1879-1955

Scientific Research

Nietzsche 1844-1900

Freud 1856-1940

Eastern Practices Almaas

Contemplative Inquiry

Locke 1632-1704

Rousseau 1712-1778

Jefferson Adams USA 1776

Abolition of Slavery

Suffrage for Women

Overthrow of Patriarchy

Democracy

Smith 1712-1723

Keynes 1883-1946

Friedman Hielbroner Henderson Korten

Free Markets

Marx 1818-1883

Mao 1993-1976

Socialism

Industrialization

Globalization

Muir 1838-1919

Carson 1917-1964

Naess 1912-2009

Ecological Movements

Religious Revolt

In the West some very early revolts took place against empire and theocracy. English Theologian John Wycliffe (1328–1384) and Czech Catholic priest John Huss (1372-–1415) inspired significant revolts. In the sixteenth century, Martin Luther and John Calvin provided a deeper religious foundation for this revolt. One effect of the Protestant Reformation was to split the Holy Roman Empire into Nation States. These States were also imperial in their basic structures and qualities; nevertheless, empire and theocracy had been dealt a blow from which it never fully recovered. In the wake of Luther and Calvin appeared figures like Jonathan Edwards and John Wesley whose movements laid foundations for democracy and for the separation of church and state. The Quakers were even more radical in their commitment to democracy, communal forms, and the abolition of slavery. The Quakers initiated decision-making practices that were more democratic than those embodied in the US Constitution.

Although mainline Protestantism as well as Catholicism retained many imperial qualities, the impetus of the Protestant revolt has continued through the centuries to produce fresh critiques of the style of empire. In the nineteenth century the Christian existentialist philosopher and theologian Søren Kierkegaard gave focus to a renewal of religious revolt that flourished in the twentieth century. A number of twentieth-century Protestant theologians, including Karl Barth; Dietrich Bonhoeffer; Rudolf Bultmann; Reinhold and H. Richard Niebuhr; Paul Tillich; and many lesser-known names brought this revolt to its full fruition. Each of these theologians in his own way made clear that the Protestant principle meant living on the boundary; being social innovators; opposing nationalism, racism, and economic imperialism; and implying the end of empire and theocracy. Catholic theologians such as Teilhard de Chardin, Thomas Merton, Karl Rahner, Thomas Berry, and many lesser-known figures have also added insight to this discussion. Catholic liberation theologians like Peruvian

Gustavo Gutierrez and Brazilian Leonardo Boff also provide clear expressions of anti-imperial revolt. A growing number of Christians (Protestant, Catholic, and Orthodox) have embraced this reappearance of the "prophetic" core of the biblical heritage. These movements are an important ongoing force in the dismantling of empire and in opening the gateways for Eco-Democracy.

Similar movements have appeared within Judaism. Followers of Martin Buber and Abraham Heschel are examples. Movements within Hinduism and Buddhism are also providing spirit foundations for Eco-Democracy. Names like M. K. Gandhi, Thich Naht Hanh, and the Dalai Lama are well known. Islam also manifests a progressive element as well as its reactionary ferment. In Chart 12.2 we have cited a few Christian examples of this planet-wide religious revolt against empire. In the United States the reconstruction of Christian heritage has made and is making a large contribution to this transition and is still a crucial factor for the citizens of this and other Christianity-impacted nations. In other parts of the world, movements within other religious traditions are more important. This worldwide religious ferment can be deepening and enriching for all of us in our revolt against empire.

Scientific Research

A second long-standing revolt against empire is the love of and practice of fact-based and peer-reviewed science. The explosion of scientific knowledge and its resulting technologies have been used to strengthen civilizations and make them even more destructive. Nevertheless, the scientific attitude also breaks up tradition-based views of truth and opens the door for big social changes. Though science and technology have been used by tyrants to promote vicious empires, modern science has been and continues to be a frontal attack on the delivery of self-serving dogma from the aristocracy of hierarchical societies. The truly competent scientist is an obedient servant of a love of "reality" that is beyond the existing cultural canopy. Competent experimental science honors peer-reviewed sensory experience over the current social consensus. So practiced, science is revolutionary rather than a defender of the inherited concepts of hierarchical civilization. Names, like such as Copernicus, Galileo, Newton, Darwin, Pasteur, and Einstein illustrate the revolutionary potential of scientific research. All these and hundreds of other important figures shook up society.

Contemplative Inquiry

Alongside the scientific revolt against hierarchically imposed truth, we have experienced a resurgence of inward reflection. Such "contemplative inquiry" is also a revolt against the top-down dogmas of civilizations. It seeks wisdom for living in the core of human nature rather than in the existing traditions. Reflection on our inner being is ancient.

Around 500 BCE Siddhartha Gautama gave a profound boost to contemplative inquiry. The current resurgence of Buddhist practice within the United States is another thread of hope that is creating energy for building Eco-Democracy. Contemplative inquiry has also been given a boost by Western existential philosophers such as Søren Kierkegaard, Friedrich Nietzsche, Martin Heidegger, Albert Camus, and Jean Paul Sartre. The contemplative pursuit of truth has also been enriched by depth psychologists beginning with Sigmund Freud and including Carl Jung, Alfred Adler, Karen Horney, Rollo May, Fritz Perles, and others. The wisdom of these psychological movements has been blended with the resurgence of religious wisdom by contemporary synthesizers such as A. H. Almaas and others. Eco-Democracy is being fueled by this inward quest for the truth of our essential human nature.

Democracy

As a revolt against the standard pyramid of civilization, the democratic revolution has only begun. Democracy has ancient origins: we have defined tribal life as basically democratic.

Some Native American tribes had formed modes of democracy that were more democratic than the US Constitution.[38] And in the eighteenth century within the imperial civilizations of the Western World, European thinkers imagined revolutionary modes of democracy that were then established in the social life of the United States, France, England, and so on. The democratic element in the work of figures like John Locke, Jean-Jacques Rousseau, Thomas Jefferson, Benjamin Franklin, and John Adams constructed a significant and effective revolt against monarchy, empire, and the mode of social organization we call "civilization." In the United States the initially modest experiment in democracy has been expanded by the abolition of slavery, suffrage and opportunity for women, the labor union movements, the civil rights movements, ecological movements, and more. Democracy is an ongoing dynamic, not a static establishment. Democracy is a key thread well established in the past and potentially leading toward a fully realized Eco-Democracy. We will discuss this point further in the next chapter.

Market Economies

The development of market economics can also be viewed as a revolt against the standard pyramid of a royalty-owned-and-controlled civilization. Let us give Adam Smith his due as the initiator of the concept of a supply-and-demand market, unhampered by the micromanagement of governmental bureaucracies. John Maynard Keynes greatly enriched our grasp of these dynamics and how government can be useful in promoting workable markets. Milton Friedman illustrates how market "liberty" can be carried to unrealistic extremes. Market dynamics can be an element in our vision without succumbing to a pampering of the wealthy or a dog-eat-dog survival-of-the-fittest. Economists and writers like Robert Heilbroner, Hazel

---

[38] The widespread Iroquois Confederacy gave a vital role in decision making to all members, including women. See Jerry Mander, *The Loss of the Sacred* for further study of this topic.

Henderson, and David Korten provide us with encouraging visions of how market dynamics can be combined with programs of justice and ecological responsibility. In spite of all the perversions that have attached themselves to market practices, innovative markets within a democratic setting are an important feature in our vision of a viable Eco-Democracy.

Socialism

Socialism has been another thread in the vast transition period from civilization to Eco-Democracy. The Marxist critique of capitalism, however controversial, remains an important part of the discussion. It remains true that a market economy ruled by the wealthy classes is capable of injustices so severe that social collapse is made inevitable; however, the dictatorship of the working classes has been shown to also be an inadequate corrective. The actualization of such governance tends to become a state capitalism that creates a new sort of class society that also leads to injustices so severe that social collapse is inevitable. Nevertheless, the Marxist critique of capitalism remains one of the prophetic elements for building a viable future. We see this critique taking moderate forms in European and American labor movements and in progressive democratic governments that include many socialist elements. Economic justice, democracy, market aspects, and socialist aspects can be combined into a viable social vision for the future. More on this complex and controversial topic will be explored in Chapter 14.

Industrialization

In spite of over-industrialization and oppressive industrialization, industrialization remains another thread that leads from empire to an Eco-Democratic future. Humanity cannot and need not return to pre-industrial ways of life. Though many currently used technologies need to recede, the future will be characterized by powerful technologies, many of which have not yet been invented. Our "gee-whiz" over-optimism about technological fixes cries out to be chastened, but the ongoing development of useful ecologically friendly technologies made available to the masses of people will be an important aspect of a workable Eco-Democracy. The democracy-promoting and energy-saving aspects of the Internet development are an example. Also, a viable post-fossil fuel world depends upon key, effective, and continually improving technologies widely produced and easily available to people all across the planet. This wide-spread promotion of useful technologies is a gift of what we have called "industrialization."

The Industrial Revolution began with the introduction of the coal-fired steam engine in 1776 and can be described as essentially the replacement of animal energy (horses, oxen, men, etc.) with chemical energy: the combustion of organic matter, such as wood, coal, oil, and gas, plus fission. Thus, the Industrial Revolution essentially used yesteryears' solar energy that had been stored for us by nature in these chemical forms.

Today a second Industrial Revolution is required, which can be described as the replacement of yesteryears' solar energy with today's solar energy, not though chemicals but through wind turbines and solar panels.

Globalization

In this transition period, humanity has ceased to be isolated in separated civilizations and tribes. We now live in interrelations across the entire planet. Our economic practices, our political choices, and our cultural exchanges are planet-wide. There is no turning back on this still unfolding trend. Furthermore, our issue is not ending globalization, but choosing the type of globalization we need to advocate. Globalization in the hands of huge, profit-hungry, transnational corporations means a continuance of empire—the top-down ruthless domination that makes the rich richer, the poor poorer, and Earth devastated.

Globalization from Below is the title of an interesting book by Jeremy Brecher, Tim Costello, and Brendan Smith.[39] The key idea in this book states, "Our hope rests in promoting a form of globalization that is derived from decision making that takes place in local communities and regions."

The globalization of our lives has been a step toward a viable future for humanity, and this remains true even though the tragic colonial practices of existing civilizations have been an imperial cooption of the more positive aspects of this thread. Our experience of the entire planet has been and can continue to be a cultural as well as economic benefit to each human. Further, it will not work to isolate ourselves into small clans basically separated from the gifts of and the responsibilities for the entire planet.

Ecological Movements

None of these threads of progressive change are more important than the ecological movements. Ecological challenges affect the entire planet as a viable home for humanity. We need to give special thanks to those who have so recently built momentum on this front. The many movements toward ecological sanity owe their inspiration to persons too numerous to mention. As symbols on chart 12.2 we name John Muir, Rachel Carson, and Arne Naess. Ecology has become a popular topic, but the depth of the ecological vision is still hugely revolutionary. Every aspect of human society needs an ecological transformation. Though ecological movements are the most recent of these many threads into the future, ecological competence is a foundation stone upon which the entire building of Eco-Democracy must be built. Responsible ecological decisions and behavior must become an integral part of our economic system—not a volunteer virtue alongside old practices. We have only begun the ecological component of this transition. Nevertheless, we can take hope from this beginning.

---

[39] Jeremy Brecher, Costello T, and Smith B, *Globalization from Below* (Cambridge, MA: South End Press, 2000)

* * * * * * * *

In the following chapters of Part Two we examine how the threads of this transition period can come together into a viable, workable, just, and desirable society. In Chapters 13 and 14 we will examine how ecology, democracy, market freedom, and socialism are traditions that can enrich each other rather than fight each other. We will show how avoiding ecological doom depends upon an appropriate balance between market freedom and socialism. In Chapter 15 we discuss how a union between scientific research and contemplative inquiry can move toward fresh agreements on social workability. Then in Chapter 16 we discuss how thinking beyond the box of civilization gives us a new set of political positions. The aim in each of these chapters is to envision the next social mode of human organization as something new and yet something woven from threads that have significant histories. We live in a period of transition in which the old mode of social organization (called "civilization") is undergoing its terminal decay. Nevertheless, many social inventions that were conceived and built in the civilization era are gifts for the future. These gifts are like batons that need to be passed to the next mode of social organization. We face a huge sorting out of the past as we build a very different future.

The many aspects of this vast transition from civilization to Eco-Democracy are taking place within the house of civilization. This is different from the transition from tribal societies to civilizations. Civilizations came into being alongside tribal societies. They either swallowed these smaller societies or forced them to move to out-of-the-way places. But post-civilization societies are emerging within civilizations. Civilization is being dismantled piece by piece, while Eco-Democracy is growing inside the body of civilization like a butterfly in its caterpillar. Eco-Democracy will need to take flight sometime in the next century. The caterpillar of civilization is dying, but it is also the mother of and compost for Eco-Democracy.

Chapter 13

Democracy as an
Unfinished Revolution

When we say that democracy is a core element in the Eco-Democracy mode of social organization, we do not mean a static image of "democracy." We do not mean a mere honoring of the US Constitution. As we have already noted, US democracy has been improved over the centuries, especially for women, African Americans, Native Americans, and laboring people. We are currently broadening our democracy for Hispanic immigrants, same-sex couples, gay and lesbian individuals, and more. Nevertheless, these ongoing improvements (as well as the basic tenets of democracy) are being threatened by a backlash of in-group bigotry and by big-money rule over our democratic institutions. The fight for democracy, true democracy, is far from over.

We are awakening to the need for broadening and deepening democratic practice. Meaningful participation by more people at the grassroots level is key. An informed citizenry who talk to one another about the serious issues of the day is a necessary state of affairs for a fully realized democracy. But the style of our busy rat-race society afflicts us with too much work in order to make ends meet or sustain some economic status. This desperate busyness is exploited by the wealthy and power-hungry few who want to make all the decisions. The busy masses are bombarded with carefully crafted media messages that distract and profoundly misinform citizens. The misinformed vote on issues they do not understand and do not feel they have time to understand. Invisible sources use our television screens to beam crafted lies as if they were valid positions. These clever lies appeal to popular prejudices and dismiss the most promising possibilities. This is not democracy.

Fresh democratic structures are required to truly involve the citizenry. New institutions must replace and/or transform the current *major media*—print and broadcast—currently owned and controlled by mega-corporations. We are seeing the demise of competitive newsgathering, aggressive investigative reporting, and appropriately critical editorials and commentaries. Most of the readily available "news" is highly filtered and shaped to suit the establishment.

Jim Rough has proposed a *fourth branch of government* that emphasizes consensus building by ordinary citizens at every scope of governance.[40] We need to open our minds to some fresh imagination in this direction. Suppose that at every governmental level twenty-four registered voters were selected for duty the way we now select people for a jury panel. These citizens would be paid to take a week or more of time from their busy lives for talking through relevant issues and publishing their findings for the rest of the voters at that governmental scope. This would not be law making, but it would be consensus building. It would enrich the consensus and provide some additional context within which to choose representatives who would more accurately represent the people in the work of detailed lawmaking. Such a branch of government would augment the people power of labor unions and nonprofit organizations.

Here is another important democracy-promoting innovation: *more meaningful political districts*. The political subdivisions with which we are saddled today in most parts of the United States are almost entirely anachronistic. They were typically defined in a bygone time for reasons that today are

---

[40] For further study of his idea see Jim Rough's book *Society's Breakthrough! Releasing Essential Wisdom and Virtue in All the People* (2002).

irrelevant. Voting districts are often entirely absurd. Instead of these gerrymandered weird-shaped districts created for some political party's power purposes, we could establish districts in a manner that emphasizes communities of people. Such "districts" would, over time, build communal feelings, sensibilities, values, and common directions.

Let us also emphasize building *community with all the life-forms and with all the geographical features* in our home regions. With these expanded "home feelings" we could allow and encourage citizens to focus on how these regions need to be responsibly cared for by the people who live there.

In this short chapter we do not presume to spell out the details of a restructured democracy, but we do want to emphasize this point: *democracy is not a finished product*. Democracy is an ongoing development of ever-new systems of government that ever more completely embody the vision of government of the people, by the people, and for the people. We don't need to apologize for not knowing fully how our new democracy will look. We are building something that has not existed before. We won't fully know how it works until we are working it.

Unless we can build genuine democracies that include active local community participation, effective consensus building, and processes that are exciting for most people, everything else we are saying in this book becomes unworkable.

Chapter 14

Ecology, Democracy, Market Freedom, and Socialism

As we make ecology and democracy primary, we set a fresh context for our economic considerations. We need to probe deeply into how ecology, democracy, market freedom, and socialism are threads that can be woven into common features of a new style of economic life within this new mode of social organization we are calling "Eco-Democracy." These four threads of ongoing change are already in motion, but deep tensions exist between them. Nevertheless, they can be reconciled into an overall pattern of social life. Viewed separately these four threads can appear conflictual, even irreconcilable. But if we take a longer view, we can see how these threads can reinforce each other and check each other's exaggerations and incompletions. No tension is greater than the free-market/socialism rift.

The Market-Freedom/Socialism Rift

A huge rift has existed between the loyal followers of Adam Smith and those of Karl Marx—that is, between the proponents of market freedom and those of socialism. But if we take a longer view, we can see that both traditions are dealing with the role of government—with the role that government needs to take in a post-medieval society. Both traditions claim to be democratic. Both traditions struggle with themes of justice and equity. Both have opposed the vicious perversions exemplified by Adolph Hitler, Benito Mussolini, and other modern advocates of absolute monarchy.

At the same time both socialist and market societies have spawned their own versions of vicious top-down governance. Joseph Stalin was a prime example of this occurrence within socialist history. We can also include the various horror stories of Eastern Europe. Socialist theory has claimed the high road of justice and "economic democracy." But in practice such idealism was too often compromised; the "dictatorship of the proletariat" became an all-powerful oligarchy that forbad dissent. Perhaps Marx, Engels, and Lenin were correct to assume that extremely firm governmental structures were needed to put wealthy aristocratic tyrants in their place. But once this was done, the resulting centralization of power easily created a "new class" of governmental autocrats.

The neoconservative government of George W. Bush symbolizes a "free-market" type of vicious top-down oligarchic rule. This administration illustrates the antidemocratic inclination within market economies that encourage entrepreneurial freedom. Though masked by an overlay of democracy, this brand of governance maintained the rulership of a moneyed aristocracy over every hint of democratic populism. The second Bush administration also resisted legal restraints on what right-wing ideologues called "the unitary executive." This phrase is a cleaned up term for "autocrat," and it needs to be exposed as a regression from the core principles of the US Constitution. In other words, the second Bush administration was basically dictatorial; it was not responsive to what the majority of the people wanted. It was not even responsive to the factual truth on various controversial topics. It attempted to impose its own "truth" (propaganda, spins, misinformation, lies) and then expected to be afforded the honor of having a "democratic" position worthy of public "objectivity." Such an attitude is not democracy. Our so-called "conservative" thinkers and leaders within market freedom societies have typically favored the maximization of wealth-making opportunities for the owners of great wealth. Democracy is thereby abandoned and oligarchy is promoted. The wealth owners and the top-executives are favored to the detriment of wage earners and mid-level salary earners. Furthermore, ecological issues become irresolvable in a society that supports wealth making over the common good and even the truth.

Both socialist and market-freedom economies go astray when oligarchy rather than democracy is promoted. Only when democracy is fully operative can there be a people- and Earth-friendly mixed economy that honors the best of both market freedom and socialist traditions. At their best, socialist governments have shown that many economic activities can best benefit the natural environments and a majority of the people when a sensitive and responsive government manages those activities. Sewage disposal, water supply, and public transportation are among the clearer examples. Electrical power supply could also be included. And most ecological protections and restorations absolutely depend on governmental laws and policies. Other aspects of society work best when the decisions are made in the give and take of market dynamics that decentralize decision making to the innovators and customers. The Internet revolution has been driven by innovators and customers. No government program could have done this.

Today, many democratically governed market economies have learned to be moderately socialistic in an increasing number of areas. Many European nations (for example Sweden, Finland, Denmark) have integrated socialist practices into democratic market societies. To a lesser extent this is also true of the United States. Social Security, Medicare, unemployment payments, public parks, public libraries, and public schools are all examples of integrating socialist elements into a market-enterprise democracy. The alternative to having these government-managed programs is the further concentration of wealth and privilege and the further impoverishment of everyone else.

In the Socialist Republic of China we see vibrant market processes being expanded within a still intact socialism. In Latin American countries such as Brazil, Bolivia, and Venezuela, we see a rich blend of socialism, democracy, and market freedom.

Some US observers fear Hugo Chavez of Venezuela will become a dictator, but at the present time honest democratic elections are supporting him with more than 60 percent of the vote. To the astonishment of many US pundits, Chavez is viewed throughout much of Central and South America as fresh hope for viable democratic government. Whatever be the virtue or vice of any of these experiments, they illustrate that the blending of market freedom and socialist traditions is already part of our lives. An Eco-Democratic society will manifest neither pure capitalism nor pure socialism. Some form of "mixed" economy is clearly the direction for a viable social future.

By "mixed economy" we mean a society that is willing to raise all these questions: (1) Which activities are best left primarily in the hands of the private sector? (2) Which activities are best left primarily in the hands of the public sector? (3) What regulations of the market are appropriate to ensure that market activities are conducted with equity and justice? (4) What checks and balances are appropriate to ensure that public-sector activities are conducted with equity and justice?

Adam Smith recognized that even in a society that emphasized market freedom, the government must keep the market "efficient." This has been done through antitrust laws, pure food and drug acts, truth in advertising, fair weights and measures, accurate financial reporting, prohibition of predatory pricing, etc. Recently in the United States we have seen an erosion of the enforcement of such laws. This lack of enforcement has contributed to the corruption and criminal behavior we have seen in today's corporations. The absence of firm governmental enforcement has severely weakened consumer protections and even the optimal functioning of the market. Adam Smith would be outraged by some of those who claim to be his ideological descendants. By ignoring the safeguards that Smith saw as necessary, we have created a distortion of his intention, which was to maximize social and economic benefits and optimum resource allocation.

We have seen that Smith was overly optimistic about the power of the market's "invisible hand" to produce wholesome order, but socialist thinkers need to give Smith and his market dynamics their appropriate due. If well regulated, innovative market economy decentralizes and democratizes economic decision-making. This result supports democracy. Governmental bureaucrats cannot handle the vast data involved in micromanaging a complex economy. The somewhat ordered chaos of a market economy does many things better than the often overzealous social planning by centralized agencies.

Pure socialist government tends to own and manage almost every economic function. Free-market purists want to privatize almost everything. In an Eco-Democracy we must get beyond such ideological purity. Privatizing is not right or wrong in and of itself. Government ownership and management is not right or wrong, in and of itself. The questions are: What can be managed best by a democratic government, and what can be managed best by private enterprise?

And by "democratic" we mean letting the people decide what to do and what not to do. We need to become strictly practical about these matters. Let us learn from both our capitalist heritage and our socialist heritage how to do things that might be useful in building our Eco-Democratic societies. *Indeed, let us bury the hatchets of warfare between the capitalist and socialist sides of our memory banks and start emphasizing democracy and ecology.* Let us decide that the vision of an Eco-Democracy can guide us in making appropriate socialist and market choices.

The Contribution of Ecological Primacy

Beginning with the very first chapter of this book, we have maintained that ecological responsibility is primary. In our economic discourse we need to include the awareness that the natural planet's contribution to human well-being is many times greater than the contributions being made by humanly-created economies. Both socialist and market societies have typically emphasized using the natural planet for humanity with little or no attention to the limits of the planet's ability to support an ever-expanding industrial economy. Likewise, both socialist and market societies have failed to embrace the responsibility that human societies must take for the well-being of the overall planetary foundation.

When a socialist, free-enterprise, or mixed economy neglects its ecological foundations, immense tragedies are set in motion. The entire society is distorted. Even the interior lives of people become truncated and abstracted from their natural sensibilities. The modern era of human history has been characterized by an alienation from nature, from the human body, and from a sense of geographical place and responsibility for that place. Affirming the primacy of ecology is the key progressive thread that can correct these tragic distortions.

As suggested in the title of the recent documentary *The Eleventh Hour*, we are fast approaching "midnight" for a continuing human presence on this planet. Earth will recover from its adventure with humanity; Earth has a "world of time." Humanity does not.

The Contribution of Democracy

We have named our future vision of a human society "Eco-Democracy" because both ecology and democracy are the primary corrective forces that make a society viable. Democracy in this context means the opposite of top-down, hierarchical, dictatorial rulership. Democracy means grassroots responsibility functionally organized so that every local citizen is expected to participate in decision making, and his or her participation is expected to count in the final working through of common social decisions.

If the democratic factor is weak or missing, a society cannot solve its ecological crises or meet its requirements for justice, effective social order, prosperity, freedom, and opportunity for the pursuit of happiness. Workable and thoroughgoing democracies that carry out the people's consensus on economic, ecological, and all other matters are an urgent priority. Firm governmental regulation is not tyranny if the aims and means of that regulation have been chosen through effective democratic processes by a well-informed citizenry.

Minority protections are also important not only for justice to individuals but also for the well-being of ongoing and appropriate social changes. There will always be elements of the population who will oppose the current general will of the people, and it is important to protect these minorities from the tyranny of the majority. Democracy is much more than majority rule. One could argue that majority ruled when the Nazi Party came to power in Germany. The hard part about democracy is that it must include full protection of the rights of the minority, including those who have no voice of their own.

A Bill of Rights has been an effective democratic means of doing this. Most major useful innovations begin within some creative minority. At the same time, there will always be reactionary and criminal minorities who need to be restrained by a "responsible" majority. These tensions will not disappear. Nevertheless, it is more often true than not that the general will supports a better approximation of justice and wisdom than the empowerment of any small group of "powerful people" who are unrestrained by that general will. "Power tends to corrupt and absolute power corrupts absolutely."[41] The restraint of power by the participation of the general citizenry is an essential factor in our vision of Eco-Democracy.

---

[41] From a letter by Lord Acton to Bishop Mandell Creighton in 1887.

Chapter 15
Facts, Authenticity, and Workability

The "great transition" we are discussing will require ongoing thought. It is not a finished model waiting to be put into place. It is an emerging consensus in process of being thought, revised, built, and rebuilt. Our methods of thinking, however, have a degree of permanence. If we are to succeed we will need to be scientists who seek and trust the facts. We will need to be contemplative inquirers who uncover and serve human authenticity. We will need to combine our scientific knowledge and contemplative wisdom into workable patterns of social operation that we can agree to practice together.

Many persons in the US culture, some quite brilliant, emphasize the scientific method as the exclusive approach to truth. Artistic creation, depth psychology, and interior inquiry are minimized or dismissed as arbitrary opinion or the expression of mere personal feelings, not truth. Others have emphasized contemplative inquiry in a manner that minimizes or dismisses scientific knowledge. Both of these extremes are unfortunate positions. Scientific research and contemplative inquiry are complementary approaches to truth. Both are necessary. Contemplative inquiry gives us grounding in the development of values and motives that can open our basic curiosity and guide us in our choice of topics for scientific research. Science, not contemplation, reveals to us the concrete limits and possibilities for our social vision and strategy. Though profoundly different, scientific research and contemplative inquiry are mutually enhancing, complementary approaches to truth.

Both of these approaches to truth have been and will continue to be opponents of the top-down tyranny of hierarchical impositions of truth. Both approaches to truth challenge the credibility of the repetitive assertions of tradition-based institutions. Both debunk imperialistic thinkers who support the values of the "upper" classes and use pseudo-scientists and old cultural traditions to support their lies.

Senator Inhofe of Oklahoma provides an example of this way of thinking in his arguments that global warming is a hoax.[42] He refuses to accept the views of the majority of scientists because these views imply the need for a policy of reducing our production of greenhouse gases. Such a direction does not fit with his oil company loyalties, so he looks for other "scientists" who can shed doubt on the majority view.

Inhofe is not the only politician who operates in this manner. Many scientists in forest management became infuriated with the George W. Bush administration because that administration paid no attention to their science if it did not fit with that administration's forestry policy that favored business profits over the truth of responsible forestry.

A similar mode of argument is used by many conservative Christians; they resist scientific research on the historical development of biblical literature if those scientific findings do not support their doctrines. Doctrinaire religious communities will also resist the truth of contemplative inquiry if their doctrines are not supported.

Eco-Democracy, as we envision it, is not a new dogma propagated from some authoritative "top" and imposed on the "ignorant" masses. The masses may indeed be uninformed and unaware, but the truth of Eco-Democracy is a truth that can be discerned by any person who is willing to face the facts and interpret those facts through a screen of values discovered by viewing in depth what it means to be an aware human being. In other words, Eco-Democracy is an ongoing process of

---

[42] Senator James Inhofe was chairman of the Environment and Public Works Committee until Senator Barbara Boxer replaced him.

pulling together an ever-improving consensus among people who are willing to identify with both competent science and honest contemplation.

This synthesis of scientific research and contemplative inquiry is a clarification of the quest for truth that needs to be learned by the adult citizenry of every society. This synthesis needs to undergird our educational system, our media, our personal decision-making, and our political discourse.

As this synthesis takes place, a third primary approach to truth comes into view. We can call it "social workability." However deeply we understand our essential humanity and however fully we learn the facts of our times, we still lack core guidelines for the practical operation of our society. These guidelines can come into being through effective consensus building. As citizens discern our deep humanness and understand the facts, we can find consensus on workable social alternatives.

We do not discover this "workability" alone. We build it together neighborhood by neighborhood, community by community, region by region, continent by continent. We need consensus building institutions within which to do this, and we need good methods for our thinking and working together. And most of all we need to renounce rigid ideological principles, moral absolutes, and authoritarian beliefs. "Workability" means honoring the following questions: What works for our survival and our flourishing as human beings? What works for the viable functioning of a planet that can maintain a human population? What size and quality of human population can be so maintained? These and other such questions drive our "social workability" quest for truth and appropriate action.

Chapter 16

A New Spectrum of Political Positions

As we gain clarity on the transitional era in which we live, we are witnessing the emergence of four basic political positions:

1. Save Civilization
2. It is Already Too Late to Save the Human Species
3. Build Tribal Societies
4. Build a Planet-wide, Post-Civilization Alternative

1) The first position might be summarized as "saving civilization." The other three agree that civilization/empire need to be dismantled.
2) The second position takes the view that no future for the human species is possible. According to this view, we have already gone too far with the consequences of civilization: we have already overshot Earth's capacities to sustain the human species (or we soon will).
3) The third position claims that tribal forms of human society worked well for at least a hundred thousand years and that our best hope for the future is creating an updated form of tribal society for a few billion humans.
4) The fourth position claims that neither tribal society nor civilization is a viable option for the future; nevertheless, our situation is not entirely hopeless. We can invent a post-civilization form of planet-wide society that is ecologically sustainable, viable, just, and workable for perhaps four or five billion human beings.

1. Save Civilization

The first of these political positions includes a wide diversity of sub-positions. We have called them "left," "right," and "center" and variations on each. Here is a right to left list of the most prominent of these positions:

a. Right-wing dictatorship
b. Free-enterprise, moneyed aristocratic rule with large commitments to military power, and minimal nods toward democratic processing
c. Moderate free-enterprise democratic rule
d. Progressive mixed-economy democratic rule
e. Democratic socialism
f. Dictatorial communism

All six of these political positions understand themselves as saving civilization—saving their version of civilization, of course. "Civilization" and "civilized" have become poorly defined words that are typically used to mean nothing more helpful than "good society." But descriptively and historically "civilization" reveals itself as a hierarchical, pyramidal, top-down-conducted society with vast economic differences among its members and a sense of prerogative for continuing to increase its use of the resources of the planet. When we view "civilization" in this light, we can see why many of us have suggested that the civilization mode of social organization is the core problem. And as we have pointed out in previous chapters, these patterns are unsustainable. Civilization is a mode of social organization that will carry humanity into the abyss of ecological starvation and/or into unworkable social chaos. Rather than asking humans to save civilization, both humans and the planet need to be saved from civilization.

2. It is Already Too Late to Save the Human Species

This position is a more viable position than most of us wish to admit. The dire ecological condition of the planet is the overwhelming truth that seems to support this position. It is possible that existing civilizations may conduct unending warfare for the increasingly scarce resources of fresh water, arable land, energy sources, etc. Evidence also exists for the prospect of social chaos: large pockets of grueling poverty, poor nutrition for many people, disease and pandemics, failing infrastructures, and natural disasters for which no adequate social response is affordable. All these factors combine to give this political position a realism that cannot be overlooked.

Nevertheless, part of the hopelessness of this position is rooted in a lack of imagination. This position is actually the mirror image of saving civilization. Those who hold this position typically do not attempt to envision a positive future for the current human population of the planet other than continuing some sort of civilization. Thus these persons are hopeless when confronted with the realization that saving civilization is indeed hopeless. This position will continue to be held by large sectors of the human population because it is simply true that we cannot save humanity if we believe that the only sort of humanity worth saving is a humanity that is organized in the civilization mode of social organization. So, what we have in this view is a lack of imagination with regard to a viable alternative to civilization and a means of getting *there* from *here*.

3. Build Tribal Societies

We can easily understand why many minds have taken this position. Once we face the failure and hopelessness of the civilization mode of society, we can notice that tribal society is the only other alternative with which humanity has had extensive experience.

But if we define tribal society as intimate societies comprised of a relatively small number of people who live with one another for a whole lifetime, we can see the limitations of this position. For good or for ill, all the humans on this planet have become interdependent. There is no return to isolated groups. Ecological problems, health problems, and many others problems unite all of us on a planet-wide basis. For example, we are creating a climate crisis that affects everyone. We are also united by wider perspectives, instant communication, fast transportation, and many other factors. Tribal organizations do not give us solutions to these planet-wide aspects of responsibility. Those who envision a type of tribal society that has Internet connection and other forms of high-tech support need to face up to the fact that providing such support entails a wider-than-tribal arrangement.

Then too this position visualizes only a small number of survivors. Each tribe requires room. We cannot expect twelve billion, six billion, or even two billion people living in tribal arrangements. An enormous catastrophe is presupposed here.

Most important of all, this political position offers no antidote to the continued existence of oppressive civilizations that organize extensive military power to plunder the last remaining resources of the planet at the expense of any and all tribal experiments. Some holders of this position assume that civilizations will simply crumble away because of their inherent inadequacies, but what may actually happen is that reactionary civilizations in panic to survive will take the whole human species into the abyss. We will need to dismantle every civilization piece by piece and replace it with alternatives that restrain every reemergence of these oppressive, pyramidal, human organizations.

4. Build a Planet-Wide, Post-Civilization Alternative

This is the most difficult position to describe; yet it is the most promising alternative. It combines whatever gifts the 5400 years of civilization and the 100,000 years of tribal society have to offer. At the same time it is a fresh creation, a mode of human society that has no precedent in the past. It is an ecologically obedient society, a democratic society, a decentralized society, and yet a society of planet-wide scope and responsibility. It is this vision of society we have been picturing with the term "Eco-Democracy." Such society is organized from the grassroots out to the wider scopes. These wider scopes are confederations of the smaller scopes. Through these confederations each local scope of society can take responsibility for all the other local scopes of society. These are some of the basic guidelines, but the details of making such a society work are not yet invented, and the thorny issues to be resolved are almost boundless. Nevertheless, this overall position is clearly distinguishable from the other three. It rejects the hopelessness of position two and the naive hope of positions one and three. It sees the hope for a viable future as a step-by-step dismantling of civilization and a step-by-step inventing of a mode of social organization that has never existed before.

The challenge inherent in this political alternative is the huge demand on our imagination to come up with innovative solutions, to inspire enthusiasm, to maintain clarity, and to organize the number of people required to actually build this potential future.

Conclusions

Unlike position one, position two has the gift of realism about the extent of our challenges, but position two lacks imagination about how we might meet those challenges. A core virtue of positions three and four is that they imagine a future that is different from a further elaboration of the social form we call "civilization." The virtue of position three is that it has some fairly clear images about tribal forms of organization; however, position three is not clear about the unworkability of the tribal vision on a planet-wide basis. Position four can, in principle, resolve the planet-wide workability issue, but it is harder to be clear about what this unprecedented vision actually means. Until spelled out more clearly, position four runs the risk of falling back into position one—promoting minor reforms of civilization rather than offering a thoroughgoing post-civilization solution. Position four also contains the difficulty that it calls for dismantling civilization while at the same time constructing the post-civilization replacement that contains some of the gifts of civilization. This will continue to be a source of complexity that may be confusing to many.

Nevertheless, position four is the position of realistic hope. It is our only hope because it does not take refuge in some illusory hope or give in to a lazy, unimaginative hopelessness. It faces the real conditions that must be faced to find the hope that exists in those conditions. The challenge of position four is that it requires tremendous awareness, imagination, and creativity as well as some industrious patience and hard work on the part of a large percentage of the human species. One might argue that we are not up to doing alternative four, or at least not enough of us are up to it. And it is surely true that a great number will not be up to it. The realistic hope in position four includes the assumption that the minority who now hold this position can become a workable majority through effective awakening, education, and leadership-training efforts. Such hope is never certain. But if it is our only realistic hope, it does tend to focus the mind.

Never before have humans faced such a challenge. Successful tribal societies were put together over tens of thousands of years of trial and error. The mode of civilization matured over many centuries. The transition to an Eco-Democratic society must take place one piece at a time and be fully underway in a mere century. Furthermore, it must take place through our own deliberate and well-thought-out designs. If we do not meet this huge challenge, most or all that we know and love will surely perish. Can we combine in our psyche this urgency with the patient happy work it will take to meet the challenge?

* * * * * * * *

In Part Two, our aim was to present a simplified picture of the overall turning point of our times. Obviously, much more attention to the details of this turning will be needed by those who take on the task of transformation. Following are five books we recommend for further reading on the nature of this massive turning in social organization.

David C. Korten, *The Great Turning: From Empire to Earth Community* (Bloomfield, CT: Kumarian Press & San Francisco, CA: Berrett-Koehler, 2006)

Charlene Spretnak, *The Resurgence of the Real: Body, Nature, and Place in a Hypermodern World* (New York City: Routledge, 1999)

Charles Eisenstein, *The Ascent of Humanity: The Age of Separation, the Age of Reunion, and the Convergence of Crises that is Birthing the Transition* (Harrisburg PA: Panenthea Press, 2007),

Charlene Spretnak, *Relational Reality: New Discoveries of Interrelatedness that are Transforming the Modern World* (Topsham, ME: Green Horizon Books, 2011)

Lewis Mumford, *The Transformations of Man: A Profound Interpretation of Mankind, Its History, and Its Hope for the Future* (New York: Collier Books, 1956)

Part Three:

Seeing Society Whole

Though we talk about economics incessantly in our culture, too few of us have an inclusive model of what economics is, what economics has always been, and what economics must include in any future society. In Chapter 17 we will present a model of economic processes that applies to any society past, present, or future. This model may be improved, but the reality being modeled is universal. Such a model is a guide to seeing economics whole and thus creating future solutions that are holistic.

Similarly, in Chapter 18 we will present a model of political processes that applies to any society. Political processes include more than campaigning, elections, and the work of office holders. Political processes include everything that has to do with group decision-making and the carrying out of those decisions. Seeing the political processes in a whole and universal way will assist us to overcome our obsession with one small part of political life or our animosity toward political affairs in general.

Then in Chapter 19 we will present a model of the third major aspect of any society. Cultural processes will be our name for this dimension of human society. It includes educational fabrics, media, life styles, customs, roles, languages, artistic expressions, and religious formations. It includes everything that has to do with giving form to human consciousness and the communication of that consciousness. Cultural processes have sometimes been neglected in our vision of social engagement. We will contend that they are foundational, especially in the type of long-range transition in which we are involved.

Finally in Chapter 20 we will discuss how these three major aspects of society need to be balanced. We will indicate how our imbalance toward economics is one of our key maladies, a malady that needs to be corrected to make viable a future human presence on this planet.

Chapter 17

Economic Processes

We cannot fully understand what we mean by "economic processes" until we understand how economic processes are related to the other processes that comprise a human society. Below is a model of the essential processes of a whole human society. **Economic processes** are the "taking in" or "input" dynamic of a whole society. Earth resources are gathered, produced for human consumption, and then distributed. The **political processes** are the "active" or "organizing" dynamic within society. The political is where geography is defined, social order is maintained, and ongoing decision-making is facilitated and executed. The **cultural processes** provide the underlying "purposes" or "meanings" or "conscious articulations" of the whole society. We can break that down into a society's common sense, common style, and common symbolization through languages, arts, and religious formations.

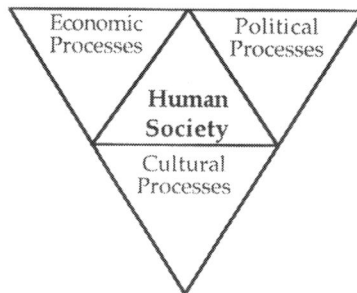

Our triangular models are built upon this basic pattern of human consciousness: human consciousness is a polarity of (1) **attention** or "taking in" reality; and (2) **intention** or "putting out" initiative. Unlike a rock, an amoeba takes in information and makes appropriate responses toward food and away from danger. A human being takes in reality much more inclusively and makes responses of greater complexity and consequence than the simple amoeba. And this taking-in and putting-out polarity is undergirded by a context of (3) **self-awareness**.

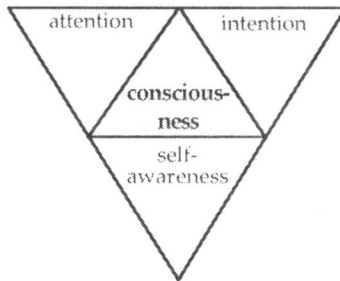

This mode of social modeling has proved extremely illuminating in describing what is basic or essential about every human society. For example, viewing economic processes within the larger picture of political and cultural processes helps us clarify that whenever we are dealing with fundamental economic issues, there can be no *merely* economic solutions. Large economic problems require economic, political, and cultural solutions. Also, this mode of triangular modeling enables us to comprehensively examine the subparts of economic processes. Following is our effort toward envisioning the inclusive subparts of essential economic processes.

Every society must pull **resources** from nature for its use, transform those resources into useful products and services (**production**), and **distribute** those products and services to the society. These three processes (resources, production, and distribution) define the overall social process called "economics." There can be other models of what comprises "economics," but this model is deeply embedded in the economic discourse of many centuries. In this chapter we will define these three economic processes in more detail; then in the following chapters we will examine how economic processes relate to the rest of human society.

Here is our model of the economic processes that are found in every human society. The institutionalizations and practices of these universal processes differ greatly from society to society, but these basic processes are essential to the nature of human society. This chart defines what we mean by economic processes. All the names on this and other charts are meant to be descriptive not judgmental. We must judge the manner in which we structure these universal processes, but the processes themselves are unavoidable aspects of every whole society.

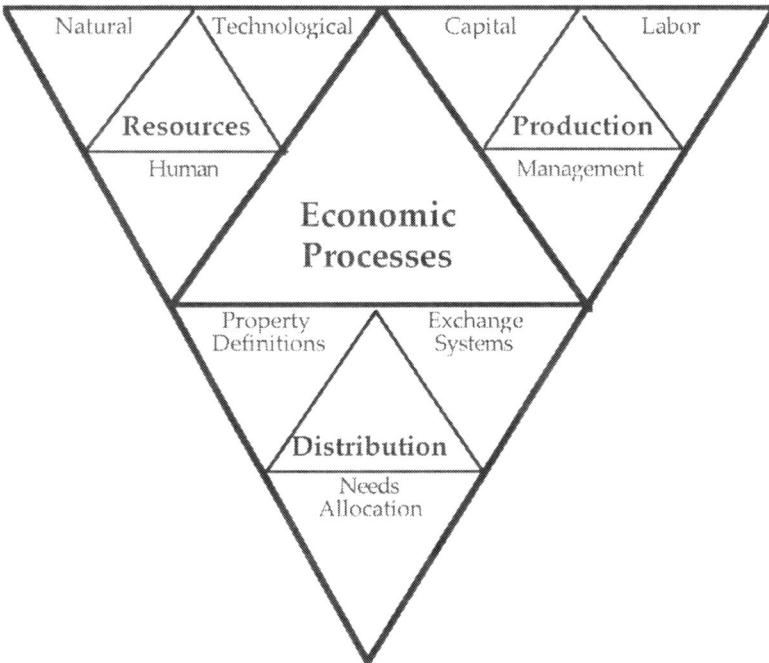

The arrangement of the elements on this chart follows the pattern outlined above: in the upper left triangle of each set of three triangles is the "taking in" dynamic. For example, resource processes take in what society needs to function. In the upper right triangle in each set of triangles is the "active" dynamic. For example, production processes transform resources into useful products and services. In the lower triangle in each set of triangles is the process that gives meaning or purpose to the upper two triangles. For example, the distribution of goods and services is the purpose of the whole economic enterprise. Distribution gives meaning to everything that goes on in an economy.

If the prepared products and services are not distributed, the human economy is entirely frustrated. Moreover, it is the need for distribution that makes meaningful what is produced and determines what aspects of nature are counted as resources. For example, iron was not considered a resource for human societies until it was discovered that useful products could be made from it. Similarly, how to repair a carburetor was not a technological resource in a stone-age society, and how to chip flint is not a technological resource of great importance today.

Like all models built by the human mind, this model of society can be improved. Nevertheless, it is important to have such a model in order to see the whole reality of economics and to view all the aspects involved in building a workable economic system for the future. The power of this manner of modeling society will become clearer as we describe it in more detail. We begin with the set of social processes we call "resources."

Resources

As a set of social processes, resources includes not only the use of **nature** in general but also the use of human beings to do society's work. **Human** beings are both elements of the society to be served by the society and resources that the society uses to produce these services and products that are then distributed.

In addition, the **technological** knowledge and skills of these human beings can also be seen as resources for the society. For example, if a trained physician leaves a society, that entails a resource loss for that society.

So here is an inclusive model of the basic processes that comprise the resource aspect of any human economy:

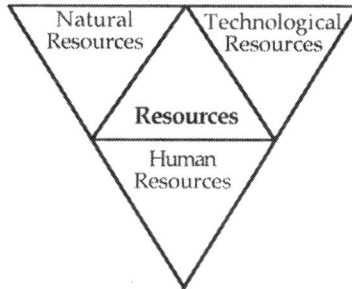

Natural resources are the resources that are taken in from outside of the society. *Technological resources* are human knowledge, experience, skills, and abilities possessed by the active members of the society. And *human resources* are the living human beings who bind the other two types of resources together into one overall resource dynamic.

Production

How might we delineate the three major sub-processes of the overall process of production? The process of production can be shown to include the process of *capital means*, the process of *managerial functions*, and the process of *laboring forces*. In order to produce something, the **capital means** of producing it must be established. This includes the intellectual designs, the buildings, the equipment, and the funds necessary to start up the enterprise. In order to produce something, **managerial functions** are needed to provide order to the production process so that the required product or service is actually produced and made available. Thirdly, **laboring forces** are those persons who carry out the actual human work of production.

In our typical industrial arrangements, capital, management, and labor are roles played by different people, and severe conflicts may exist among them. In some organizations, such as a worker-owned-and-controlled cooperative, the capital owners, the managers, and the laborers are all drawn from the same pool of persons. We are attempting to point to enduring dynamics that can be found in any human society. Though the words we use tend to take on meanings that derive from a particular mode of society, our aim here is the look beyond these limitations to what is universal. We assert that capital of some sort, management of some sort, and labor of some sort are actually present in every society. A vision of society in which one of these processes is missing is just a picture in someone's head, a picture that is out of touch with the reality of an actual human society. The terminology we use may not exist in every society, but the processes we are indicating with these words do exist in every society and elucidate the overall process we call production.

Distribution

How might we delineate the three major sub-processes of the overall process of *distribution*? The process of distribution includes the process of *property definitions*, the process of *exchange systems*, and the process of *needs allocation*. In order for a society to distribute its products and services, it needs to define what is meant by "**property**." What is private property; what is public property; what is rented property; what rights does each person have over the property they own or share or control? This process can be quite simple or quite complicated, but the basic process indicated by our term "property definitions" takes place in some manner in every society.

Also, in order for a society to distribute its products and services it needs to establish some sort of **exchange system**. This can be a barter system, a use of gold and silver coins, colored beads, a paper-money system, a system of electronic records, or something else. Exchange of goods and services takes place in every society. The exchange system is whatever means are used for doing this exchange.

Thirdly, in order for a society to distribute its products and services, it must have a way of determining what **needs** to be distributed, to whom, by what criteria, and in what quantities. Some of these determinations may be left to the workings of a supply-and-demand market process. Other aspects of a society's needs allocation may be chosen by public bodies acting on behalf of communities, states, regions, nations, or the planet. In some manner or another every society has to choose what it does and does not need. For example, this choosing process has become urgent today in the energy arena. Do we need to continue using fossil fuels or do we need to phase them out? Do we need to establish solar collectors and wind farms as our primary energy source or something else? These are choices someone makes. Perhaps these choices are made by democratic governments or by oligarchic rulers. Perhaps they are made by the producers of energy. Perhaps we allow these decisions to be made by supply-and-demand dynamics. Perhaps these decisions are made by a combination of these forces.

The whole economy is shaped by these needs allocation choices. As we will see in the more detailed discussion to follow, it is important to realize that our economy is not a product of nature or divine control or some automatic process. An economy is created through the decisions of human beings. Therefore, the dynamics of an economy can also be recreated by human beings. There are limiting and determining factors in nature and in human nature, but the freedom to choose is also a factor, and this choosing is central for understanding all economic processes, especially the process we call "needs allocation." Choosing the basic patterns of need is a key factor in shaping an economic system.

* * * * * * * *

Understanding all nine sub-processes of an economic system gives us a tool for examining the gifts and flaws of past and present economies and for noticing what we may need to save, construct, or reform in order to have a workable and optimal economy in our future. This optimal economy cannot be deduced from this model of essential processes. Many considerations come into play. But if all these sub-processes of what we call an economy are not considered and formulated for our times, we will not have a complete and workable economy.

Chapter 18
Political Processes

Political processes have to do with public decision making on behalf of a given population of humans. So defined, political processes take place within economic institutions as well as within governmental institutions. Indeed, every association of humans that makes group decisions is participating in what we are defining here as political processes.

Political processes, like economic processes, can be viewed as three inseparable arenas of social process. In a complete human society, the first of these arenas is the defining of the geography and population of humans involved. Let's call this *geographical grounding*. The other two processes we will call *social order* and *decisional participation*.

Geographical Grounding

Each society defines its regions and districts of public responsibility. Whether this is the hunting ground of a tribal society, the grazing areas of mobile herders, or the more definite borders of nations, some grasp of human-to-nature districting is essential for the political processing of public decision making. Geographical grounding is a reflection of this important awareness: every society has a boundary, a skin, a defined scope within which all the other functions of that society take place. We live together on the whole planet, yet we also live within regions of the planet, regions that are composed of communities of plants, animals, fungi, microbes as well as humans. We each live within an eco-region that might be said to have a "skin." Human communities also have skins. Nations have skins. We do not live within a world without borders, nor can any attempt to do so succeed. Geographical grounding is an essential aspect of every society. An image of globalization that seeks to erase these skins is delusional and dysfunctional. Equally delusional is any view that does not notice that these skins are porous. Social boundaries are skins, not boxes. And boundaries change. In some future era nations may be deemphasized and natural regions of life forms and human settlements will be the skins we emphasize. Whatever be the size of the society we are discussing, we need to define the scope of that society's governing body. Who are its citizens, and what land is included in its domain?

Social Order

Every society also requires some sort of articulated taboos, legal codes, laws, treaties, or taken-for-granted rules to live by. "You shall not murder" is a basic example. These ordering formats must then be applied and enforced by expressions of public response to their violation. This evolves into police forces, prisons, fines, courts, judges, and other sometimes grim but necessary functions. There is no social order until that order is enforced in some manner. Social order also includes organizations of personnel and instruments that function in the common defense of that society. Whether we are thinking of keeping predatory animals at bay, warriors of other tribes neutralized, or nations defended, we are envisioning a necessary aspect of human society. The fact that the military aspect of human society has so often been misused should not confuse us into thinking that we can simply do away with military processes. Common defense is an essential process of every society. It is not necessary, however, that this aspect of human society take the form of imperial expansion. And it is not necessary to resolve every serious controversy through violent means. The ethics of using violence as a "last resort" has been an important guiding principle for generations. It is also true that this "last resort" of violence cannot be entirely absent in any viable, long-range, whole society.

Common defense (the organization of military forces) is an important social process, along with education, health care, or any other essential social process. The option of employing violence must be present if a society is to have meaningful boundaries and an enduring peace. But the actual employment of violence needs to be viewed as a last resort. Furthermore, we err when we over-glamorize the role of military service; we merely need to fully honor this role as needed along with the roles of, for example, schoolteacher or nurse.

Decisional Participation

This process holds the core meaning of all political processes. Each society has to put together a way of making public decisions and carrying out those decisions. In a modern democracy we begin with founding agreements that may be written up in a constitution. Then we have ways of representing the population in councils of decision making that design the laws we require ourselves to live by. We need to have administrators who carry out the enactment of these laws and the overall policies of domestic and foreign action. We also need persons who interpret the laws and supervise the application of the laws to specific cases. One of the basic struggles in the decisional participation aspect of US society has been the tension between giving maximum decision-making power to each citizen rather than giving most political power to an aristocracy of the owners of the largest wealth. To resolve this struggle in favor of the people entails assuring that those who design and administer the laws and policies be accountable to the people.

* * * * * * * *

As we attempt to envision the future and make practical our vision of Eco-Democracy, it will be necessary to keep in mind these basic elements of political processes as well as the basic elements of economic processes. And it will be necessary for us to keep in mind the other processes that comprise a human society. Our name for those "other" processes is "cultural processes."

Chapter 19
Cultural Processes

Sociologists are generally clear that economic and political processes are not the only processes that go on in a human society. Often, these "other" processes are simply called "social processes." But in the model of society we are recommending, the term "social processes" will be our name for all the processes of a human society. We will use the term *"cultural processes"* for those common processes of a society that are neither economic processes nor political processes. Cultural processes give the undergirding of meaning to the political and economic processes. And they do more. They are the basic forms that express human consciousness and enable the communication of that consciousness among the members of the society.

In our master model of society we have organized the subparts of the overall cultural process under these three inclusive categories: *Common Sense* processes, *Common Style* processes, and *Common Symbolization* processes.

Common Sense

Every society has processes for "taking in" reality and communicating it to one another. The common sense of a human culture includes its scientific knowledge, its humanities, and its technologies or useful skills. Our common sense is made common by our educational means, by our public media, by everything that has to do with the development and transmission of the assembled knowledge and wisdom of that culture. A modern culture may have a wide diversity of viewpoints, differing educational institutions, and many means of communication, but in order to be "workable," a society must have enough commonality to function. Dictatorial societies create their commonality by forcing a uniform viewpoint and suppressing alternative views. Democracy includes a style of public discourse that allows wisdom to grow from a wide range of sensitive and honest persons into a consensus of common practices that benefit everyone. Democracy is also a means of restraining the stubborn lies of the rigid dictatorial impulse that can arise in any human society. Without an emphasis on developing a strong common sense, democratic discussion cannot be successful in arriving at consensus and resolving conflicts peacefully.

Common Style

Every society has processes we might call the "active" pole of culture. This includes life styles, moralities, customs, modes of association, family patterns, and roles for men, women, children, youth, adults, and elders. Everything about the commonality of a culture that can be acted out in patterns of behavior we are naming "common style." These patterns of behavior will support or not support viable, just, and ecologically sane political and economic fabrics. A modern society of national size will include a wide diversity of styles, but to be a successful home for its humanity, a society will also have important elements of commonality in its styles of living. For example, a workable democracy depends upon commonality with regard to its processes of assembly and its ways of being and selecting leadership.

Common Symbolization

Every society has processes that enable the "depth" pole of culture: this includes language systems, artistic expressions, and religious formations—everything that has to do with the elemental patterns of using the symbol-using consciousness that characterizes the human species. Most of us are aware of how the arts shape basic sensitivities among the population enjoying those arts. The qualities of our languages benefit us in a similar way. The role of religious formations is not well understood in this time of thoroughgoing critique and transformation of our religious traditions. Simply stated, religious formations are finite social processes that enable awareness of the depth of personal and natural being. The heart of a religious formation is its practices—its solitary and group practices that enable people to personally access their inner awareness of their own profound nature and the profound overall reality in which we all dwell. On the basis of this direct awareness accessed through religious practices, religious communities build their theoretics—their psychologies, theologies, ethics, and sense of history. The third aspect of religious formation is the institutions of religion that preserve and promote those practices and theoretics. Religious formation is a vast and controversial topic much too involved to thoroughly discuss here. But properly defined in a non-sectarian manner, religious formation has always been and always will be a part of human society. The deep perversions we notice in current religious practices, understandings, and institutions should not cloud our minds to the essential nature of religious formation in human society.

* * * * * * * *

Culture, defined as common sense, common style, and common symbolization, is an essential part of our overall study of human society. Culture is a key factor in our social engagements to change society. Culture is a profound reality that is poorly understood by many people. A band of chimpanzees or great apes has a sort of culture along with its polity and economic activities. Complex patterns of communication take place in such a band, but the social qualities of other primate groups are not yet culture in the human sense. This leap into human consciousness was attended by and enabled by the dawn of symbol-using intelligence, a capacity that expressed itself in language, art, and religious formations. The dawn of these elemental cultural processes enabled a more nuanced patterning of common life and the accumulation of formalized traditions of memory. With the dawn of writing these formalized memories became libraries of accumulated wisdom. These basic cultural processes enabled the human species to create more complex political and economic processes than those that characterize the other primates. Human society has some similarities and some roots in pre-human societies, but in its overall quality, human society is very different from the commonalities that characterize the group life of the other existing species.

Noticing the uniqueness of human culture enables us to notice more fully the primacy of cultural processes in human social development and in producing social change. In conducting deep social changes, we will point out that making changes in culture is prior to the development of new political and economic ways of living. For example, education is always a crucial strategy in making any far-reaching social change. Before far-reaching changes in political and economic patterns can take place, we must develop changes in people's understandings and attitudes. Only if we keep the cultural aspects of society in mind, will we be able to think comprehensively about social change. We need a model of society that pictures the whole of human society in order to envision viable future forms of society and move toward them. An extensive transformation in any part of society will entail transforming all the processes of that society.

Chart 19.1 (see following page) is a triangular model of all the economic, political, and cultural processes that we have described in these three chapters. This model may be improved, but it is a model about the essential processes that are present in every human society. It is a model with which we can view the gifts and flaws of past societies as well as a model that is useful for designing the qualities of any future society we wish to build. This model cannot tell us what those new structures and systems need to be. The model only tells us the basic arenas that are included in any whole society. When we propose to give leadership to the overall transformation of human society, we need to give consideration to all of these aspects.

Chart 19.1

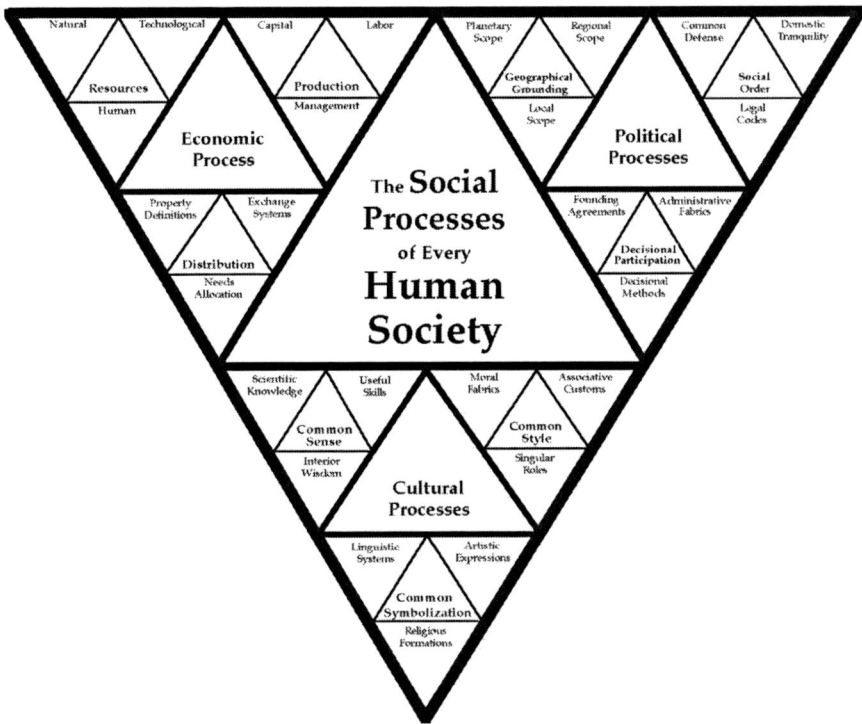

The Social Processes of Every Human Society

Chapter 20
The Rebalancing of Society

In our industrial civilizations we often find an unhealthy collusion between wealthy business organizations and political bodies. This collusion tends to ignore other stakeholders in the society. An ingrown collusion between business and government tends to become insidiously corrupt. A government that is owned and controlled by its richest business institutions is way off track. Such a government is focused on serving business interests above general well-being, environmental responsibility, the welfare of working people, the welfare of consumers, the nobility of a foreign policy, and even the infrastructure of the economy itself. These essential values cannot be properly supported through the bargaining and secret collusion that takes place between business institutions and governmental elites. When this business-government collusion represents the primary power structure of a society, we have an oligarchy that is contrary to both the spirit of democracy and the beneficial functioning of a market system. Such government undermines whatever progress toward democracy has been achieved by that society.

In most industrial civilizations, we see a corrupting imbalance of power being given to economic institutions. Political institutions become the lackeys of economically defined bodies, especially large and wealthy corporations. Then the cultural institutions and life practices tend to be tyrannized by both the economic and political aspects of the society. For example, the basic direction of university research in the United States is often determined by what is paid for and directed by corporations and a corporation-controlled government. Medical research is likewise shaped by what will make a profit for some corporation, rather than by what will bring affordable health care to the citizen body. Furthermore, most of the mass media becomes mere propaganda arms for businesses and for governmental bodies that are in collusion with businesses. Finally, even most religious institutions, art galleries, symphony orchestras, and other cultural institutions end up catering to the desires and wishes of big money.

Such external imbalances impact the internal life of citizens. Industrial civilizations typically produce citizens who are preoccupied with economic matters: economic growth, economic survival, business building, stock investing, property owning, conspicuous consumption, economic status, old age security, bigger salaries, more economic power, and so on. Such economic matters have their place in a balanced society, but the emphasis upon economic matters in industrial society has become all-consuming.

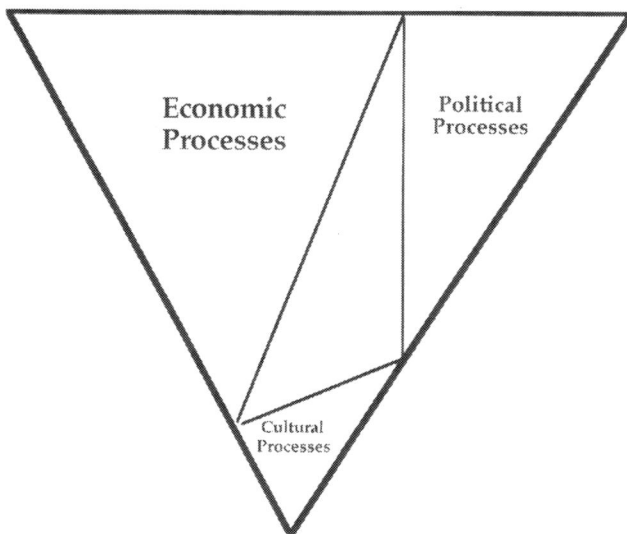

The above diagram depicts the warping that is present in contemporary industrial societies. The economic processes are oversized, the political processes are reduced in independent power, and the cultural processes are almost crowded off the "page" of serious attention. In the United States the economic processes clearly draw excessive time, energy, and resources from our political participation and our cultural enrichment.

If the economic warping of society is not corrected, our society will remain out of balance with both the ecology of the planet and the well-being of individual persons. A deeply warped society is not only oppressive; it is vulnerable to complete collapse.

How can this imbalance be corrected? The cultural dynamic needs to be strengthened with effective institutions that are independent from the economic and political institutions. These strengthened cultural institutions can then strengthen and democratize the political institutions, thereby making them more independent and thus capable of limiting, disciplining, regulating, and reducing the inordinate power of the economic institutions.

We are so used to the economic rule of our lives that we may find it difficult to imagine a balanced society. The US society following the innovations of Franklin D. Roosevelt, we enjoyed more balanced society than the society we have in the United States today. The extent of this imbalance is the underlying complaint of the Occupy Wall Street Protests that are taking place as this book is being prepared for publication.

The societies of Medieval Europe were imbalanced in the cultural direction. The institutions of the Roman Church inordinately ruled over the political and economic life of that era. How our post-civilization or Eco-Democratic societies will manifest balance is a vision yet to be filled in, but many good books have been written on this topic of overcoming the imbalance. David Korten illuminated this problem in his book

When Corporations Rule the World.[43] This will be one of the key
themes underlying the elements of strategy outlined in Part
Four. Corporations are a human invention. They were originally
given charters for the purpose of serving the needs of people in
particular ways. In a balanced society these institutions would
either be replaced or be returned to their primary purposes—
namely providing a service to customers and a return to their
investors. *Running governments and shaping public policy would
not be permitted to these publicly licensed bodies.*

In a rebalanced society it would be the job of the political
institutions to set the overall policies for the economic playing
field and then fairly and firmly regulate the economic players
who opt to operate in the markets that this society provides.
Further, these political institutions would be responsible to
all of the people, and not merely to those who financed the
election of the governing officials. Without such rebalancing
there is no hope for a full measure of justice or for appropriately
making the ecological decisions that have now become first
priority. It is not necessary for economic institutions like
General Motors, Exxon-Mobil, Halliburton, or Goldman Sachs
to survive. Our imperative is the survival of a planet that can
remain a viable home for humanity and for a large percentage
of the other existing species of life. This will be possible only
if we take measures to rebalance the basic social processes of
our society.

---

[43] David Korten, *When Corporations Rule the World* (San Francisco, CA: Berrett-Koehler Publishers, & Bloomingfield, CT: Kumarian Press, 1996). Also see
David Korten, *The Post-Corporate World* (Berrett-Koehler Publishers & Kumarian Press, 1998); and *The Great Turning: From Empire to Earth Community* (Berrett-Koehler Publishers & Kumarian Press, 2006). The writings of Jerry Mander,
Charlene Spretnak, Noam Chomsky, Naomi Klein, Thomas Berry, and many others also emphasize this theme.

Part Four

Eco-Democracy: How Do We Get There from Here?

In Part One we explored what it means to be aware of the "here" of our social life. In Parts Two and Three we explored "envisioning" a "there" toward which we need to move. Both explorations will improve as more relevant facts and contemplative insight enter our awareness. Nevertheless, we have enough clarity to ask the next question: How do we get there from here? This will be the question addressed in Part Four. We will call the answer to this question "strategy." Strategy is the "road" from our problematical "here" to our visionary "there."

Our overall strategy for this transition can be broken down into these five sub-questions:

1. How do we utilize electoral politics?
2. How do we expand citizen education?
3. How do we use nonviolent noncooperation?
4. How do we empower local communities?
5. How do we construct appropriate global institutions?

We will clarify why all five of these questions must be answered and how those answers relate to one another. Another

193

question comes into play: Who is the "we" who is going to do all this controversial work? Obviously no one of us can be competent and active in all five of these strategic arenas. Each of us will need to find our own small role in the overall task of lifting this massive weight. It will take millions—in the end billions—of us to complete this transition. Who are we? How do we strategize and work together in some way? How do we build together a common view of the strategies required to get "there" from "here"? The feasibility of this entire transition depends upon having a convincing sense that there is a viable "road" from "here" to "there." We begin with some images of feasibility.

Chapter 21

The Plausibility of Radical Change

A strategy for social change is first of all just a mental picture. It is not a to-do list. It is just a picture of how it is feasible to move from "here" to "there." The construction of our strategy depends upon both our vision of where we want to go and our grasp of the present situation. Strategy is a mental picture that answers questions such as: What are the overall moves that need to happen to arrive at our vision? What needs to be done first, second, third, and so on? In the mind of the strategist, strategy links vision with hardheaded knowledge of the given situation. Strategy pictures a plausible sequence of transformations from the present to our vision of a possible future.

Strategic thinking is down-to-Earth; it discerns the factors in the current situation that block movement toward our vision. Taking those blocking factors seriously, we ask ourselves realistic questions about how to overcome them: Do we remove them, dissolve them, go around them, drive through them, or neutralize them? Our strategy is whatever actually works in overcoming what is blocking movement toward our vision.

Strategic thinking plays a middle role between our vision and our detailed action. Strategy is not our vision of where we want to go, and it is not our specific actions. Strategy is a fabric of thought that takes its place between our vision and our action. We do our specific actions in order to implement our strategies, in order to reach our vision. Strategic thinking is motivational in the sense that it gives us a picture of how our action can be a plausible road from here to there.

The challenges we have discussed in the first three Parts of this book include both a vast external transformation and an equally vast internal transformation of the social imagery within each and every human being. This internal transformation begins with those of us who are going to lead the vast transition. If we are to provide leadership for the external transformation "from Empire to Eco-Democracy," we must become inwardly detached from being civilized. Let us see ourselves as the first fruits of a post-civilizational mode of social organization. And let us create the strategies that allow us to see with our own eyes how this transition is plausible for the world at large.

Building feasible strategies will be an ongoing task. Our strategies will undergo constant changes to meet the ever-new circumstances that we will face. So, who is going to do this imaginative work and teach these effective yet-to-be-created, winning strategies to the billions who will be required to carry them out? The work begins with those of us who see the necessity of the vision we are discussing. This includes persons who have become disillusioned with and detached from the half-truths of those who want to merely repair civilization. And it includes those who have become disillusioned with the half-truths of those who see no hope for civilization, yet cannot envision an alternative. This state of inward detachment is not merely an intellectual viewpoint; it is a deep quality of consciousness. A viable future for humanity on planet Earth calls upon us to access our essential freedom and creativity. Such astonishing creativity can spread to billions of people and be continued for a century or more until the horrific crises that we confront are fully met.

When we envision a social transformation of such historical magnitude, we quite naturally feel overwhelmed. So let us admit this feeling—this state of "Oh my gosh!" that is quite inescapable. Let us learn to live with this feeling and use it as fuel for our ongoing thought and action. Let us not allow the immensity of the task to be an excuse for inaction or for hanging on to old-style thinking. "Overwhelmed" need not mean panicked or hopeless. It is true, however, that feeling overwhelmed can become a pit of despair unless we have images that enable us to visualize the plausibility of actually achieving the vast changes we are proposing. The metaphor of "avalanche" provides one such hopeful image.

The Avalanche Metaphor

Large social changes happen through a gradual buildup and then a huge slide of alteration. Let us consider the metaphor of snow building up on a mountainside. The buildup is gradual until all at once an avalanche of snow slides down the mountain.

Applying this metaphor to social change, we notice that transformation forces must patiently build up "the snow," perhaps for a long period of time. Many forces are currently building up social pressure for big changes, some consciously doing so, some unconsciously doing so. It is difficult to anticipate the avalanches of change that may go into effect with surprising suddenness.

Who among us anticipated the sudden end to the Cold War and the removal of the Berlin Wall? Who among us anticipated the sudden end of apartheid in South Africa and the election of Mandela to its presidency? These changes were small in comparison to the vision of change we are considering, but they seemed huge to most of us at the time they happened.

And avalanches continue to happen. Ralph Nader writes: "What could start a popular resurgence in this country against the abuses of concentrated, avaricious corporatism? Imagine the arrogance of passing on to already cheated working people and the jobless enormous corporate losses? This is achieved through government bailouts and tax escapes. History teaches us that the spark usually is smaller than expected and of a nature that is wholly unpredictable or even unimaginable. But if the dry tinder is all around, as many deprivations and polls reveal, the spark, no matter how small, can turn into a raging inferno."[44]

---

44 Ralph Nader, "Waiting for the Spark," CommonDreams.org, April 19, 2011.

We, the visionary strategists of massive transformation, can take initiatives to start avalanches when the time is right. We can do so by finding that small ingredient of action that catalyzes a big shift. With regard to an avalanche of snow on some snow-rich mountainside, perhaps a small whistle of the right pitch and loudness is all it takes to start vibrations among the right snowflakes and thus initiate the avalanche. Planning to start an avalanche of change requires an intense study of the whole mountain of "snow" and a careful construction of the initiating actions. Such study of the situation includes identifying what we will call a "whistle point"—the place in the snow bank of potential change where a right pitched action can start an avalanche of change. Presently, we will suggest where whistle points may be located in our current society. We will discuss how to occasion avalanches that can slide toward Eco-Democracy. But first, we will provide some examples of whistle points and avalanches of change in the past.

Past Avalanches of Change

The Reformation of Christian practice and of European society in the sixteenth century is a well-documented example of an avalanche of change. When Martin Luther posted his propositions for discussion on the Wittenberg Cathedral door, he did not realize what a "whistle point" this was destined to be. In the century or so before Luther, there had been a long buildup of critique of a medieval European society in which ecclesiastical tyranny was at the heart of the corruption. There had been pre-reformation explorations in religious innovation, translations of the Scripture, movements among the population, and encounters with whole new continents and peoples that challenged long-held assumptions about human history, human nature, and human possibilities. Nevertheless, the old tyranny had remained stuck, the innovative movements had been contained, and many of the forward-looking innovators had been slain. Luther's actions sounded the right note to set theologians, monks, nuns, peasants, kings, and noblemen on the move. What we now call "the Reformation" was not merely a religious debate among theologians; it was a social avalanche, a multifaceted and rather chaotic movement of social forces that no one fully controlled. Luther himself was swept along, having to make huge and sometimes horrendous decisions in his attempts to shape best-case outcomes from the enormous chaos of fast-moving change. And Luther was not alone. There were many other very creative persons moving and attempting to shape the movement. Luther had sounded an extremely pertinent whistle in the midst of a very dark hour of social tyranny. The arrangement of social forces was ready to slide into a new ordering of the social life of Europe.

The Gandhian movement for the independence of India provides a more recent example of an avalanche of change. Gandhi's whistling was heard by millions of village peasants and urban citizens. He had a genius for intuiting what would provoke the rise of overwhelming social forces the British could not defeat. His salt march is an example. The British law against making one's own salt from sea water was patently ridiculous, yet it was part of the entire British attitude of selling manufactured products for profit to a controlled population. So when thousands disobeyed this law and marched to the beach and made salt, a whistle was sounded. This and other such whistles initiated an avalanche of change that neither the British, nor Gandhi, nor others could control.

Here is an example that is even better known among US citizens, especially those of us who lived through the 1960s: **the movement for African American equality** sparked by Martin Luther King Jr., Bayard Rustin, Malcolm X, Fannie Lou Hamer, James Farmer, John Lewis, James Baldwin, and thousands of others. The Montgomery bus boycott is an example of a whistle point that initiated an avalanche of change. That story has been well told, and it remains a glorious story of how a small and quite local happening contributed to building social momentum of a truly awesome magnitude. Much buildup had already happened, but the avalanche began when the spunky revolutionary Rosa Parks refused to move to the back of the bus.

Then came the persistence of the African American community in refusing to ride the busses, finding car pools to work, fighting racial insanity every inch of the way until some of the established patterns gave way. The bus boycott established the leadership of Martin Luther King Jr. and inspired much else that followed.

Each of these examples of a whistle point was complex. Each entailed ready-to-move situations built up slowly over time. Each included the presence of remarkable leaders who initiated and then persisted in doing the necessary work of shaping positive outcomes from the avalanches of change that were initiated. Much can still be learned from each of these examples and many more. But perhaps we have said enough to illustrate the basic dynamic of whistle points and avalanches of change.

Looking backward is far easier that looking forward. What are the ready-to-move accumulations of snow on the mountainside of civilization that are poised to shift toward social manifestations of Eco-Democracy? What are the whistle points that might start those avalanches?

Current Whistle Points of Action

Here are three key "mountain slopes" already gathering snow that may be ready for avalanche: (1) citizen resurgence, (2) alternative energy fueling, and (3) local community empowerment.

1. Citizen Resurgence

In his book *Supercapitalism*, Robert Reich points out how deeply the role of citizenship in the United States has eroded since the time of Franklin D. Roosevelt and his New Deal. After World War II we had a period of balance between the power of the citizenry and the power of economic managers and big investors.[45] Reich calls this "The Not Quite Golden Age." Without idealizing that also-troubled period, Reich

---

[45] Robert B. Reich, *Supercapitalism: The Transformation of Business, Democracy, and Everyday Life* (New York: Alfred A. Knopf, 2008)

makes his case that democracy in that period still had the power to restrain the large banks and corporations. But in the following decades citizenry power and democratic governing deteriorated. Indeed, the US population has been reduced to individualistic consumers and individualistic investors with almost no power except what we citizens can do with our money. The voting booth is now almost entirely ordered by the big money forces of society. We quite often are called to vote for the lesser of bad choices provided for us by huge powers, seemingly beyond our control.

Furthermore, we the citizenry are not organized into popular movements with sufficient clout to challenge the wealthy status quo we need to oppose. With a few exceptions we find ourselves alone and powerless with only our meager checkbook as our means of social change. Hundreds of progressive organizations that are doing fragments of good work fill our mail boxes with requests for monetary support. Disquiet about this powerlessness is building, but it is not yet an avalanche of change. It is just a slow building of thoughtfulness and anger amidst the flood of big money violations of our lives. The revolt of government unions and their friends in Wisconsin and elsewhere are a hopeful development. So also are the Occupy Wall Street and other Occupy Movement protests.

President Obama's election might be viewed as a small avalanche of citizen power. At least a large number of us got out to vote and expressed our disgust for the incompetent, corporation-controlled George W. Bush administration. In part we accomplished this by outspending the opposition through millions of small contributions. Such a practice is not sustainable, especially with increasingly unemployed and financially strapped citizens. But it was a hopeful sign. We progressives enjoyed seeing a citizen movement move to victory against the grain of the status quo. This was a bigger change than most people noticed. Like the citizen shift that ushered in the New Deal of Franklin D. Roosevelt, we can feel the possibility of a buildup of citizen revolt that has the potential to undo the "bad deal" that began with Ronald Reagan and continued all the way to the end of the George W. Bush administration. The buildup for a full citizen resurgence avalanche has not yet reached its full potential. The irrational and erratic reactivity of conservative forces to the Obama administration signals that even this small violation of status quo attitudes touches deep nerves. Much more progressive citizen power will be required to restrain and break through this reactivity.

The Obama administration is only moderately progressive relative to the vision we have summarized in this book. Perhaps historians will conclude that Obama's task was simply to save industrial civilization from immediate collapse. We are proposing a much more fundamental change: replacing civilization with a long-range sustainable mode of society. But "saving civilization" is an important secondary step, provided that this step salvages some of the better features of the civilization era. Even the moderate initiatives that Obama promotes meet formidable opposition from the big money forces who say "No" to any change—modest or visionary— upon which a truly alternative direction might be built.

In spite of the increased citizen enthusiasm evident in the 2008 elections, a full third of US citizens still do not even vote, and of the two-thirds who do vote, only a fragment are what we might describe as fully informed. We do not yet have a large, informed citizenry capable of resisting the misinformation purchased and expertly packaged by status-quo wealth. We do not yet have tens of millions of citizens ready to make significant sacrifices, as needed, for a massive social transformation.

The reason for this passivity is not that US citizens are apathetic by nature. No, US citizens have mobilized before. They can mobilize again. But no one has yet blown the whistle that touches the motivation that is mounting in the hearts of US citizens.

So what is the whistle that needs to be sounded in the arena of citizen resurgence? Where is the snow piling up? What is the trigger that will start the desired avalanche moving?

Finding the answers to such questions will require some trial and error, but here are some informed guesses. We need more clarity with regard to our enemy. We will not win fundamental changes with polite, friendly, bipartisan, rational conversation with the status-quo forces that we are confronting. The enemy we will have to defeat is devoted not only to opposing the future we envision, but is also actively undoing the relevant steps already made in the last eight decades. We are in a life-and-death conflict with entrenched and suicidally panicked forces that are desperately attempting to preserve the unpreservable. Our primary battle is not a conflict with "Islamic extremists." They are only a tiny part of the forces that are clinging to an obsolete past. *We are called to battle with the ideology of a supercapitalism that claims that every value can be monetized and traded on the world market.* The ideological rigidity of this economic establishment is seductive in its appeal, and it is powerfully established. They have mobilized the reactive forms of Jewish and Christian religion to assist them in their even more dangerous reactivity. Our core conflict is with the vast majority of the large for-profit corporations and their governmental patsies. We can experience resonance with the symbolism established by Occupation Wall Street—the 1 percent with inordinate wealth and the 99 percent who are being oppressed.

We are called to battle against the notion that unregulated markets will make everything work out fine. We are called to battle against the notion that unregulated markets and democratic freedom are the same thing. We are called to battle against the notion that corporations are basically providing what we need. We are called to battle in support of the truth that corporations, while sometimes useful, are also dangerous institutions that must be carefully watched and restrained by coercive democratic governments that are truly responsive to citizens' needs and the planet-wide crises. We are called to battle in support of the truth that huge transnational corporations can in many instances be replaced by better institutions. And our battle with the old patterns needs to include building the new patterns. In order to win we will have to build community in local places. We will have to deal with local food provision and

affordable homes and healing art and well-formed gatherings
and creative citizen co-creation from the grassroots to the
treetops of society.

The reigning establishment is a formidable enemy, but
it is an enemy that is vulnerable to an avalanche of citizen
resurgence. A whistle point for US citizenry is a passionate
dose of clarity about who our real enemy is. Unless we are
clear about the core enemy we will continue moving in circles
of frustration and cynical complaining. When the true enemy
is identified within ourselves and within our social life, then
we, the citizenry of the United States will move. We will endure
such obvious tyranny no longer. We who are fearful, compliant,
overworked employees of industrial institutions will revolt
when the awareness of who is oppressing us and cheating us
takes up lively residence in our minds.

Eco-Democracy will not come about without many
avalanches of citizen resurgence over the next several decades.
Progressives will need to learn how to blow correctly pitched
whistles that clarify the enemy and the issue, and provide a call
for action to those citizens whose ears are beginning to hear. We
must not underestimate the potential of citizen resurgence.

2. Alternative Energy Fueling

One of the very first things the emerging millions of "moving"
citizens can effectively do is build an alternative energy system,
an alternative to the current fossil-fuel-fired system. We might
look for our first avalanche in the coal industry. Popular
disapproval of coal-fired power plants has already reached a
high level of clarity. A whistle point in the coal arena may be
found in promoting a rapid expansion of citizen realization
that coal-fired plants can be shut down, that all such plants can
be phased out by strong citizen revolt against them. No new
coal-fired power plants need to be built. Citizens are already
mobilizing on this point.

Stopping the pipeline from the Canada tar sands to the Gulf
refineries is another vulnerable and very important place to
begin the revolt against the old energy system.

The extensive nuclear disaster in Japan (combined with a sharpened sense of the danger that all nuclear power plants pose) can issue in another avalanche of change. Already, millions of citizens do not trust the propaganda that this energy source is safe.

Another avalanche of change we might spark is a massive investment in solar and wind energy provision. This is a job-producing, global-warming-moderating, clean-air-providing, highly popular direction of change. Millions of citizens support it; however, these citizens need to be more clear that it is the oil, coal, and natural gas companies as well as tire and automotive companies that are actively undermining such developments. Being clear about those enemies can become another whistle point in the area of alternative energy fueling. The existing energy institutions control a huge coalition of money, managed by money and power obsessed managers. But once investment money begins to move in the direction of alternative energy sources, more money will shift. The vast majority of investors don't care where they make their returns. The big pension funds and big investment funds are equal-opportunity investors. Enormous amounts of money can shift quickly toward alternative energy if citizens insist upon supporting those energy sources. The current energy giants can be boxed out of the decision-making on this issue.

3. Local Community Empowerment
In our disempowered local communities, small avalanches of change are already happening, and other avalanches are building. There is a growing disquiet about the fact that most of the major decisions that affect local community life are made in national and state governments or in far-away corporate boardrooms. This makes local community life vulnerable to huge upheavals; insecure and unsafe food provision; air, water, soil, and economic degradation; needless profit-making developments initiated by far-away profiteers; and so on. Many people feel powerless to do anything about these matters that affect them so personally. Many are also awakening to

the absence of meaningful conversation with fellow citizens about these concerns. Some typical conversations among local citizens have become little more than empty talk that assumes that undependable politicians and business managers must take the necessary actions. But this can change.

There is a growing readiness for change in the community arena, even though it will take some imaginative whistling to overcome the habits of cynicism and apathy that have been practiced for so long. Local communities will move when such movement can be shown to make a difference. The whistle points that set change in motion will probably be small and subtle and specific to each community. In rural communities local organic food projects have promise for giving international food corporations and huge agri-business conglomerates some serious competition. Community gardens in inner city communities have also been successful strategies, but urban communities may have even more urgent needs (e.g., housing, mortgages, water use, and education) around which community empowerment can build. Suburbs may not experience disempowerment so directly, but their isolation from the rest of the world is a kind of disempowerment. The skills of suburban people are being misdirected in support of the status quo rather than toward the support of community empowerment everywhere.

Whatever community we are considering, empowerment will begin with groups of deeply concerned citizens in well-led meetings of serious talk about actually doing something that participants can see will make a difference in their lives. The movement called "Transition Towns" illustrates this promise. This movement is described in a book by Rob Hopkins, *The Transition Handbook: From Oil Dependency to Local Resilience* (Padstow, Cornwall, Great Britain: Green Books, 2008). As the subtitle indicates Hopkins advocates more independence from the global economy and more local resilience, by which he means a complexity and variety of life that makes a local community more capable of recovery from various jolts. Hopkins's book analyzes the peak oil and climate change contexts that we all face and then focuses on a new style of local community as a big part of the solution to those challenges.

Likewise, Douglas Rushkoff has emphasized local community engagement in his book *Life Inc.: How the World Became a Corporation and How to Take It Back* (New York: Random House, 2009). Rushkoff emphasizes how each of us has been disconnected from our real lives by the corporatism that rules the world. We are even disconnected in our attempts to correct the situation; we are depending too heavily on our financial gifts to good causes, electing better government officials, and promoting better behavior from the corporations, rather than getting fully engaged in transforming society from the bottom up, community by community. Whenever people are ready to move, the local community is an opening in the structure of things. Almost no one is giving the energy and leadership to this arena that it needs. Our efforts here can create movement. And many communities acting together comprise a force that the cloud-dwelling corporation masterminds cannot stop.

* * * * * * * *

So who is going to design and blow these whistles? Who will do this work? Who will start these avalanches of change and shepherd them to positive results? The next chapter is about these forces of transformation.

Chapter 22

The Forces of Transformation

"Antidisestablishmentarianism" is reputed to be the longest word in the English language. This word came into being to name a way of being a force of social change. Two other ways of being a force of social change have more familiar names: the *proestablishment* and the *disestablishment*. The first is basically "for" the current establishment of society, the second is basically "against" the current establishment of society. Antidisestablishmentarianism points to a third way of being an active force within society. For this third way we prefer the term *transestablishment*. The third way, as we will define it, is not only "anti" or against the other two but also "for" an inclusive vision of social transformation. The pro-establishment and the disestablishment are bound to each other as being for (pro) or against (dis) the same thing, the establishment. The transestablishment transcends both of these groups by envisioning and promoting a thoroughgoing, alternative social system. The transestablishment forces of transformation are central and crucial for realizing the vision of Eco-Democracy.

Following is a diagram of six basic types of social response. Contemplate this diagram for a moment to seal in your mind these names and the relations between them. Each of these terms stands for attitudes potentially found in all of us and also for groups of people in whom one of these six attitudes predominate.

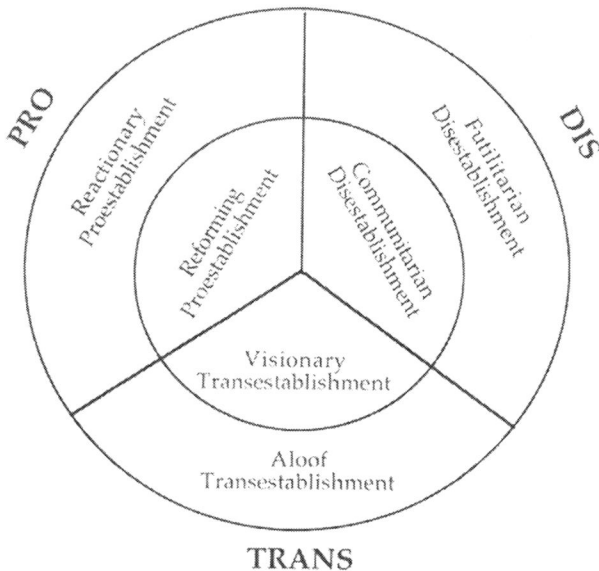

The Proestablishment

Proestablishment forces come in two versions: (1) the **reactionary proestablishment** who want to move the established society back to some vision of a former society before society was "ruined" by "liberalizing" changes; and (2) the **reforming proestablishment** who want to keep the established structure but make repairs upon to it. The George W. Bush administration is a recent illustration of the reactionary type of proestablishment. The Barack Obama administration is an illustration of the reforming type of proestablishment. Obama does not promote a radical vision of social change, but he does see that deep repairs are needed on the basic frame of the existing society.

The Disestablishment

Today's disestablishment can also be divided into two types: (1) the **communitarian disestablishment** and (2) the **futilitarian disestablishment.**

The communitarian disestablishment reject the established society and seek to drop out of it into some sort of alternative experiment in social living. This may take the form of a thoroughgoing alternative community, a return to the land, or a high-tech version of tribal life. Or this "dropping out" of established civilization may be more partial: an alternative school, an alternative mode of housing, an off-the-grid hermitage, an antiestablishment religious body, a local money system, and so on. Such communitarian projects may be useful as parts of the wider transestablishment vision that we have been describing in this book, but the communitarian disestablishment is characterized by a lack of inclusive vision and a lack of a comprehensive program of action. Without inclusive vision, even very fine communitarian projects tend to become an escape from the overall challenges of the planet. If these overall challenges are not met, partial communitarian projects will eventually be destroyed by the desperate attempts of the established society to survive. Also, an inclusive vision of social transformation will change the quality of a communitarian project, making it part of a new whole and a support for that whole.

The futilitarian disestablishment are more thoroughgoing in their rejection of the established society. They anticipate the entire collapse of the established social order and counsel people to prepare themselves to be content with riding this doomed social vehicle to its grave. This futilitarian attitude finds a kind of comfort in facing up to what they view as the inevitability of total collapse. These persons expect the collapse of industrial civilization and perhaps also the collapse of planet Earth's capacity to support even a remnant of the human species. This futilitarian attitude may take the active form of awakening people to the truth of collapse and assisting people to survive or at least ride out the collapse more happily. There is also a more passive form of futilitarianism—those who simply do not see anything they can personally do about the immense issues swirling around them.

Both forms of disestablishment tend to be like the fuzz on a tennis ball. While they are separating themselves from the basic ball of established society, one end of their being is still attached to the existing ball. They are attached to what they are rejecting because they do not have a comprehensive vision of a whole new ball of social organization. The communitarian disestablishment are trying something that will fail. The futilitarian disestablishment are more lucid about impending failures, but they simply accept failure and choose to ride it into the abyss. Disestablishment activists vary widely, because their sensibilities tend to be directed toward different basic flaws in the establishment. In so far as they have a vision of the future, it is fragmentary—merely an effort to correct or not correct their most clearly perceived flaws. In general, disestablishment activists tend to be more clear about what they are against than what they are for.

The Transestablishment

The transestablishment can also be said to have two versions: (1) The **visionary transestablishment** and (2) the **aloof transestablishment**.

The visionary transestablishment are those who have been grasped by a viable alternative form of society. They are like the woman who in a night dream saw herself swinging out from the top of a tall building on a rope that was hanging from the sky. When she came to the end of the swing she let go of that rope and grabbed a next rope, which swung on to a next building from which she now views the old building with new eyes. Unlike the disestablishment person who swings back to the old building, the visionary transestablishment person views the establishment from the perspective of a whole new social building. This means both a rejection of the established society as well as a detachment from the bonds of animosity toward the established society. From a position of fresh footing within a viable alternative mode of society, the visionary sees the old establishment objectively, sees its glories and its flaws.

In contrast, the aloof transestablishment swings in empty space never touching the old social building or a new social building. A person of this perspective simply rejects historical engagement. Rather than being a visionary transestablishment whose detachment from the establishment is rooted in a vision of a comprehensive alternative society, the aloof transestablishment focuses on interior qualities, including a thoroughgoing detachment from the ups and downs of history. Their focus is individualistic and ahistorical. Some forms of mystical religion illustrate this attitude. As a retreat from historical engagement, the aloof transestablishment shares features with the reactionary proestablishment and the futilitarian disestablishment. The reactionary proestablishment rejects the actual historical challenges, lies about them, and retreats to the illusory safety of some past that never was. The futilitarian disestablishment is caught up in animosity toward the status quo but lacks the imagination to work toward a viable, progressive outcome in history. In its exclusively psychological focus, the aloof transestablishment rejects the need for any serious grappling with sociological processes.

* * * * * * * *

The outer ring of the previous diagram pictures the pro, dis, and transestablishement as three forms of escape from dealing with the actual challenges of the historical situation. The inner ring of this diagram pictures the pro, dis, and transestablishment in various forms of engagement with the historical challenges that are actually being confronted.

There are strong tensions between the three types in the outer ring (the reactionary proestablishment, the futilitarian disestablishment, and the aloof transestablishment). And there are strong tensions between the outer ring and the inner ring. There are also tensions between the three types in the inner ring (the reforming proestablishment, the communitarian disestablishment, and the visionary transestablishment), but the tensions among the inner three are creative tensions. All three of these forces manifest an attitude we might call "those who care"—those who love justice and fight for it, who build up the snow for social alteration and start the avalanches of progressive change.

A Historical Example of These Six Dynamics of Social Response

We can observe all six of these dynamics in the fight for the independence of India from Great Britain. In this story Gandhi and his movement illustrate the visionary transestablishment. A political outcome was uppermost in Gandhi's vision, but his vision also included an economic transformation emphasizing village industry and a cultural transformation emphasizing respect for rural people, practical truth, and a universalism that sought reconciliation between Hindu and Muslim adversaries as well as between adversarial relations among the casts. Gandhi used nonviolent noncooperation as an innovative means of social change. All these elements were visionary within his situation.

In this story the proestablishment are the British and their native collaborators. Some of them were reforming proestablishment persons who held out for compassion and conscience in their dealings with the independence movement. Others were reactionary proestablishment persons who were at times willing to engage in mass slaughter rather than allow significant changes to occur.

Similarly, the disestablishment was present in both communitarian and futilitarian forms. There were those who proposed less comprehensive programs of change than the visionary Gandhi. There were those who had given up on the possibility of a thoroughgoing change, including independence from British rule. To a large extent Gandhi succeeded in giving inclusive shape and effective method to the fragmentation offered by the various disestablishment thrusts. He won many disestablishment communitarians to his more inclusive visioning. There were futilitarian holdouts who scorned the Gandhi movement, and there were other futilitarians who found hope in the vision and persistence that Gandhi presented.

Finally, especially among deeply conservative Hindus, there were those who manifested the aloof form of transestablishment detachment from any form of historical engagement.

In every story of significant social change, all six of these dynamics may be observed.

Where is Today's Visionary Transestablishment?

The Gandhian independence movement was not primarily focused on ecology or the energy crisis or the rule of corporation wealth over democracy. These are historical awakenings taking place in 2011. There are overlaps between Gandhi's vision and the vision of today's visionary transestablishment, but different times require different inclusive visions. We have proposed that the end of civilization/empire and the building of Eco-Democracy defines the core vision of the visionary transestablishment today. Whatever vision we visionaries now have will improve as we seek to enact it over the coming years.

Do visionary transestablishment forces actually exist today? How large is their number? Are they doing something? Are they coordinating with one another? Is it realistic to see this portion of our contemporary society as an effective force for long-range social change?

Visionary transestablishment forces certainly do exist. Their numbers may be small, but their impact upon the course of history can be great if we become clear about the avalanches of change and how whistles can be blown at the whistle points of the building snow. What make the visionary transestablishment powerful is their grasp, articulation, and enduring commitment to the truth. Truth can win in the end. Millions can be motivated to live the truth no matter how powerful the opposition to truth may be.

Today's visionary transestablishment agree with today's disestablishment view that civilization is not a sustainable mode of social organization. But visionaries disagree with the futilitarian disestablishment view that human survival is hopeless. Visionaries also disagree with the communitarian disestablishment view that humans can get off this fast-moving train that is heading toward the abyss and build small communities of survival. Those who attempt to get off or pretend to get off will only succeed in feeling righteous while they perish. Our doom-headed social vehicle is going to carry all of us with it. If we want humanity to survive and thrive we will have to alter the basic mode of the planet-wide social order. The decaying mode of social order (civilization) can and must be transformed. Each piece of this fast-moving train has to be replaced or altered to form a workable, viable, survivable, planet-wide social vehicle. Perhaps "moving train" is not the best metaphor for a human society, for we humans not only ride in our so-called "social vehicles," we are also parts of our society like cells in a living organism. So, we might speak of our visionary transestablishment strategy as tearing the guts out of the civilizational mode, gut by gut, while at the same time we replace those discarded organs with the new organs of the next society. And we need to do this operation without killing the patient. Clearly, this is a tricky task, requiring more imagination than most humans have volunteered to provide.

Today's visionary transestablishment agree with the reforming proestablishment that the inherited society is not all bad, that we need to honor and build upon civilization's best elements, that repair is possible, and that repairing established society is worthwhile even though this old social vehicle is wearing out and is destined for the junk heap. At the same time the visionary transestablishment has different work to do than the reforming proestablishment who, like Barack Obama, work within the current crunch and ambiguities of historical power for some viable repairs on a dying social order. The visionary transestablishment honors these repair technicians, for when civilization passes the baton of social power to Eco-Democratic societies, it is good to have the best gifts of civilization in good repair.

Today's visionary transestablishment has little or no agreement, however, with today's reactionary proestablishment. Those who defend the established corporate rule and its imperial relations with the human world and the natural planet are enemies with whom little or no cooperation is possible. We who identify with the transestablishment vision cringe when we watch the Obama administration attempt bipartisan cooperation with reactionary members of the political elite. Even the modest repairs that Obama is pushing meet scorn and defensive panic from today's reactionaries. These reactionaries have formed a cabal of "No" to any meaningful changes in our disastrous status quo. These reactionaries must simply be denied power to reverse or delay urgent repairs and transformations. Indeed, these reactionaries need to be sidelined from the conversation about how political power is to be employed. Their only positive contribution is to be a foil of idiocy that helps awaken the masses to ever-clearer wisdom.

Today's visionary transestablishment is also in deep tension with the aloof transestablishment. While visionaries share with the aloof a thoroughgoing detachment from the status quo, visionaries are detached in order to be profoundly engaged. In being merely detached, the aloof transestablishment is seeking escape from the horrors of time. Visionaries see engagement in the historical drama as an essential part of authentic living.

The Awakenment Task of the Visionary Transestablishment

An ongoing task of the visionary transestablishment is to increase their numbers through the awakenment of persons currently operating in the other groups.

The awakenment task includes enabling the reforming proestablishment to see their strategic flaw—the impossibility of avoiding the end of the civilizational mode of social organization. The transestablishment rejection of the viability of civilization is grounded in the horrendous problems already discussed: the end of cheap oil, climatic disruption through our vast carbon-fuel burning, a food system that depends upon fossil fuels, billions too many people for this planet, the increasing rate of species extinction, the acidification of the oceans, soil erosion, air pollution, increasing poverty, a widening income gap, the dysfunctions of hierarchy and patriarchy, the disintegration of democracy, the threat of an even more complete control of government by the moneyed few, and so forth. The basic hierarchical arrangements of civilization are antidemocratic and anti-ecological. Since civilization is now global, its inevitable self-destruction will touch almost everyone on the planet. Civilization cannot be simply repaired; it must be replaced. Those who build the replacement will be those who have given up hope that repairs will be enough. An inward death to being civilized is required for the reforming establishment to join the community of the visionary transestablishment. This includes detachment from the long-practiced patterns of being sustained by unconscious comfort-fostering assumptions as well as detachment from addictions to consumerism, cheap fuel, and shallow expectations.

The awakenment of the reactionary proestablishment is harder. Perhaps the task is simply helping them to notice the gross craziness of their resistance as well as the lack of empirical truth that supports their increasingly desperate actions. For the most part these dangerous members of our society must be ruthlessly exposed, sidelined, and excluded from the conversation about the future.

The awakenment of the communitarian disestablishment includes enabling them to see their strategic flaws. In the end it will not work to abandon civilization to its inevitable ruin and start over in small out-of-the-way places. This is a doomed strategy because these new islands of society will be destroyed by those who stay on the civilization train. What sort of human society could even a billion humans create in the presence of five, six, or seven billion humans starving to death in dysfunctional social arrangements? Such a situation is unimaginable in its potential for terror, criminality, corruption, and unrestrained murder. If some local group succeeds in its efforts to feed itself and order its life, the increasingly desperate civilized power holders will confiscate its resources, bleed it dry, and discard the lifeless remains. Eventually, as the civilized train continues its momentum down the track of doom, it will take with it all the conditions needed for human survival anywhere. Victory for a viable future for humanity on this planet includes dealing with the creative dismantling of civilization and its thoroughgoing replacement.

The awakenment of the futilitarian disestablishment includes enabling them to see a vision of hope for actually creating a viable human presence for this planet. While the futilitarians are awake to the peril of civilization and the wrongheadedness of the civilized mode of living, futilitarians are unaware of the full power of the human imagination to create answers where answers are currently not even dreamed. In spite of great lucidity and passionate rejection of what must be rejected, futilitarians remain bound to the establishment they resist. They are like a rebellious son who cannot move beyond his pattern of rejection of a controlling father. Rebellion binds futilitarians to the society they reject. To become full visionaries, futilitarians need to complete their departure from civilization through commitment to a next mode of social organization. In addition, futilitarians need to be challenged to moderate their animosity toward the repair-minded proestablishment. Unlike the futilitarians, the visionary transestablishment provides support for the most forward-looking repair-minded proestablishment. For example, this might mean giving support to the moderate work of an Obama administration, even though the transestablishment vision advocates going much farther. Visionaries often find Obama's proestablishment compromises heartbreaking. Nevertheless, such repair is valuable. It buys time. It allows civilization to last long enough to build a replacement. Futilitarians have a hard time accepting the flexibility of the visionaries and their long-term vision of a dismantlement of civilization and a step-by-step replacement of civilization with something better.

The awakenment of the aloof transestablishment may be the hardest of all, for these persons are in one sense close associates of the visionaries. They have embraced half of the visionary attitude: a complete detachment from the current social order.

They omit, however, the other half of the visionary attitude: the grim joy of engagement in the bloody, ambiguous successes and failures of actual historical accomplishment. It is understandable why being aloof might seem preferable. But aloofness finally rests on the delusional desire to escape the historical struggle. The visionary transestablishment acknowledge the futility of escape from history and see that the true fulfillment of being human is found in historical engagement, an engagement that knows that historical results will never be permanent, that every achievement is only a ledge for the next engagement. In their detachment the aloof transestablishment might be viewed as a step toward the visionary transestablishment, but without historical engagement the aloof remain halfway toward full relevance.

A key quality of the visionary transestablishment is a willingness to work with all the other groups to whatever extent possible to create avalanches of change. The visionary transestablishment joins with the reform-minded proestablishment in support of relevant repairs. Visionaries join with the disestablishment in their radical social critique. By honoring the gifts of proestablishment and disestablishment, the visionary transestablishment tends to bring the proestablishment and the disestablishment closer together. Typically, the proestablishment and the disestablishment work for each other's defeat. But the transestablishment seeks to unite the gifts and passions of both these groups into one overall effort toward creating a viable future for humanity and the planet as a whole.

The Friends of Visionary Change

In spite of the differences in perspective between the visionary transestablishment, the reforming proestablishment and the communitarian disestablishment, the latter two groups are friends of the visionaries in producing progressive change.

The reforming proestablishment can provide the numbers that the visionaries lack. While these numbers vary from society to society and from time to time, it is not unrealistic to expect these three groups (reformers, communitarians, and visionaries) to form a majority of the society. Such majorities will be required in electoral politics to sideline the reactionary proestablishment.

The communitarian disestablishment can provide the visionaries with the most likely candidates for additional visionary transestablishment membership. The communitarian disestablishment as well as the reforming proestablishment are already people who care. They are not running away from social engagement. They only lack a fully inclusive vision of what is possible and what is necessary.

Further, the reformers and the communitarians can provide insight and information to the visionaries. The communitarian disestablishment's critique of society is priceless and easily integrated into the visionary perspective. In addition, the communitarians provide most of the people who pioneer new forms of community life. The communitarians typically put their lives on the line in the empowerment of local communities and in opposition to the oppression of state and national power structures. The visionary transestablishment joins the communitarian disestablishment in viewing the empowerment of local communities as an important strategy.

The reforming proestablishment can provide insight and information to the visionaries with regard to the necessary transformation of national and transnational institutions of governance and economy. They see and preserve the good held by these institutions and realize the step-by-step manner in which these institutions can be changed or replaced. Finally, this body of people is the central force for holding the reactionaries in check.

Relative to the inner life, the *communitarians* can help the visionaries be clear on the magnitude of the necessary transformation—the inability to resolve the most crucial issues with mere repairs.

And the *reformers* can help the visionaries be optimistic about the possibility of actual changes in the established fabrics of society. Through their example reformers teach the visionaries that patience and persistence are key to keeping social change in motion. They protect the visionaries from drifting into aloofness.

It is important for us who identify with the visionary transestablishment to recognize our friends and how they can enrich us. It is also important to know how the visions of the other groups are limited and how they can be enriched by our special gifts of consciousness, insight, and presence.

Our goal as visionaries is to bring our vision to fruition. For this we need friends, lots of friends, powerful friends, talented friends. Indeed, we need people, some of whom will take from us the baton for visionary work in the next generation.

The Enemies Without

Not everyone is our friend in the sense of providing a measure of help toward achieving the transestablishment vision. Even our friends will sometimes fail us and disappoint us, but the reactionary proestablishment is out to stop us, discourage us, defeat us, and perhaps even kill us. The futilitarian disestablishment may also manifest deep anger toward us for challenging their cynicism and lack of imagination. They will call us naive for working with the reform-minded. And many of them will have the intellectual power and cleverness to convert some of us to their futilitarian cop out. Similarly, the aloof transestablishment will, in a more subtle and gentle manner, tempt us to give up our hope for visionary change.

We cannot count these groups among our mission-minded friends. They may teach us important lessons about how to see and how not to see reality. Some may be personal friends, even relatives, even people we love and are committed to for personal reasons, but we cannot trust them to share in carrying out our core thrust toward visionary social change. They remain our enemies. They embody those reigning "principalities and powers" that must be defeated. Most of their policies and all their suppression of the policy debate must be opposed. Our love for others must always be tough as well as generous, and our love for the reactionaries, futilitarians, and aloof will require an exceedingly tough quality.

The visionary transestablishment must unrelentingly oppose the reactionary establishment's corporatism; admiration for aristocratic monetary power; and failure to support the weak and the poor against the top-down organization of political, economic, and cultural forces. Nevertheless, our opposition to these reactionaries needs to use nonviolent and electoral means except in the most extreme cases where full blown fascism has taken over and commits to all-out war to defend itself.

The visionary transestablishment must unrelentingly oppose futilitarian cynicism and mental frameworks that limit the futilitarians' capacity to envision possibilities and to access the deep human capacity to invent fresh possibility where none seems to exist.

The visionary transestablishment must unrelentingly oppose the aloof for their idolization of inner states of being and their use of these states as an escape from historical responsibility. A full appropriation of our inner glory as humans includes our capacities to care deeply and engage thoroughly in the activities of the historical drama. We become less than our true selves when we allow ourselves to drift into the comfort of aloofness.

The Enemies Within

The reader of this chapter may have noticed that each of the six types of social attitude occurs inside each of us. Though we may identify deeply and fundamentally with the visionary transestablishment, we may also find within ourselves a capacity to be more aloof than we might like to admit.

We may even come upon ourselves being a pro-establishment reactionary on some topic or another. For example, the men among us may encounter visionary women who expose our addiction to the patriarchal patterns that still corrupt our unconscious or half-conscious use of inappropriate speech and behavior.

We may find ourselves being disestablishment futilitarians who are settling for a thoroughgoing hopelessness as we face the enormity of our challenges.

We may also slip into being disestablishment communitarians who believe (on, say, Wednesday or Friday) that our well-conceived inclusive vision is too much to ever be achieved by humanity. So we conclude that perhaps it is enough after all to simply create a small alternative community somewhere and let the rest of this awful world go by.

And finally, we may find ourselves being reform-minded proestablishment activists who conclude that civilization may be workable after all with a few well-chosen repairs.

Truly, this entire drama is going on within each of us. It turns out that the persistent visionary is someone who knows that in spite of everything, there is always a fresh start for each of us and for all of us.

Overcoming the Enemies Within

It takes initiative to overcome the enemies within, but it is not the initiative of self-incrimination. It is not the initiative of some invasive operation that tries to remove these enemies as if they were cancers. Rather, the initiative required is the initiative of simply noticing the presence of these interior enemies, noticing the function they serve in providing comfort rather than truth. When we notice that our enemies within want to avoid being noticed, we are opening to our visionary potential. Perhaps we have made a vow to remain a visionary for the rest of our lives, but tomorrow and the next day and the next it will not be the vow, but the noticing, that will overcome the enemies within.

Communities for Overcoming the Enemies Within

As we master our own inner enemies, we will be able to assist others in their handling of their enemies within. They will have to do their own noticing, but we can assist them to notice. We can build communities of assistance in which we assist one another to become aware of and overcome the enemies within. What a person may not see in himself or herself, the caring companion may see. Such communities of mutual assistance will prove to be of major importance in creating the forces that can overcome the enemies without. A strong transestablishment movement will need to create ways to meet with one another and provide nurture and encouragement to one another. The human being is a communal being. If we are to win our fight with the vast illusions of the social establishment, we will need our own communities of visionary support.

Chapter 23

The Role and Limitations of Electoral Politics

Electoral politics is a key arena of action for overcoming the destructive forces that are carrying humanity to premature extinction. As a strategy of action, electoral politics is necessary, but it is not a sufficient mode of action. Some count too much on this strategy, expecting from it more than it can produce. Others become discouraged with electoral politics and thereby expect too little. So what is electoral politics? What is its role, and what are its limitations?

Law and Order

Governing has to do with law and order and with the use of coercive force. Political process is about who makes, judges, and enforces the laws and how they do it. Political process is about who carries out the administration of social order and how they do it. Political process is about who applies "legal" coercive force and how they do it. Law is a blunt instrument; the best ethical choices can never be limited to the current laws of any society. At the same time, without law and order humanity's worst impulses go unrestrained.

Law is a huge improvement over the capricious rule of a king or CEO or other alpha-dog figure. "Law," when it means something more than a king's arbitrary promulgations, is a huge advance in human affairs. When law means a set of clear, rational agreements made by a large number of persons, law dethrones the capricious king or queen. When we say that our president is not above the law (that the law applies to him or her like anyone else), we are affirming a huge advance in human affairs.

Democratically arriving at laws that are then fairly and firmly enforced is a key feature of an effective progressive strategy of social change. We must avoid these two pitfalls in our social thinking: (1) the illusory individualistic overemphasis that chaffs at having to be ruled by law; and (2) the use of law by a ruling class to oppress claims for justice by the disempowered. Both an idealization of law and a contempt for law are detrimental views of social functioning.

Progressives must not surrender the law-and-order apparatus to the reactionaries. US right-wing ideologues oppose government in its role as a disciplinarian of the economic institutions, claiming at times that the least possible government is the best government. Yet these hypocrites also insist on running the government and on enlarging the government toward further enrichment of the rich, further robbery of the poor, plus buying of a massive military outlay and supporting its excessive use. Progressive forces need to champion an increasingly democratic quality of government that thoroughly excludes these crass right-wing attitudes.

Good law and order is needed. Even a somewhat obsolete establishment of law and order has value: it preserves values that we need to keep, including an orderly process of governing in which progressive social changes can be proposed, explained, spread, and finally enacted as part of a next law and order.

The Limited Role of Government

Nevertheless, what can be accomplished with law and order and the coercive force of government is limited. What does it mean to take a balanced view with regard to the strategy of electoral politics?

One of the core limitations of electoral politics is that electoral politics is about the empowerment of majority positions. This means that achieving electoral victory is not the first stage of any far-reaching social change. In fact, electoral victories come late in the social-change process. For example, Abraham Lincoln's famous Emancipation Proclamation was not the first stage in the abolition of slavery, but the next-to-last stage. The last stage was using the law-and-order apparatus of the US government to restrain a stubborn minority who still resisted the end of slavery. The first stage was represented by people like John Woolman, Sojourner Truth, Harriet Tubman, William Lloyd Garrison, Frederick Douglass, and other abolitionists who served this cause during many earlier decades. All this work was done before a US president had the opportunity to outlaw slavery.

In 2011 the issues current in the US Congress are not new. Health-care reform, energy transformation, and banking regulation have been much discussed for decades. These long overdue changes are coming into governmental play after much social awakening. Furthermore, current visionaries will tend to be a decade or more ahead of what an Obama-type administration will be politically able to carry out. Perhaps we are approaching the time when electoral politics and government action on some long-postponed issues are possible, and perhaps not. Perhaps more preparation of the population is needed before government can act. In any case, visionaries must not wait on government power to lead social change in the most forward-leaning arenas. Visionaries must move the citizenry into new contexts and then use citizen clout to demand that politicians function in those new contexts. Visionaries must not wait on governments to do their visioning, education, and organizing for them.

At the other extreme, many citizens tend to despair altogether of the usefulness of electoral politics. They tend to rank all the political players as equally dedicated to preserving the status quo. This attitude is visible when progressives who are disappointed with the moderate policies of Barack Obama rank him in the same category as George W. Bush. His modest accomplishments are scorned. His compromises are grieved.

These feelings are understandable, yet a thoroughgoing mistrust of currently empowered government is unwarranted. A moderate government is better than allowing government to sink into extreme reaction. And any government is better than no government at all. Effective politics is the art of the possible; great statesmanship entails building majority consensus and making deep compromises in order to enact the good that is possible for now. Though this realization may seem deeply disappointing to we urgent visionaries, we visionaries need to embrace the challenge to create the as-good-as-possible democratic governments at local, regional, national, and international scopes of governance. This tedious electoral work is part of our winning strategy. Winning entails working with the existing governmental institutions and with the laws that we have, while also working to change the whole context in which laws and governmental institutions can be improved.

The established government typically functions as a barrier that needs to be overcome in making the next sequence of progressive changes. Established government is both friend and enemy to visionary causes. The current government can preserve earlier progressive changes and an improved government will be needed to finish the next set of progressive changes in the years to come. This paradox (however grim it may seem) is simply part of the natural process of human history.

Therefore, a visionary transestablishment strategy in electoral politics includes supporting the best possible empowerment within the current governing institutions in order that old gains can be preserved and completed, and in order that a more open social order can be provided—one that permits the next set of progressive gains to be developed in the consciousness of the citizenry who (hopefully) will later become the next majorities of established democratic governments.

Many disestablishment persons tend to minimize or ignore the importance of cooperating with the existing political institutions or with the existing majorities of people who support these institutions. Some disestablishment perspectives even minimize the importance of all coercive governmental force in human affairs. But the visionary transestablishment supports government as a power structure using specific rules of law and order, punishments, and coercive force (where needed) to enforce the consensus to which democratic discussion has already arrived. And the visionary transestablishment views the firm enforcement of law as an educative service that changes the perceptions of people, and thereby deepens or widens the consensus that undergirds and further liberates the making of the next series of needed laws.

This wholehearted support by the visionary transestablishment for existing government (including its use of coercive force) is supplemented, however, with a strategy of vigorous citizen education. We will discuss citizen education in the next chapter. One of the aims of citizen education is to deepen and transform the democratic discussion and thereby to further empower the democratic, consensus-building process against the tendencies toward oligarchy and obsolescence.

Viewing the Whole Drama of Progressive Change

As already noted the role of government in the drama of progressive change is the role of carrying out the "next-to-last" stage of progressive change. The first task in any profoundly new way of doing things is "progressive witness," the picturing of what can and needs to be done. The second task is the spreading of this fresh breakthrough in societal practice to a full majority of the citizenry. Then comes the next-to-last task of electoral politics—namely, putting this societal breakthrough into law and establishing the social order and the use of coercive force needed to carry out the last stage of the progressive change, namely forcing the still-resisting minority to play within the rules of the newly established legal game.

With this drama in mind we can see that those who count too much on government tend to neglect the work of progressive witness and citizen education. Perhaps they do so because these two forms of social action entail risks. Challenging the current illusions of the established order will usually occasion defensiveness, and this defensiveness may be furious. Changing the perspective of the general citizenry on hotly contested topics requires skill and determination. Furthermore, such educational work requires a basic understanding that people can change, that their habits of living are just that, habits that can be broken and replaced. Human society, in order to be a good and strong society, must accommodate to natural, genetic, biological, and physical factors, but society is not ultimately determined by natural factors. Human society is chosen by humans within the restraints that natural factors provide. Therefore, human society can always be re-chosen by humans. In order to take the risk of doing progressive witness and citizen education, we rely upon this freedom-to-change that constitutes the essence of being human. Those who count too much on government tend to be those who flee from the challenging work of citizen awakening, education, and organization.

Those who count too little on government are those who do not properly fear the potential for human defensiveness, foolishness, and malice. A primary responsibility of good government is to restrain the worst impulses of human beings. Whenever a social order becomes extremely weak, we see an increase in open looting, murder, rape, gang rule, pressing young boys into military service, genocide, and a general dysfunctional chaos. We see a need for more government, not less, in many poverty-stricken nations. And a need for more government can also be seen in the United States (as well as other "well developed" places).

Recent US news stories bear witness to the fact that wherever the coercive power of government is not strong enough, we see an expansion of greedy business practices, incredible billion-dollar Ponzi schemes, trillion-dollar banking fiascos, untenable ecological damage, and so on. Those who want government to be "so small you can drown it in a bathtub" are either libertarian fools or wealthy "greed-heads" who do not want their greed to be limited. Those who think we can flee from the law and order of coercive governments to some pleasant island of unstructured loving fail to notice that human beings carry their capacity for foolish meanness with them to those fair islands. Also, such naive social planners do not notice that there are no islands, that our seven billion humans (if unchecked by law and order that is coercively enforced) will destroy all the innovative islands of proposed innocence and safety.

For all these reasons transestablishment strategies include building a serious partnership between themselves and government unless government has lost all touch with democratically constructed law and order. When a thoroughgoing oppressive dictatorship is the social situation, armed revolution may be necessary to establish enough democratically constructed law and order to proceed with a transestablishment electoral strategy. But when we have a quasi-democratic situation as we do have in the United States in 2011, a partnership between transestablishment forces and such moderate government is appropriate. And this remains true even though the institutions of that government and the laws being passed by that government are in need of vast changes.

The Obama administration provides a clear example of a better-than-usual but not-yet-good-enough government to satisfy a fully progressive vision. While progressives are justly disappointed with what the Obama administration has been willing or able to do, we still have some momentum toward building progressive outcomes. One of the gifts of this administration has been competent governing in comparison with the cronyism so rampant in the previous eight years. The steps made in health-care reform, inadequate though they are, were sorely needed changes. Many politicians have at least crystallized an acknowledgment of the need to restrain the abuses of for-profit health insurance companies.

Another change has been serious concern toward shoring up the laws that govern banking industries and other loose-canon organizations. Opposition to this has been very strong and progress very weak, but the principle has at least been maintained. Also, we are seeing modest steps toward government programs that bring resources to the needs of the underclasses rather than further enriching the aristocracy and promising that never-arriving trickle-down for the rest of us. Support for a post-fossil energy transition is currently meager, but it holds promise to expand rapidly over time. Also, we have seen some closing down of the unrestrained and arrogant "our-way-or-the-highway" nationalism. We have already seen steps being made toward a companionship of listening and consensus building among the community of nations. So huge was the need for this shift that Obama's speeches alone resulted in a Nobel Peace Prize, even though little substantial change was evident at that time. We have also seen long postponed civil-rights advancements such as the elimination of the "Don't Ask, Don't Tell" policy in the US military. These and other changes put in motion by the Obama administration illustrate that electoral politics can produce accomplishments. The fact that these changes are meager from a fully developed transestablishment or disestablishment perspective does not make them unimportant.

Even the most elemental qualities of good government can be crucial steps toward enabling significant change. The lack of governmental competence is horrifically destructive. For example, let us recall the handling of the New Orleans disaster during the George W. Bush administration. Behind all the excuses that were made was the appointment of unqualified persons who were not up to the tasks involved. We who resonate with the transestablishment perspective want much more than the minimal changes we are seeing from the Obama administration. At the same time, we need to recognize that politicians are required to work within the limits of citizen awareness as well as within the limits of the existing structures and the necessity to work with the currently elected officials. Obama has sensitivity about pragmatically working within an expanding citizen consensus rather than following some rigid set of ideological principles. This skill makes him a far more appealing partner for the transestablishment than the rigid ideologues who wish to replace him. Finally, Obama might be led into more progressive actions by those who are able to lead a majority of the citizenry into increased realism.

The Core of Transestablishment Politics

The core of transestablishment political action is electing ever more progressive candidates to public office and building the electoral constituencies that can elect them, sustain them, and pressure them. By "progressive" we mean supportive of the Eco-Democracy vision being described throughout this book.

In order to adequately carry out such electoral strategies, we need to sense what government can and cannot do in the near term, as well as what we want government to do a decade from now.

For example, in the short term the democratic fabric of our society can be rescued from the inordinate power of the super-wealthy. Also, the US government can help our economy move with ever-increasing speed on the energy transition. Immediate government action could prove to the skeptics, cynics, and fossil-fuel fans and profiteers that rapid change on this front can take place. Any politician on the status-quo side of this issue can be convicted of destroying the planet and can be removed from office in all but the most backward districts.

Transforming the US health-care system is another important and illuminating example. Health-care costs have been wrecking the economy and pricing health-care out of reach of many people. This is the fault of an unworkable system. Canada, Great Britain, France, Cuba, and many other places have proved that the solution to these problems entails replacing for-profit insurance companies with a single insurance agency administered by government. We don't have to rewrite the US Constitution to do this. All we have to do is enact and enforce new laws.

But in the United States such a direction meets huge resistance. The for-profit health-care insurance companies fought to eliminate even a moderate government-administered insurance option. Perhaps they are admitting by their actions that a private insurance company cannot compete with a well-run government option. Price-gouging pharmaceutical companies also fear the government's capacity to bargain for drug price reductions. The nature of the resistance of these business institutions shows why the current system is failing. Too much of our health-care spending is going for outlandish salaries and corporation profit taking.

Single-payer advocates know that a government option within a mix of private company options is not a full solution to the health-care crisis. Sooner or later the maze of high-cost, unjustly administered private health-care insurance companies must be closed down. Such companies are the main problem; they cannot be part of the solution. The managers of these antiquated and predatory institutions claim that a single-payer solution is socialism, and they mean this as a criticism. But government management of some social functions is the best solution. Parks, public libraries, police departments, armies, etc. do not work better when run by for-profit organizations. In country after country health-care insurance has proved itself a member of that list.

Neither Left nor Right

Transestablishment politics is neither left nor right but out in front. It is neither capitalist nor socialist but post-civilizational. Capitalism and communism (as well as the various forms of socialism and the various liberalized versions of capitalism) are ways of ordering now-declining industrial civilization. The transestablishment vision sees beyond civilization to a new mode of governing. A transestablishment vision of political order takes from the free enterprise heritage and from the socialist heritage whatever works to solve each practical issue within a post-civilization era of social order. Radical as this vision may seem, it is already happening throughout the world. Most nations now have "mixed economies." The terms "capitalism," "socialism," and "communism" have become increasingly meaningless terms. This is true in the United States, Canada, France, Russia, China, and so on. Pure communism may still exist in North Korea. Pure capitalism exists nowhere. Transestablishment politics must not get trapped in the old left-right arguments.

Our arguments need to have a very practical focus: for example, the restraint of US managerial elite, their boards, and big investors who insist on being unlimited by government with regard to anything they want to do. They even want to be bailed out by government when their wild schemes fail. So blatant have these arrogant forces become that the population is beginning to get very angry. Corporation executives must be corralled, disciplined carefully, and sometimes jailed. Fining a corporation as if it were a person makes a mockery of the law. It only penalizes the shareholders, who are guilty of nothing more than having bought stock. Corporations don't decide to violate laws, managers and executives do. Jail them and it will stop.

Over the long haul we need to require the management of each and every corporation to distribute to their stockholders every dollar they now spend on lobbying government. If they want to organize their stockholders into a nonprofit organization to lobby government, that should be legal. But if we really want a democracy, we will need to make illegal the spending of other people's money (investors' money) to influence public policy. For citizen organizations to lobby and financially support public policies is different. These are citizens who are spending their own money rather than investment money. Corporation executives are spending other people's money. This needs to be a core plank in transestablishment politics—disenfranchising the corporations and enfranchising the citizens. Of course this direction is being vigorously opposed by powerful forces, even five members of the US Supreme Court; nevertheless, citizen insistence can force this change, even if a Constitutional amendment is required.

Clean Elections

The transestablishment political action list also includes clean election legislation that strengthens the relations between citizens and their elected officials. This includes public financing for all accredited state and national candidates plus the institution of instant runoff voting. These innovations need to be combined with voter registration procedures and balloting procedures that are squeaky clean, devoid of any rules that discourage voting or any openness to corruption by existing governmental officials.

The two-party system that has grown up around the necessity to raise huge sums of money to run for public office is part of the corruption. Vast financial power is used to exclude third-party perspectives from even participating in the discussion as well as from significant political power. All candidates are forced to give more time and thought to money raising than to law making. Changing this system is a win-win direction for both voters and politicians, but incumbent politicians tend to side with "those who brought them to power," and in most cases that means the interests of huge corporations, banks, wealthy individuals, and related money pools.

The details of publicly financed political campaigns can be worked out in many ways. It is clear that candidates must prove some measurable level of viability before they are included in public funding. It is clear that the many ways of loop-holing the public financing laws have to be handled. It is probably true that some Supreme Court justices have to be replaced or the Constitution amended. But the difficulties of doing this nationally or locally are not an excuse for inaction on this core topic.

Instant runoff voting laws also need to be carefully crafted, but the basic idea has great potential. Here is the basic idea: give each voter two votes, a first and a second choice, for each office. This enables the voter to use her first vote for the candidate she favors most, and still have a second vote to assure that a perceived worst-case scenario does not transpire. For example, a voter might have voted for Ralph Nader first and Al Gore second; this practice might have avoided the Florida fiasco and eight years of reactionary government under George W. Bush. In a properly operating instant runoff voting system, we would probably have seen most of the second votes of the Nader voters going to Al Gore. There would also have been a lot more first votes given to Nader, and his overall message would have had more impact on education of the citizenry. All these are good results, unless one is a reactionary who fears the sort of big changes that a fully democratic process could and perhaps would accomplish.

Without these electoral-process changes, long-range solutions cannot be achieved and sustained for many crucial ecological, economic, justice, and foreign policy issues. Continuing with the current system means turning the US government into thoroughgoing oligarchy. We can expect these simple electoral-process changes to be vigorously opposed by big money interests. Incumbent politicians who have sucked their power from this corrupt system will be frantic about finding ways to block progress on these matters. Politicians know and big-money people know that clean-election changes open legislative directions that they oppose. The Democratic Party as a whole would find its true interests met if they supported these changes. But many Democratic politicians are also captive to their big money donors.

Clean-election changes will have to be powerfully insisted upon by the voting population. In general, the population is not yet fully informed about the nature of and need for clean election legislation. We need some citizen education that is separate from electoral campaigning. Opposition to these changes will continue to be great, so the voting population will likely need to resort to other means than voting to change the voting system. Citizens will need to construct clever, effective, nonviolent noncooperation strategies that shut down critical portions of the society until these electoral changes are made.

Party Prospects for the United States

As already noted, Barack Obama is a different kind of proestablishment politician than the Bush-Cheney type. The latter are reactionaries who want to move the US society away from many of its deepest and most characteristic US traditions toward policies that support a narrow vision of this nation, a more oligarchic and less democratic society.

In current "media speak" Obama is characterized as a left-of-center liberal or even a radical socialist. But perhaps he actually functions as a right-of-center moderate. And as the Republican Party continues to shift toward extreme right-wing desperation, the upcoming political environment will reveal that Obama is what we might call "a true conservative." The Democratic Party under the leadership of the Obama administration is leading us in a truer conservation of the US Constitution than those on the right. He is for the conservation of the rule of law and order; the conservation of a conscience about torture; the conservation of effective, competent, well-organized government on behalf of the whole people; the conservation of dialogue with all the elements of society in a democratic fashion; the conservation of a respectful and cooperative foreign policy; the conservation of honesty and care for one's neighbor; the conservation of a regulated market economy that works; and the conservation of a big role for government as the spender of last resort in an economic downturn. Obama is not asking for the dismantling of industrial civilization. He is a reformer of civilization. And his reforms conserve gifts that will be important contributions to a post-civilization reordering.

The current leadership of the Republican Party is moving backward toward now-discredited reactionary policies that have proved disastrous in the past. Their image of conserving is conserving tax cuts and tax shelters for the wealthiest citizens, conserving military expenditures that are no longer needed (assuming that they were ever needed for anything except enriching Republicans), conserving an over-reliance on military means in our foreign policy, conserving questionable means of interrogation, conserving unregulated banking systems that coddle corruption and permit theft from the entire global economy, conserving no-bid and hard-wired government contracts for political cronies, conserving the lie that corporation managers know best and that governmental regulation and labor unions are mere impediments to economic growth, conserving racism and religious bigotry, conserving the belief that telling lies often enough and long enough makes them true. Such strategies can now be viewed as reactionary, not conservative. Though some Democrats and Independents have also supported these reactionary directions, "true conservatives" of whatever party will continue asking, "Why must 'conservative' mean support for these untenable directions?"

While the Obama administration's accomplishments have been understandably disappointing to those with a more radical vision, the Obama administration is doing this nation a service by restraining the reactionary Republicans. Obama embodies a form of conservatism that progressives can work with. This is why the Obama administration may still become the beginning of a major change in US leadership. Obama may at least veto the worst ideas. And if pushed hard enough he may promote some transestablishment directions; he has the intelligence, skill, and pragmatic openness and flexibility to make this possible. But we may have to content ourselves with the blessing that the Obama administration's tour of duty merely enables the social mode called "civilization" to last a decade or two longer, giving us time to rally citizenry for something better. In the end, the core issues of civilization are too great for a mere "repair" of civilization to remedy. If we want political leaders who will empower and preserve a shift from civilization/empire to Eco-Democracy, we will need to do more than electoral politics can accomplish. We will need to do a better quality of citizen education, do some well-designed and massively supported nonviolent noncooperation actions, create thousands of empowered transition communities, and achieve some very influential creativity in global affairs.

Doing all, not some, of these transestablishment strategies can bind together enough voters to elect people who can pursue a vibrant dialogue with the Obama-style "true conservatives." Such dialogue can result in meaningful compromises that move US democratic governing toward an ever-more progressive role in human affairs. Such ongoing political dialogue will enable the population to neutralize the political power of the reactionaries. Such dialogue will enable US democratic government to play an appropriate role in establishing and protecting the shift from Empire to Eco-Democracy.

* * * * * * * *

Hundreds of good books have been written about US politics. For further reading on this topic we have selected these four provocative titles:

Bill Moyers, *Moyers on Democracy* (New York: Doubleday, 2008)

Jim Rough, *Society's Breakthrough: Releasing Essential Wisdom and Virtue in All the People* (Bloomington, IN: Jim Rough, 2002)

Brian Tokar, *The Green Alternative: Creating an Ecological Future* (San Pedro, CA: R. & E. Miles, 1987)

James K. Galbraith, *The Predator State: How Conservatives Abandoned the Free Market and Why Liberals Should Too* (New York: Free Press, 2008)

Chapter 24
The Never-Ending Task of Citizen Education

We have already indicated the need to awaken millions of people to the overall transestablishment vision and strategy outlined in this book. The topics covered in this book show a beginning, but only a beginning, of what citizen education needs to include. In addition to developing and communicating a broad vision of the positive potential for our era and the overall strategies for reaching that vision, citizen education needs to include imparting a working knowledge of our own local part of the planet and our local social conditions. Further, we need honest, timely reporting on state, national, and world events, and these events need to be insightfully interpreted in relation to the contexts we are discussing in this book. All this needs to be delivered to a broad array of citizens in forms that are accessible to them.

Citizens of the United States have been "dumbed down" socially and ecologically by ineffective high schools, colleges, and universities; by backward-looking radio, television, Internet, and news magazines; as well as by dogmatic, moralistic, and sentimental religious institutions. There are wonderful exceptions: wise professors, bold news magazines, progressive religious institutions, realistic TV commentators, great websites, and more. Many of these "exceptions" do excellent work and strongly assist citizens who actively seek out these sources.

Nevertheless, we must do much more, especially in rural, inner city, and other neglected places. The overall problem of an uninformed and apathetic citizenry remains huge. A full third of US citizens do not vote in even the most important elections, and many of those who do vote are grossly uninformed. Robert Reich in his book *Supercapitalism* affords evidence that many members of the US population are well informed and well practiced in being investors and consumers but have lost their hold on being informed citizens. We fail to notice that the managers of the huge corporations use our expenditures and our investment money to overwhelm our votes and shape the policies of our government in favor of narrow issues like company profits or market share. Their policies neglect our true interests, our health care, our living environments, and the long-range well-being of our grandchildren. We citizens are part of the problem. Too few of us forcefully and frequently communicate that, "We are not going to take this any more."

Also, we need a new quality of education. We need methods that bring home the existential urgency and concrete, practical relevance of the challenges that we face. People need to be trained to recognize lies, propaganda, and advertising for what they are. Describing such a task is bigger than one book—bigger than a whole library of books. The task requires an awareness of being human as well as being profoundly informed about the basic content of this historical period and its potentialities. This sort of education is never complete. It is ongoing, never-ending, and ever-deepening. We need a permanent process of citizen education, not spasmodic efforts. We need lasting institutions of citizen education in every community.

While some visionary transestablishment citizen education has been taking place for decades, the scale is too small. The audience is too restricted. Our aim in writing this book is to communicate this vision and strategy to a wider range of people. We also hope to deepen the dialogue on these topics among the many persons already engaged in progressive actions.

Books are only a small part of a complete citizen education strategy. Citizen education includes hands-on training and experience as well as many sorts of media exposure: news magazines, newspapers, documentaries, television programs, e-mail messages, Internet dialogues, conferences, workshops, research assemblies, town-hall meetings, political party discussions, nongovernmental trainings, pageants, parades, plays, and this list goes on.

We envision an upgrade in the quality of these activities. We envision a coming together of a visionary transestablishment consensus about what needs to be clarified and how to do it with a wide range of people. We look for our means of communication to be improved. We look for the number of people skilled in effective means of communication to increase.

So, what are effective means of communication? How do we think through what it takes to enable miseducated, undereducated, and apathetic human beings to become inspired, visionary agents of change?

Some Raw Wisdom on How People Change

When we encounter people who desperately cling to delusory perspectives on what is real, reinforced by a refusal to consider contrary evidence, how do we assist them to open themselves to the truth of their lives? First of all, we have to assume that people can change. We need to notice that their resistance to change is rooted in deep personal anxieties. Any deep change in basic perspective amounts to a kind of death to security systems, to long-held sensibilities about what is real, and to comfortable associations with other people who hold similar views. This may be a formidable fortress of defense. It can take time, patience, and good methods to melt these prison walls and set these prisoners free.

Nevertheless, people can and do change. Each of us knows that people change when we reflect upon our own life history. Almost none of us now see life as we did even one decade ago. With a bit of assistance, each person has the capacity to discover for herself or himself what is true. Transestablishment education is not about imposing dogma, but about pointing out reality. Reality is a powerful force. We need to work with reality rather than impose upon reality our latest ideas about reality. We need to point out reality, rather than shout down opposing opinions.

So how do citizen educators provide the assistance needed? We will need to learn how to breach the walls of defense mentioned above: (1) security systems, (2) long-held sensibilities, and (3) comfortable associations with others who hold similar views.

(1) Security Systems

Everyone has a passion to be secure in what they know or think they know about life. Our practices of living are based on this knowing. Our many fears have been temporarily set aside by our systems of "secure" knowing. Deep change means that each changing person has to experience those suppressed fears and admit that no one is really secure, that everyone is ignorant about life, always has been, and always will be. To be of help to people, the transestablishment educator needs to communicate that she or he understands such feelings from personal experience and has, nevertheless, moved beyond them into the wide-open spaces of recognizing that mental security is not needed, that there is no such thing as a lasting ideology or any other form of intellectual security. When this basic ignorance is seen, we can point out that people might as well walk out onto the wild waters of intellectual insecurity and find happiness within things as they actually are—always mysterious, always unfolding, always requiring of us new thought.

(2) Long-Held Sensibilities

Everyone has a sense of reality, and this sense of reality includes some validity and some illusory qualities. In order to move beyond a given sense of reality, a person needs to sort out what is true and what is not true within his or her existing sense of reality. Assisting people to do this takes time, patience, and some understanding of other people's current perspectives— both the gifts and the flaws of those perspectives.

(3) Associations with Others

Everyone except the most courageous truth tellers among us requires communal support. If we expect people to hang on to a new view of things, we have to provide them with a community of support for that fresh viewpoint. If we don't, they will return to their old communities and their old views. This is why most of the detailed work of citizen education has to take place in local communities where awakening people are provided ongoing community with other awakening people. However daunting such a program of care may seem, it is clearly one of the keys to citizen education. Keenly awake people tend to hang out with keenly awake people. Citizen education is going to involve awake people hanging out with those who are still awakening and who need support in doing so.

The Education Challenge

These brief descriptions of effective citizen education methods are only a scratch on the methodological surface, but perhaps we have said enough to support two conclusions: people can change, and deep change is not easy to assist. Furthermore, the education challenge does not reside in other people and their unbelievable stubbornness. Their stubbornness is not unbelievable; we all experience it in our own lives. The education challenge resides in "we" who have volunteered to be the educators who awaken the stubbornly sleeping.

Consider a family member who is still asleep in bed when it is time for breakfast. The responsibility for remedying this situation is not in the hands of the sleeper but in the hands of the awake family member. The person who is already awake has to awaken the sleeping. The sleeper, without knowing it, is waiting to be awakened.

Appealing to the Profound Person

Those of us who are initiating citizen education need to appeal to people's deepest grandness—their trust in reality and a willingness to open to it, their freedom to see the truth and act upon it, and their compassion for others. People by nature do care for everyone; compassion is built into our essential nature. Alerting people to their own suffering is a means of awakening compassion for themselves. Alerting people to the deep suffering taking place in the world is a means of accessing this same compassion for others. The educator will also be required to counter silly excuses, skillfully distributed by status-quo supporters. The educator will need to point out to people that being compassionate includes more than enriching our one-on-one personal relations. A thoroughgoing and deep compassion includes altering the social fabrics that care for everyone. Changed individuals create changed social structures, and changed social structures entrain changed individuals. Though changing social structures may seem like impersonal work, it is deep love that has consequences in the lives of persons.

Some people flee from the slow, sometimes cruel work of changing social structures. They feel more comfortable working with one-on-one relations. Other people flee from intimate relations into working exclusively on changing the social fabrics. Both intimate relations and structural change are needed, and each of us is called upon to participate in both. A complete picture of a truly visionary and effective educational strategy includes both one-on-one care and enabling transformation of the overall social structures. The visionary educator must champion both, even though she or he may tend to specialize in one of these two areas of contribution.

The Content of Transestablishment Education

Transestablishment citizen education focuses on awakening persons to their own sense of truth, and it also has specific social content. Transestablishment educators are already building new stories for remembering the past and anticipating the future. The master story shared in this book includes: (1) the promotion of a profound reconnection with the natural planet – (e.g., a love for the rocks, rivers, oceans, species, atmospheres, and soils); (2) a dedication to a viable humanity for this planet; (3) a knowledge of cultural, political, and economic processes and how these processes change; (4) a realization that we are in a period of massive change from civilization to something better; and (5) the strategic wisdom we are discussing in Part Four of this book. Strategy is part of the content that needs to be communicated. People need to learn the importance of designing and carrying out effective strategies. Finally, the ongoing process of social change will constantly re-inform us about what citizen education needs to include.

Even the best educational processes do not automatically lead to social change. Education must be followed up with opportunities for participation in social change actions. Quality education includes instilling the motivation and the confidence to participate in the ongoing work of social change. Citizen education not only precedes citizen participation, it also continues during that participation. Citizen education needs to become part of the rhythm of life that characterizes our whole pattern of social engagement, becoming an ongoing component of the new society that we are building.

Citizen education is a factor within each of our five social change strategies. Politicians and their supporters can educate the public with their speeches and their actions. Nonviolent noncooperation actions are educational events as well as pressure for change. Local community projects demonstrate the sort of social practices we are asking people to understand, tell about, and build. Fresh, populist-oriented global institutions must be fought for and supported by educating citizens to be educated citizens. As visionary educators our words, our actions, our presence becomes educative through the many human contacts that each of us has and arranges to have.

Finally, we need to be able to state the content of our transestablishment education in simple sentences. Here is an example:

The core task is to overthrow hierarchy and patriarchy with the power of full democracy and full ecological responsibility. This does not mean going back to tribal society. It means going forward beyond what we have called "civilization." We can learn from pre-civilization societies and from civilized societies, but we are inventing something different and better.

Following is a slightly longer rendition of the core educational message.

Rescuing Humanity from Extinction

We live in a time of serious threat, a threat so serious that we don't want to even notice it. And if we do notice it, we don't want to believe that we can do something about it.

This threat is first of all an ecological threat. The unleashed and undisciplined impulse to grow industrial civilization ever upward and onward has reached the limit of this planet's capacity to support it. So our first appropriate response to the overall threat may be to shut down our fossil-fuel use and move toward solar power, wind energy, geothermal energy, and other non-carbon-dioxide-producing fuels. This direction is strongly resisted by companies that profit from the current practices, by workers whose jobs are involved, and by those who prefer the familiar to any thoroughgoing change. The promoters of our current energy system are willing to lie and spend millions of dollars lying and buying media and politicians to lie for them. In such a confused social environment, the plain and simple truth becomes something controversial and spurned. Nevertheless, we need to proclaim this truth and act upon it.

Secondly, we need to face, understand, and alter a serious threat to our US democratic roots. We are facing a wealthy oligarchy that masquerades as a viable option for dumbed-down and duped voters. The entire US Republican Party and a large portion of the Democratic Party are addicted to serving the wealthy segment of our society. Patriarchal relations toward women and nature are woven into this hierarchical pattern. These hierarchical/patriarchal relations can only be dissolved by awakening citizens who take their citizenship seriously. Electoral politics is part of that seriousness, but it is not all. To be serious about what we actually face, we awakening citizens will need to go to the streets, shut down companies and governments, block railroad tracks to coal-fired power plants, or whatever is required to present the powers that be with a deal they cannot refuse. We need to insist on having state and national governments that restrain the greedy and lawless forces of our society and thereby permit the local changes we need.

Thirdly, we awakening citizens need to empower the local communities where we live against the centralizing power of corporate boardrooms as well as state and national governmental bodies dedicated to corporate rule. We need to decentralize power to the citizens. Citizens live in local communities. If we do not have the power to determine what takes place where we live, we are powerless. We are slaves to the huge and thoughtless forces that are shaping every local community on the face of the Earth.

Fourthly, we need to drastically reform our international institutions. The World Trade Organization, The World Bank, The International Monetary Fund all stray from benefiting the worldwide community when they are controlled by wealthy corporations and their bought political leaders. As we empower our local communities, reform our state and national governments, and alter our ecological and personal habits, we also need to build a new set of international institutions that are responsive to the citizens of the world rather than to the corporation wealth pools and their bought governments.

If this task sounds overwhelming, the actual details are so overwhelming that most of us don't even want to know them. As an old song says, all of us long to find "a sweet little nest somewhere in the West and let the rest of the world go by." If we do not admit this longing, we are not likely to resist it and do something meaningful with our one life.

* * * * * * * *

For further reading on the citizen education topic, every book we have recommended could apply. We have selected below three books that are especially useful for ten or twelve sessions of small group study:

Robert Jensen, *Citizens of the Empire: The Struggle to Claim Our Humanity* (San Francisco, CA: City Lights Books, 2004)

Sam Smith, *Why Bother?: Getting a Life in a Locked-down Land* (Los Angeles, CA: Feral House, 2001)

Robert B. Reich, *Supercapitalism: The Transformation of Business, Democracy, and Everyday Life* (New York, NY: Alfred A. Knoff, 2008)

Chapter 25

The Need for Nonviolent Noncooperation

The Gandhi independence movement in India and the US civil rights movement led by Martin Luther King Jr. are good illustrations of the nonviolent noncooperation means of social change. Most labor union activities also illustrate nonviolent noncooperation. Strikes sometimes turn violent, but this is usually the fault of the employers. Rarely has union activity included beating people or killing people.

No human organization can function without the cooperation of its members; therefore, nonviolent noncooperation is a potentially powerful strategy. Passing and enforcing laws may be less messy and more permanent, but when laws cannot be passed or are not being enforced, nonviolent noncooperation is an effective way to stop something, slow something, start something, or expand something. Transestablishment forces are almost always working from a minority position. So, for well-organized minorities, nonviolent noncooperation can be an effective strategy.

Nonviolent noncooperation is often costly to its participants, and it is an extremely costly strategy when the social context is an authoritarian government that is willing to use unlimited violence to oppose any dissent. When facing such a government, nonviolent noncooperation may result in little more than revealing to that government who they need to slaughter first. Effective nonviolent noncooperation presupposes the presence of a somewhat democratic government and a population with a conscience about the issues in question. Nonviolent noncooperation honors such a government as a partner in its actions. When employing such strategies we expect to move democratic governments farther and faster than they might otherwise move. Nonviolent noncooperation is also an educational method, because it constructs a newsworthy social drama that reaches many people with a more profound view of the chosen issue. It tends to rock a population out of the standard views being propagated by the established media and carried out by established institutions.

The work of Gandhi and Martin Luther King Jr. has left a strong following throughout the world. Some exaggerate the usefulness of nonviolent noncooperation methods, considering them to be almost always the best tool for deep changes. Others are offended by these methods, especially illegal actions that challenge taken-for-granted laws or moral comfort. But the authors of this book place nonviolent noncooperation actions in our core list of visionary transestablishment strategies. We do so because we believe this means of action fills an important gap in the need for effective overall strategies of social change.

Whenever an established social order is stuck in a rut of bad practices and that social order is not amenable to political action or even normal education, the nonviolent noncooperation mode of social action may be the best available strategy. It also needs to be said, however, that carrying out nonviolent noncooperation in a competent fashion requires careful thinking and patient endurance by the acting forces. To be effective such action must be more than a catharsis for pent-up anger. Anger is a wholesome emotion, but to be an effective motivator of social change, anger must be skillfully channeled.

Examples

Gandhi's salt march is a vivid example of a thoughtful assessment of the historical situation combined with persistent, careful, imaginative planning. The British oppression of the economy of India included a ridiculous law that prevented people from making their own salt. This provided Gandhi with an opportunity to stage a massive drama of noncooperation with the governing authorities. He did so in a way that amused and challenged the conscience of the British oppressors. Thousands of people showed up on the beach, lit fires, and made salt from seawater. The police were overwhelmed by the numbers, the law was ridiculous in the first place, and a massive portion of the population was standing up for themselves and indicating to the established powers that their cooperation with further tyranny was not assured.

The Birmingham bus boycott is another vivid example of how masses of people can persist in noncooperation with ridiculous laws until the governing authorities are forced to negotiate change. This glorious story is told in detail in Clark Johnson's documentary film *Boycott*.

The India campaign for independence and the US civil rights movement may now seem like ancient history to many people. Perhaps we need more recent examples to fully visualize the potential of nonviolent noncooperation methods. An inspiring but little-known example is told in the documentary film *Pray the Devil Back to Hell*. It is the story of ending fourteen years of civil war in Liberia. The dictator, Charles Taylor, and forces opposing him had turned the entire society into a battlefield. Each day the Liberian women who operated the markets had to face the risk of theft, rape, and death as well as having their sons kidnapped for military service. A Christian churchwoman, Leymah Gbowee, reluctantly discovered that her disgust, clarity, and communication skills were selecting her for leadership. She and other Christian women organized and then extended their organization to Muslim women. These women knew where the next battles were going to be fought and showed up in silent protest. When peace discussions were being held among the Liberian male leaders in neighboring Sierra Leone, many of these women traveled there and blocked the exits of the negotiating hall until the men worked something out. Later, the women and men of Liberia elected Ellen Johnson Sirleaf to be the first woman president of an African nation.

Another inspiring example is told in the documentary film *The Take*. It is the story of Argentine manufacturing workers who took over mismanaged and shut-down plants at which they had been working. They claimed that the property and the equipment were owned by them because of unpaid wages. They managed the plants themselves, produced and sold their products, and endured the attempts of the managerial elite to have the government give the plants back to the failed managers.

In 2011 US television covered the massive protests in Egypt that removed Mubarak and opened doors for a more democratic government there. A key element in that story is that the Egyptian military refused to violently put down the protests and thus supported the working out of a nonviolent transition. At this juncture we see a further conflict with the military to enable the promised fair elections.

As we go to press, the Occupy Wall Street and Occupy Movement protests are growing nationwide and worldwide and promise to have a significant impact. They will further educate us on the nature and importance of the strategy of nonviolent noncooperation. It may be that we are seeing the beginning of a generation-long sea change in US economic policies.

Principles of Nonviolent Noncooperation

"Truth power" was an important principle of Gandhi's nonviolent philosophy. The social truth is an underlying power that can be counted upon and summoned by a competent nonviolent noncooperation action. As the social truth becomes powerfully exposed to the consciousness of a population and its leadership, oppressive lies can be defeated. In the end, truth is a power that can win over established lies. Lies have to hide something true in order to endure. Exposing these hidden aspects of truth is a core ingredient in the effective use of nonviolent noncooperation as a means of social change.

Nonviolence is also a key quality in this social change method. Whenever violence is used, the legal structures of the social order are granted authorization to respond with violence. This is their job, to maintain social order with coercive force. As a means of social change, violence is only appropriate when the entire social order must be replaced. Hitler's Nazism endures as a prime example. Arguments that Hitler's fascism could have been defeated with nonviolent noncooperation are unconvincing. But when social change is desired within a semi-open social order, nonviolent noncooperation can be an effective means of social change. Nonviolent actions respect the overall need for social order while undermining the existing social order. Nonviolent noncooperation may be met with violence from the social order, but this tends to discredit the social order and reveal to a wider portion of the population that the existing social order is doing a misordering of the society. When nonviolent forces are willing to go to jail as a testimony of their support for social order (but not the current social order), they undercut the charge that they are simply criminals or advocates of social chaos. They know that they are disobeying laws and that laws need to be enforced. But the laws they are disobeying are the laws that they wish to change, laws that they want the population to see are laws that need to be changed.

In order to be effective, this mode of social action needs to be *well planned* and crafted to transform society toward clearly stated outcomes. Painfully awake and angry people need to be trained to acknowledge and channel their anger into useful actions. Nonviolent noncooperation is not for cowards or for loose cannons. It requires a thoughtful and courageous discipline.

The Future of Nonviolent Noncooperation

Some have lost their trust in nonviolent noncooperation as a means of effective social change for the future. While massive protests were eventually effective in closing down the Vietnam war, the massive protests that took place even before the Iraq war began were not effective in avoiding that war. The protests were scorned by the US government, minimized by the press, and largely ignored by the general population. Why was this so? It may be that these protests did not focus clearly enough on the core lies that supported the Iraq war. The question of "best focus" applies to other protests as well. We examine below how nonviolent noncooperation can be effective in some of the key areas—with war protesting, but also with protesting for equity against the Wall Street oligarchy, for a post-fossil-fuel energy transition, and for clean elections.

War Protesting

Some protesters against the Iraq war seemed to communicate that all war is bad. This does not resonate well with a nation that still prides itself on its war for independence, its civil war to end slavery and preserve the union, and having made heroic sacrifices to defeat fascism in World War II. Not all protesters against the Iraq war were pacifists; many were even war veterans. But the claim that this particular war was uncalled for may not have been made powerfully enough to make headway against a population still consumed by anger, fear, and feelings of "patriotic revenge" fostered and enflamed by the misleading claims of our national leaders after the 9/11 attacks on the Twin Towers and the Pentagon.

So let us imagine what might have happened and still might happen in our war protesting if we focus on something other than "War is hell." Most people already know that war is hell, and they also know that war can be an action of last resort. So let us imagine what might happen if we focus on how the particular war we are protesting does not qualify as a last resort—that, for example, it is not taking the moral high ground to go to war to make the world safer and more profitable for US business interests. Most Latin American, African, Middle Eastern, and Asian nations no longer cooperate with being controlled by US business interests. But a majority of US citizens, knowingly or unknowingly, cooperate with a business-oriented US foreign policy and with the use of military means to enforce business interests. Most citizens do not acknowledge that their nation is using these imperialistic practices to provide an already advantaged US citizenry with cheap products and larger investment returns. The Iraq war was clearly related to cheap oil availability, not revenge or homeland safety as claimed. So our protests against that war might have been more effective had we more clearly charged our leaders with using the patriotism, excellence, health, and lives of our military personnel in such a shamefully greedy cause. This is the sort of social truth that can reach deeply into the US conscience.

Here is another illusion that our war protesting might expose: the assumption that the military and economic power of the United States is strong enough to control the twenty-first-century world. We might have learned through the Vietnam experience that when a majority of a local population is willing to die for their vision for their nation, a distant nation like the Unites States could send every able-bodied person to that war and still not win it. Also, the United States can destroy its own economy by overextending itself in such wars.

Though war entails a huge cost in lives, psychological wreckage, and financial treasure, US citizens are willing to justify such enormous sacrifices on the grounds of national defense or creating a safe world. Such a willingness to sacrifice can easily be viewed as heroic. War protests will not win in the United States as long as we insist on protesting war itself rather than the specific wrongheadedness of each specific war.

Wall- Street Oligarchy Protesting

What might be the most useful acts of nonviolent noncooperation with regard to our broken fiscal systems? Many books have already been written on how we need to close down the Wall-Street economy and build a Main-Street economy.[46] What

---

[46] For example, see David Korten's *Agenda for a New Economy: From Phantom Wealth to Real Wealth, Second Edition* (San Francisco: Berrett Koehler, 2010)

would it mean for us to devise effective ways to nonviolently noncooperate with the Wall-Street economy in favor of building a Main-Street economy? As this book goes to press the Occupy Wall Street protest is growing in numbers and places around the nation. Clearly this action is awakening people to the depth of the inequity and oppression of the 99% by the 1% Perhaps this can eventually include devising ways to put some criminal bankers in jail and breaking up the big banks. Perhaps masses of people will need to pull deposits and credit card accounts out of the big Wall-Street banks and use that money to establish cooperative community banks that loan money to build our Main-Street economy—our solar panels, our wind turbines, our locally grounded, job-producing economic order. Most of us do not have the wealth to make a difference through investing, so we would probably need to make our contribution to fiscal-system changes through buying locally made products; organizing local businesses and food cooperatives; starting organic farms, barter clubs, and whatever might help move the center of economic gravity away from the global-profit addicts to where people actually live in daily association.

We will discuss local community actions more fully in the following chapter on community empowerment. Nonviolent noncooperation and local community empowerment are closely related strategies.

Energy Transition Protesting

On the energy front we can use nonviolent noncooperation in a coal moratorium, an ongoing protest already in motion. The coal moratorium movement is assisting communities to be clear that coal use is the nastiest aspect of our obsolete energy system. We could do more to mobilize response to the horrific mountaintop-removal mining practices of coal companies in Appalachia. We could do more with protests against government agencies that fail to enforce compliance with the laws being violated by coal mining companies. When coal companies threaten higher prices, the coal moratorium movement can explain that making coal more expensive to use, transport, and mine is one way to end the use of this dirty fuel. Another way to raise coal prices is to insist on enforcing laws that require mining companies to pay for the full repair of the environments they damage. Coal companies could be required to pay for the employment of those who do the repair. This would also help relieve the unemployment situation caused by the phasing out of coal mining jobs.

We could also organize a protest club in every community that lives in the same county with a coal-fired power plant. We could fight against not only the licensing of new plants but also insist on closing down the old ones. Those of us who use the energy are in a position to decide how we do and do not want that energy provided. For example, we need to critique the ridiculous notions of "clean coal" and "carbon capture." (Carbon capture might play a small role in minimizing coal damage as coal is being phased out, but as a reason for retaining coal use it is bogus.) Our overall slogan might be "Leave Coal in the Ground, Not in the Air." Such a goal may seem impossible in terms of current practice, but it is exactly the direction we need to go. Right now, educating the population on this specific aspect of a new energy direction is more important than any particular coal plant or coal-mine victory. Basically, we need to be organized in a massive way and be relentless on this topic until coal use is more scandalous than cocaine use. And the tar sands production of oil needs to be outed as even more scandalous than coal use.

Clean Elections Protesting

On the clean elections front, especially on the public financing of campaigns for national and state offices, we can use nonviolent noncooperation to make clear the imporatance of needed changes in this area. This has become especially urgent in the wake of the recent Supreme Court ruling that allows unlimited corporation money into the electoral process. We need to call public attention to the money-addicted politicians who oppose clean elections and to unelected Justices who support big-money rule. We need to find ways to thoroughly embarrass any legislator or congressperson or justice who votes or rules against clean election reform. We need to dramatize the truth that they are holding ordinary voters in contempt in order to pander to big-money rule. So what do we actually do? How do we interrupt the current trends in dramatic ways? The status quo cannot persist without cooperation from the population. We need to find ways to withdraw that cooperation. We need to find the ways in which our cooperation counts, that no voting machine can miscount.

Merely dealing with the fund-raising of the politicians does not deal with the corporate money that goes into issue-advocacy TV and extensive lobbying. For a while we are not going to have laws against using corporation treasury money to influence public policy. Even if Congress and the President crafted such laws, the current Supreme Court would rule them unconstitutional. So our protests may need to include and perhaps emphasize the stigmatizing of five members of the US Supreme Court as the most vicious, antidemocratic oligarchs in our common life.

* * * * * * * *

Even though it will take a great deal of careful planning and work to make nonviolent noncooperation protesting effective in the current United States, we need to keep employing our creative minds toward realizing the social awakening potential of this strategy.

For further reading on this topic we recommend the following:

Saul D. Alinsky, *Rules for Radicals: A Pragmatic Primer for Realistic Radicals* (New York: Vintage Books, 1989)

Starhawk, *Webs of Power: Notes from the Global Uprising* (Gabriola Island BC, Canada: New Society Publishers, 2002)

Roy Morrison, *We Build the Road as We Travel* (Gabriola Island BC, Canada: New Society Publishers, 1991)

Workplace Democracy and Social Change, ed. by Frank Lindenfeld and Joyce Rothschild-Whitt (Boston: Porter Sargent Publishers, 1982)

Chapter 26

The Strategic Importance of Local Empowerment

Building a post-civilization mode of society (Eco-Democracy) requires more than an upgrade in electoral politics, effective progressive citizen education, and illuminating nonviolent noncooperative campaigns. Bringing about the massive transition that we have described will also require the detailed work of empowering local communities. Community empowerment is required for its own sake and also because local empowerment will be necessary as a means of forcing the state, national, and international power centers into constructive paths.

Local communities in the United States are currently disempowered because the large decisions tend to be made by state and national governments or in boardrooms and managerial offices of the largest corporations. Local communities have become accustomed to being small, powerless subparts of their state and nation. In general people don't even know what "local community" means. Do we mean a county, a city, a neighborhood, or some larger region? Most of our electoral districts are gerrymandered monstrosities that have no human meaning at all. Our zip code districts and telephone districts are also meaningless to the communal sensibilities of local citizens.

To empower a local community means a huge change and a huge challenge to those larger structures that have assumed all the power. It is also a huge challenge to those local citizens who have given up on being communally powerful and resigned themselves to function as individuals or single-family units struggling to survive and prosper in this competitive dog-eat-dog world.

So, why bother with local community empowerment? To start with it is necessary as a means of winning the overall victory we are envisioning. The emergence of a genuine democracy must take place locally. Most citizens live in some local place. Only through identification with that place and the people who live there can each citizen begin to experience a sense of responsibility and a meaningful role in the shaping of history.

Some have given up on finding a place of influence within a local community. Instead, they have opted for a place of influence within some corporation. Having a role in a corporation can feel powerful if one is a "higher up." But there is usually someone who is still higher up; therefore, even strong executive roles are vulnerable. Even a chief executive who becomes too innovative will tend to get fired by those who comprise the real rulership of that corporation. Also, a corporation is a limited-scope organization. It is not a whole cultural, political, and economic organization. It is an economic organization that strives for cultural and political influence to support its economic emphasis. It is also an antidemocratic organization, a bit of feudalism left over from the Middle Ages. There may be a use for a few corporations in an Eco-Democratic society, but democratic empowerment is not one of those uses. No matter how many worker-participation innovations are made, a corporation is not a fully democratic institution.

Community Organization

Local empowerment, often called "community organization," has been taking place for many decades and in many different ways. Barack Obama has "community organizer" on his resume for political leadership. Though this experience was scorned by Sarah Palin, Rudi Giuliani, and others, community organizing is now and shall be for the rest of the century one of the most important elements of the grand transition to Eco-Democracy.

Obama was a community organizer in South Chicago under the tutelage of a tradition of community work set in motion by Saul Alinsky, whose book *Reveille for Radicals* remains a classic on community organizing. His description of the qualities needed for the effective community organizer can remain a guide for community work throughout the coming century. Here is a list of community organizer qualities spelled out in Alinsky's second book, *Rules for Radicals*: curiosity, irreverence, imagination, a sense of humor, a vision of a better world, an organized personality, flexibility, a doer, and a free and open mind. We need hundreds of such people.

In the 1960s the Institute of Cultural Affairs began another mode of community organization on the West Side of Chicago in a small area of African American neighborhood. Titled "Fifth City," this project included the training of about two hundred local citizens in a set of methods that resulted in a community organization that endures to this day. These methods include working in a small, circumscribed area, analyzing all the problems (cultural, political, and economic), and creating ongoing programs such as preschool education, housing reconstruction, and a community center for local business promotion. Included as a central part of this project was paying attention to the need for shifting the interior images of local people from victim to responsible citizen. These methods were so effective that they have been widely shared and applied in many other places around the world.

Recently, we have seen another movement in community empowerment that emphasizes "transition towns." As mentioned in Chapter 21, a book has been written on the philosophy and methods of this movement: *The Transition Handbook: From Oil Dependency to Local Resilience* by Rob Hopkins, founder of the transition movement. Central to the philosophy of this work in community empowerment is the master context of global warming and fossil-fuel depletion. According to this view, these planet-wide challenges need to be met town by town, community by community through weaving resilient fabrics of living.

The work of the *bioregional movement* provides another illustration of the focus on local community empowerment and transition. Here the emphasis is on seeing humans in community with their natural regions of plants, animals, microbes, soils, atmospheres, aquifers, watersheds, lakes, rivers, streams, and land formations. Humans are urged to see their home place in this wider ecological context and to forge cultural, political, and economic patterns that are appropriate for their local region or their small "gully" of planetary geography.

We will not attempt to summarize further the vast wisdom contained in these illustrations of community empowerment work. Furthermore, there are other methods and efforts being made toward community empowerment. We believe that the many efforts toward community empowerment can reinforce each other, rather than compete with each other. We recommend learning from all these traditions how best to proceed with this important strategy for social change. The recently published *Relational Reality* by Charlene Spretnak is an amazing book of specific suggestions for local community empowerment.[47]

Why is Community Empowerment Important?

The reason this question needs to be asked is because most of us cringe before the detailed learning and years of hard work that community empowerment entails. If there were some easier way to bring Eco-Democracy into being, we would all be in favor of it. But local community empowerment is unavoidable, since Eco-Democracy means the overthrow of top-down images of social organization and the establishment of grassroots decision making that spreads outward to regional, continental, and planetary scopes of governance, acculturation, and sustenance. Community empowerment is a basic strategy for getting from our miserable *here* to the vital and workable *there* of a viable humanity for planet Earth.

---

47 Charlene Spretnak, *Relational Reality: New Discoveries of Interrelatedness That Are Transforming the Modern World* (Topsham, ME: Green Horizon Books, 2011)

Also, the national and international realms of human governance, culture, and economy will not change without pressure from local communities that have recovered their clout and use it effectively. Local community focus is not an escape from the problems of the wider world, but a means for the solution of these problems. Our vast planetary challenges must be resolved from the grassroots to the furthest shores, mountains, and plains. We now live on one intensely interrelated planet, and no local community is a separate island uninfluenced by faraway events. We must either pick up the challenge to renew all communities and all relations between all communities, or let failure be our outcome.

Planetary interrelatedness does not and need not mean that each local community cannot have its own unique quality of culture and other social practices. Uniformity is an ideal and a social pressure built into the top-down, hierarchical mode of social organization we call "civilization." But Eco-Democracy need not and must not espouse uniformity as an ideal or a practice. Perhaps there will be standards of measurement that many local communities agree to use. Perhaps there will be ecological and justice policies that are widespread. But lockstep, authoritarian sameness must become a thing of the past if responsibility is to begin in local places and spread outward to planetary solutions. Empowered local communities will need to insist upon this, for the forces of uniformity are still strong. Local citizens are still tempted to simply go along with supposed "experts" rather than develop their own expertise and responsibility.

In spite of all the work and thoughtfulness that is involved, local empowerment can also be fun, satisfying, and ennobling. Indeed the term "empowered" has all of those meanings. Powerlessness is a condition that most of us want to overcome. Powerlessness feels bad. It is a pain. Though we may feel glad sometimes to be just a sponge that soaks up life from the powers above, when trouble arises that we are powerless to do anything about, we experience pain, a pain we do not wish to endure long term.

The empowerment of our local patterns of life is also the empowerment of individual citizens. Without the meaningful reconstruction of local community, democracy is a joke. Democracy becomes a scam perpetrated upon us by oligarchic forces of greed obsessed with exaggerated views of their importance, wisdom, and power.

Practical wisdom and care for others originates in relationships between people who live in some local place and who create together what practical care for others means in that place. Without local communities who have the clout to make a difference in the life of their own place, we do not have the grassroots energies needed to complete our overall planetary shifts. Indeed, the gathering of momentum toward horrific catastrophes will continue uninterrupted unless there are communities of people who present group resistance to the destructive trends.

Cultural Consensus as Fundamental

The so-called "culture wars" are the first order of engagement in local community empowerment. People cannot work through the core political and economic choices when their views of what is good and valuable for society as a whole are too diverse. Total agreement on every topic is not possible, necessary, or advisable. But an overall perspective about basic ecological values, good democratic processes, economic justice, and social workability is required. Rigid ideological principles of right, left, or center are enemies of effective consensus building. People need to learn to be open to truth arriving from whatever direction. People need to learn to think for themselves in the context of openness to and love for truth as opposed to clinging to rigid certainties based on faraway authorities. We will have to be patient with people who are making deep changes, and we will need to be persistent. We will need to invent ways to be persistently present, assisting people with all these changes.

And who is the "we" that will do this patient, persistent work? First of all, the "we" are community organizers—awake Eco-Democratic community organizers. These community organizers need not be paid professionals. In most places volunteer workers are what we will have in the beginning. Volunteer arrangements may prove effective for the long haul. But if paid staff are needed or preferred, volunteers will have to finance it. We do not need to have one recipe for success that applies to every community. Nevertheless, there is a body of wisdom about community organization already built and being built. This wisdom can guide us as we continue doing community organizational work. Community organization does not just happen. A core of people has to do it and commit to doing it for the long haul. We who are the "we" who do this, will learn as we go.

We Are Talking Long Range

Local empowerment is urgent, and it is a long-range strategy. Electoral politics is short range—two years, four years, six years. A local, culture-based transformation of communal life requires at least a ten-year perspective. In the first years, empowering local community may not provide major impetus for political and economic innovation. The necessity of this slow and patient task of changing local communities is bad news for those who expect to resolve all problems through the election of the right president or governor. It is also bad news for those who expect some technological invention to sweep us into a workable future. But over the long haul, a vital and progressive politics and a thoroughgoing economic transformation absolutely depend upon the cultural transformation of basic community life.

This does not mean, however, that economic and political issues can wait until the local cultural work is done. Rather, we will need to begin now with cultural, economic, and political work, but our political and economic work cannot be fully radicalized until the cultural underpinnings for it are established. We can expect political and economic changes in the right directions to be incremental, perhaps disgustingly so. To make big changes we will need huge majorities of awakening people who insist upon the deep changes we are proposing. Nevertheless, while we are building these vast majorities, we will need to work to prevent our overarching political and economic arrangements from moving backwards into ever more brutal global feudalism. Our local communities will need to be trained to understand and respond to statewide and nationwide political and economic emergencies even while they work long range in their local place to shape minds and hopes in more long-term directions.

Part of our cultural transformation will be teaching the importance of cultural as well as political and economic responsibilities. We can begin now with incremental political and economic changes, even while the more radical processes of change are being held up by the lack of cultural transformation at the local community level. We cannot have a radical transition without the awakening of vast majorities of people to the tasks of comprehensive and radically future-oriented options. And we cannot sustain such a new society without the popular forces to sustain it. This slow grassroots work may seem painful to those accustomed to rapid top-down modes of change, but such top-down modes of change cannot be fully radical.

The fun of long-range cultural work is that it can be fully progressive. Political work tends to move forward with disappointingly small compromises. And much of our progressive political work will be to preserve the progress already established from slipping back into oligarchic greed and silliness. Political choices for big future-oriented changes come rarely and toward the end of an intense struggle with the status quo. Let the 2011 events in Tunisia, Egypt, and Libya be our illustration. Local community empowerment is the building of the forces that can make those big public moves when the time is right for them.

Fresh economic changes can be fostered in local places and spread widely, but eventually these changes encounter the established economic/political establishments that resist the changes. Further benefits have to be forced through by popular majorities. For example, we already have technologies to create a post fossil-fuel energy system, but the explosion of investment in the newer technologies is being blocked by the energy establishment with its billions of dollars that are available to defend its stake in the future. At some point masses of awakening people have to apply the force necessary to leave all tar, most coal, and some of the oil in the ground and move on.

Local communities get ahead of the planet-wide energy transition by beginning now to make their energy systems more and more dependent on sun, wind, and conservation. Local communities can lead rather than follow the national and international changes. Many communities are already leading. Other communities will be holdouts to the end for the obsolete ways of hierarchical empire. Each of us who count ourselves "progressives," wherever we take up residence, can assist our community to be one of the leaders, rather than a caboose at the end of the train of the great change from empire to Eco-Democracy.

* * * * * * * *

For further reading on this topic we recommend the following volumes:

Judith Plant & Christopher Plant, *Putting Power in its Place: Create Community Control!* (Gabriola Island BC, Canada: New Society Publishers, 1992)

Charlene Spretnak, *Relational Reality: New Discoveries of Interrelatedness that Are Transforming the Modern World* (Topsham, ME: Green Horizon Books, 2011)

Rob Hopkins, *The Transition Handbook: From Oil Dependency to Local Resilience* (Padstow, Cornwall, Great Britain: Green Books, 2008)

Peter Block *Community: The Structure of Belonging* (San Francisco: Berrett Koehler, 2008)

Sustainable Agriculture and Resistance: Transforming Food Production in Cuba, edited by Fernando Fiunes et al. (Oakland, California: Food First Books, 2002)

Chapter 27

The Reshaping of Global Institutions

People who see the relevance and possibility of carrying out the strategy of community empowerment often have difficulty participating in the electoral politics of their nation and/or doing practical thinking and action with regard to international affairs. Locally focused persons tend toward this limited perspective: "If I am engaged in community empowerment, I am already doing all I can. To apply my mind to national and international affairs is too much."

International work can also seem hopeless. What can one person do? Indeed, what can one re-empowered community do in relation to the vast scope of international problems? Furthermore, the global institutions are currently managed by national governments loyal to the huge, wealthy, transnational corporations. These forces are very strong, and they oppose the most meaningful changes. Action in the planetary arena can seem like fighting an unbeatable foe.

Faced with such difficulties at the global scope of action, we need to explain why we have included reshaping global institutions in our list of the five basic strategies for moving from Empire to Eco-Democracy. First of all, change is going to be difficult at the local and national scopes as well as the global scope of action. Progressive change in any one of the three arenas assists the other two, and the lack of progressive change in any one of the three arenas creates difficulties for the other two. Those of us who are committed to local empowerment will sooner or later face the realization that a reactionary national government can undo all of our local empowerment accomplishments any time that national government feels threatened by our local empowerment and feels capable of getting away with shutting down our local work.

Also, it is currently possible for global institutions controlled by transnational corporations and enforced by national treaties to rescind popularly supported and enacted laws of nations, states, and local communities. A California law against selling gasoline with an additive that harms the California water supply was undone by a complaint made to NAFTA (North American Free Trade Association) by the Canadian manufacturer of that product. It is shocking that an international agency controlled by corporations could rescind a US state law enacted by citizens. The law was undone through the enactment of an unpayable fine against the California state government. We need to reshape our international institutions and trade relations so that our progressive work at national, state, and local scopes cannot be undone or prevented by powerful global organizations.

The Current Problem

What is the core problem with our current global institutions? The United Nations, the World Trade Organization, the International Monetary Fund, the World Bank, and other planet-wide organizations came into being to meet perceived needs for living as a world community. As we criticize these institutions and their practices, we need also to acknowledge that the existence of these institutions is a witness to the need for organizations that enable our "one world" humanity to function. In this one chapter we will not attempt a detailed critique of the current international organizations, but we will explore the core flaw that we believe all of us need to confront in these organizations. These institutions tend to be controlled by national governments that are dominated by huge transnational corporations. In effect, we have a corporate rule of the world assisted by and defended by these existing global institutions. We have what we might call "globalization from above." We have a top-down rather than a citizen-driven, democratic approach to world affairs.

Jeremy Brecher, Tim Costello, and Brendan Smith have written a thoughtful book entitled *Globalization from Below: The Power of Solidarity.* They make the case that the issue is not globalization itself, but the style of globalization that we create. Rather than global institutions organized by and for the interests of an elite group of wealth holders in corporation board rooms and in governmental agencies captive to these corporations, we need global institutions that are answerable to the local citizenry of the planet. The polity of our global institutions must be turned upside down.

So how is such a huge change to be accomplished? At the present time two tasks are doable: (1) continuing firm and detailed criticism of our current global institutions, and (2) organizing citizen-supported shadow bodies alongside the established global institutions. We already have groups of non-governmental organizations working alongside the global bodies that are authorized by nation states. These NGO meetings forge and promote alternative directions from those commonly taken by the establishment bodies. The work of these associations of NGOs can be strengthened, and it is important for us to do so.

Also critical for progressive changes within our global institutions is the strategy we call "electoral politics." Winning more progressive national governments is key because the corporations that control our global institutions rely on the coercive force held by national governments to enforce their will. National governments have the clout to maintain the status quo or instigate the changes that are needed.

What Global Institutions Do We Need?

Long before we have citizen-controlled national governments that are willing to assist in a radical global restructuring, we need to begin envisioning what global structures are needed and how they would function in a workable planetary Eco-

Democratic arrangement. Peter G. Brown and Geoffrey Garver have authored a book entitled *Right Relationship: Building a Whole Earth Economy.* They approach the need for new global political institutions from a solid ecological and democratic perspective, and they come up with the need for these four institutions:

1. **The Global Reserve,** which meets the need for the "comprehensive monitoring and analysis of information on the ecological limits of the earth, in a way that can be applied to keep the economy within those limits."
2. **Trusteeships of Earth's Commons**, which serve as a "means to protect the global commons in a fair way."
3. **The Global Federation,** which serves as "a means of passing enforceable laws and regulations."
4. **A Global Court,** which provides an "independent judicial review of the performance of these institutions and compliance with global rules."[48]

Brown and Garver spell out in more detail the nature and purpose of these four institutions and show how they are a viable and adequate replacement for the institutions that we have. Perhaps the four institutions that Brown and Garver describe can serve as a model toward which we can reform the current institutions. Perhaps we will need to start over with new institutions. We will spell out the Brown and Garver vision more fully.

The Global Reserve deals with the issue of providing well-researched facts and the best of scientific knowledge unshaped by the monetary interests of various corporations or nations. Without the facts, citizens are left with the propaganda of various ruling interests. The Global Reserve builds consensus on critical ecological topics, a consensus that is fact-based and workable. Such research is ongoing—pulling together the most competent scientific work being conducted.

48 Peter G. Brown & Garver G, *Right Relationship: Building a Whole Earth Economy* (San Francisco: Berrett-Koehler, 2009), p. 111.

The Trusteeships of Earth's Commons are action bodies assigned to specific global crises such as fisheries, forests, CO_2 levels, fresh water preservation and distribution, etc. These bodies design viable solutions to these ongoing crises and inform political leaders, business leaders, and citizens with the means by which planet-wide solutions can be achieved.

The Global Federation fills the need of restraining those nations and businesses that refuse to abide by the common good as laid out in laws and regulations built through planet-wide consensus processes. The Federation also organizes the enforcement of those laws. This is not world government in a top-down sense. It is a federation of national and local seats of power working toward the common necessities of living together on this one planet.

A Global Court, like national and local court systems, provides judicial review of contested global cases. We have already experimented with World Court actions, but most nations have not yet ceded sufficient power to such a judiciary to enable a true administration of justice. Many nations, including the United States, resist being governed by even the most obvious forms of international law. Some super-nationalistic elements within the United States scorn even the existence of the relatively weak United Nations. Furthermore, US citizens who strongly support the United Nations often oppose international law when it is applied to the United States.

We will not attempt to summarize the functions of such bodies in more detail. It is enough for our purpose to say that democratically ordered bodies of consensus-building human beings will make wiser decisions than a chaotic world market ruled by our most greedy economic organizations. It is a mistake for citizens to abandon the international playing field to the Earth-destructive and democracy-bypassing narrow concerns of the transnational corporations. We are envisioning the empowerment of world citizens, *not* a planetary imperial rule that more fully reduces ordinary citizens to powerless cogs in the machinery.

How Do We Move Toward This Vision?

Step one is further clarifying our global vision, and step two is organizing citizen-powered planetary movements that can focus on the global issues as representatives of the multitudes who do not yet understand these responsibilities. Step three is educating a wide swath of ordinary citizens not only in the civics of their communities and nations, but also in their responsibilities as Earthlings, as "citizens" of the planet, as agencies of power who can insist upon workable global organizations of human care for Earth and humanity. Step four is enabling a deep inward change in personal attitudes toward Earth itself and toward fresh global institutions and their workable practices. Such global changes will be a long-range task, for it is a profound shift for humans to cease seeing themselves as separate persons and isolated groups who are seeking their narrow interests in competition with everyone else. In order to realize a true identification with and love for the Earth, we will need to challenge our species to reclaim its glory as creative cooperators who can foster more and more cooperation from all members of our species in facing and creatively answering the huge challenges of our era.

* * * * * * * *

For further reading on this topic we recommend the following:

Jeremy Brecher, Tim Costello, & Brendan Smith, *Globalization from Below: The Power of Solidarity* (Cambridge, MA: South End Press, 2000)

Peter G. Brown & Geoffrey Garver, *Right Relationship: Building a Whole Earth Economy* (San Francisco: Berrett-Koehler, 2009)

John Ralston Saul, *The Collapse of Globalism and the Reinvention of the World* (Woodstock, NY: The Overlook Press, 2005)

Chapter 28
Step-by-Step Strategy

The above five master strategies are not programs that are done, and done at once. A strategy is not a program, but a master picture of how we can envision a massive transition over a period of time. To actually accomplish this transition we must move from here to there step-by-step.

Step-by-Step in Place and Time

Strategy is place-and-time specific. To illustrate what we mean, let us assume that the time is now and the place is the United States. What might be the step-by-step strategy for dealing with the critical energy transition discussed earlier in this book? Here is a suggested sequence of actions:

Step 1: Through local community action, refuse to allow the licensing of any new coal-burning power plants. Use every administrative and nonviolent noncooperation means necessary for opposing new coal plants. Make it a movement across the nation. Rouse the population to the absolute necessity of preventing the expansion of this poisonous and most carbon-spewing means of energy production. Fight down the farce of "carbon capture" and "clean coal." Explain to the public that the only way the carbon in coal can be safely and permanently stored is to leave the coal in the ground. This step can also include fighting the horrifically wrongheaded proposal to build a pipeline from Canada to the Gulf of Mexico to transport tar sands oil.

Step 2: Phase out all old coal-fired power plants. Shutting down the old coal-fired plants can build upon the success in preventing new ones. And shutting down the old ones may be easier than preventing new ones because the old ones are dirtier plants and are also wearing out.

Step 3. End all subsidies and tax loopholes for fossil-fuel production, and use that wealth to build a new energy infrastructure. Not only could this innovation be a jobs program, it could encourage the turn toward solar and wind energy sources and the development of a needed hydrogen-use infrastructure.

Step 4: Tax existing nuclear plants to cover the entire expense to the government for nuclear waste storage as well as the cost of police protection and the insurance of communities against accidents and terrorism. Such taxation would end the open and hidden government subsidies for nuclear energy. It would reveal that using nuclear energy to produce electricity is now, has always been, and will remain economically expensive and perhaps entirely uncompetitive with solar and wind energy production.

Step 5: Enact a stiff national carbon tax that gets stiffer each year. This is administratively easy but politically hard. As a way to handle part of the political opposition, we could use most of the proceeds of this new tax to provide income tax rebates for those whose lives are being pushed toward poverty by the increase in transportation and heating expenses. Richer citizens can afford the increase in energy costs, and they are those who most need to reduce their use of energy on behalf of humankind. Perhaps we could name such legislation the "Energy Transition and Assistance Bill." However we frame it, a stiff carbon tax is the best way to use market dynamics to smooth the transition from carbon fuels to alternatives. A voluntary approach by citizens or businesses will never work: it is simply an excuse for failure. For making this huge transition, it is a farce to propose a voluntary approach.

Step 6: At the national level outlaw the mining and importing of coal as well as tar sands oil. This completes the curtailment of coal use and tar sands use initiated at the local level as Step 1.

Notice that these six steps include no government subsidies to biofuel production, hydrogen energy transfer, solar, wind, or any other promising energy source or transfer means. Once cleared of its carbon and nuclear biases, the market may be able to handle the complexities of the vast energy transition better than government administrators and politicians. The technological and economic complexities of an alternative energy economy are so vast that no one can accurately predict how the details of energy provision will sift out.

Although creating the political will for these steps or something similar may seem daunting within our present cultural environment, such steps are doable and can be effective in reaching the goal of a post-fossil-fuel, post-nuclear energy system. The limiting factor for carrying out these doable steps is the need to increase popular understanding and demand for these strategies. Citizen education is therefore a parallel strategy alongside these more direct steps it takes to resolve the energy transition. The capture of political power from the current energy establishment by an informed citizenry is a core part of the energy strategy. For example, citizens and their politicians must stop outdoing one another in complaining about high gasoline prices. We need to make high gasoline prices a virtue right up there with pothole repair and reinforced bridges. Oil products cannot be phased out by keeping oil prices artificially cheap. In fact, gasoline taxes in the US should be increased many fold as a means of discouraging gasoline use. Many developed countries have done this for decades.

* * * * * * * *

Next, we will illustrate the nature of step-by-step strategy in relation to the development of an informed citizenry operating through clean electoral processes. The goal here is promoting an expanding movement of dedicated citizens who have the ability to exercise political power. Such power is necessary to restrain and defeat those forces who are willing to use their massive economic resources to curtail or slow the needed transitions.

Here is an illustration of what step-by-step action in the area of informed citizenry and clean elections might look like:

Step 1: Increase effective educational programs and media events that awaken people to their loss of democratic power, and awaken people to doable steps that move toward the recovery of popular political empowerment. Here is a core slogan we need to place in every household: "Government of the people, by the people, and for the people rather than government of the money, by the money, and for the money." This might be a refrigerator magnet stuck to the refrigerator in the home of every clear-thinking citizen. The current Occupation Wall Street protests are already doing this step. Thousands of people are talking to one another about empowering the 99 percent against the tyranny of the 1 percent. This is a vast educational program as well as a power move.

Step 2: Widen the progressive wing of the US Democratic Party. All but a very few Republicans are locked into league with the moneyed aristocracy. The centrist half of the Democratic Party has also chosen to ally itself with big money in order to compete with the Republicans. Third parties trying to operate within current US election laws are prevented from achieving majority power. So the hope of achieving progressive majority power in the near term is with the progressive wing of the Democratic Party, however distasteful that may be to those of us who have been disappointed with the lack of boldness by even this segment of the political leadership. The development of this political power block within the Democratic Party must include grass roots organization. Democrats in each town, each county, each city, and each state need to be educated and organized in accord with the basic vision and strategy outlined in this book.

Step 3: Establish public financing for all campaigns for public office. This requires a democratic and simple means of assessing candidate viability. It also includes free television time provided by all TV outlets as part of their rent for using the publicly owned airways. Though the details of free TV provision may be complex, no other direction will deliver elections from big money rule. As long as big money rules the TV outlets and candidates must buy their TV time from such money-controlled outlets, we cannot have a full democracy.

Step 4. Establish a consistent, well-operated program of instant runoff voting. This widens the discussion of issues, enables a meaningful role for third parties, and further restrains the influence of big money.

These four steps are easy to understand and administer. And such changes will have enormous consequences. Therefore, they will be resisted with fanatic opposition from those who do not want those consequences. The key to the accomplishment of these steps will be a vigorous insistence on this agenda by huge, outspoken, and insistent sectors of the US citizenry. We will need a large body of talented people to put their bodies on the line for citizen education and citizen motivation to access the courage to win this fight for clean elections.

* * * * * * * *

The above lists of steps are only an illustration of the process of step-by-step strategy. Other series of steps can be imagined for other aspects of the overall transition. And the various series of steps will tend to reinforce one another. There is no permanent strategy that can be written down in 2012. Strategy is an ever-moving development, created by the movers who are leading the move from empire to Eco-Democracy.

Chapter 29

The Ever-Unfolding Vision, Strategy, and Action

So far we have focused on the vision of Eco-Democracy and the strategy for getting to a realization of that vision. We have viewed these dynamics from the perspective of living in the United States in 2011 and 2012. Clearly, we are in a massive social turning from what we have traditionally called "civilization" or "empire" to something radically different. Eco-Democracy is our code word for that something different. The details of that vision of the future will be enriched as time moves on. Perhaps we will see more clearly what aspects of the current social order are salvageable and what parts are dispensable. Nevertheless, we believe that the main outlines of our vision for an Eco-Democracy style of social organization will hold for decades to come.

The same stability cannot be assumed for our strategies of movement from here to there. As the social situation changes (whether progressively or regressively), our strategies will need to be corrected. In our discussion of strategy our core aim has been to counter the deeply wrong view that our situation is hopeless—that there is no viable way forward for anything as far-reaching as the Eco-Democracy mode of social organization. Strategy is our picture of how that way forward is possible.

We have not yet discussed action at the tactical or implementation level, except by way of illustrating the specific meaning of our various strategies. Here is a review of these three layers of social thinking:

Vision: Vision is where we want to go or how the world could be different. In this case our vision is Eco-Democracy and all the working parts of that possibility.

Strategy: Strategy is how we get from our messy "here" to our hopeful "there." In Part Four we laid out a master picture of the overall movements required to reach our vision of Eco-Democracy.

Tactics or "implementaries": Tactics are the day-by-day, week-by-week actions that workers in the field enact to carry out overall strategies. Tactics (implementaries) are where the physical bodies of the progressive actors touch down on the roadway or soil of actual Earth history.

Tactics are the day-to-day, place-specific implementations of the strategies that have become clear in the minds of a large number of willing actors. It is these active people, in all their specific places and roles, who will actually create the tactical/ implementary actions on a daily, weekly, quarterly, and annual basis.

This view of tactics brings us to an insight not yet fully developed—namely, the need for ongoing strong communities of transestablishment visionaries who rebuild their consensus about action week-by-week, year-by-year. It is these communities of actors who will choose the steps that they can best take in each geographical area and social position within this complex society.

In this chapter we will merely illustrate what we mean by "tactics" or "implementaries." Obviously, the following examples are location specific and do not apply to every place. We have selected examples from a place in rural Texas with which we are familiar. It seems true that if these kinds of tactics can be done here, they can be done anywhere.

In the county of Fannin in northeast Texas, a small group of people instigated and still sustain an organization called CORE (Citizens Organized for Resources and Environment). This group came into being as part of a statewide effort to stop the introduction of new coal-fired power plants, one of which was in Fannin County. This effort was largely successful, though such work is never entirely over.

CORE then turned attention to other issues in this rural county. It shows films, leads discussions, and makes plans directed toward a local food system that will connect local food growers with local food eaters, people who want fresh, organic, safe food grown within a seventy-mile radius. These actions address a key set of problems: current eaters are subjected to food sources they cannot entirely trust, and current farmers are oppressed, cheated, and enslaved by huge agribusinesses, food marketers, fertilizer and equipment corporations, and so on. Working on such specific issues in this rural county provides a means of liberating citizens from the herd instinct of trusting the huge, distant, and often ruthless powers that are operating in most areas of their lives. The work of CORE illustrates tactics that carry out the overall strategy of community empowerment discussed in Chapter 26.

In north Texas we have an organization called the "Upper Blackland Bioregional Council." This group meets quarterly for reflection and fun directed toward the goals of convincing about six counties of people that animals, plants, insects, microorganisms, soils, water, air, and humans are all parts of one community of beings and that the humans who live here need to find their role and responsibilities within this whole region of Earth. This group has so far had very little influence on its region, but over the long haul, it has a potential to become a base for calling together ecological groups, county commissioners, mayors, and others to brainstorm the ecological issues of this region. Such work can shift citizen perspectives toward a fresh practice of loving the Earth, a practice that sustains us in ongoing dedication toward the building of an Earth-compatible society. Such tactics carry forward both citizen education and community empowerment strategies.

Another educational effort is conducted by a small group of Fannin County writers and editors who write and publish a monthly e-mail magazine titled *Citizens' Call*. The purpose of this effort is citizen education on social and political issues that tend to be confusing to the current and potential Democratic and Independent citizens of Fannin County.

Also in Fannin County is a group that does dinner theater that dramatizes local community life using the "EcoTheater" methods of scene writing and improvised drama. The scenes are interspersed with appropriate songs and a fine meal. Another group promotes house concerts that bring liberating folk music into this local cultural environment on an almost monthly basis. These quite popular programs can be understood as tactics or implementaries for carrying out the overall strategy of citizen education discussed in Chapter 24.

In spite of a certain wonder that surrounds these simple actions in Fannin County, much more needs to be done. More people, more imagination, more depth of action is needed.

There are thousands of places where interesting and effective progressive actions are in process. Literature already exists on many of these efforts. Our aim in this chapter is to merely illustrate the implementary level of conducting the vast planetary transition. The key to further enriching these tactical/implementary actions is understanding the winning strategies outlined in Chapters 23 to 27 and doing the creative thinking that is needed to apply these strategies to a local place or a role in society.

Coda:
The Challenge to Each of Us

The aim of this book has been to lay out a picture of the master *"Road"* toward a flourishing humanity compatible with planet Earth. Obviously, the overall work of following this road will entail millions of actions that no one person can ever even know about. To make this vast transition to Eco-Democracy, it will take, in the United States alone, at least fifty million people working every week, every month, every year toward this goal. We need to be realistically overwhelmed by the vastness of this shift in world affairs. Yet we also need to recognize that each of us can only lift one small corner of this huge weight. And we can only be motivated to do our small but perhaps difficult part when we see the big picture: the vision and strategy that makes clear to us that our small part is indeed part of a meaningful whole of viable social transformation.

The aim of this book has not been to leave its readers stunned with the overwhelming scope of the current social transition. Nor do we expect every reader to master all the details referred to and further developed in the books we have recommended. Our aim has been to clear the way for action by each and every reader, action that counts for something in meeting the actual challenges that humanity faces.

Only action can lead us into the still further experiences and reflections that we need. If we feel called to be truly realistic persons, we are called to walk this *Road from Empire to Eco-Democracy*. Each of us will have to find our own sidewalk or dirt path on this overall road. Each of us will have to decide what roles are most appropriate for us and what programs of further education and preparation are needed.

Nevertheless, this road is not a lonely, all-by-myself thing. We are called to join the relevant progressive communities that are most befitting for us. Social transformation is a group thing. We are not supermen or superwomen who can do amazingly significant rescues of the entire planet with little or no help. This road we are discussing is for millions of pedestrians, ordinary people who place one foot in front of the other for weeks, months, years, and decades. Just like any road that was ever constructed, from the Appian Way to Route 66 to the first trip to the Moon, the construction of this road will require the backbreaking but glorious work of millions of workers working at a thousand different tasks, but all with a common vision

We owe ourselves and our companions a glorious happiness about this work. We are putting our bodies on the line for a truly championship game. This is it. Winning in this game is a matter of survival and flourishing of the next and the next and the next generation of humans. It is indeed an interesting time in which we have been born. This is our chance to live deeply. This is our chance to contribute significantly. Most of us will not live to see the full results of our labor. But those who do see the importance of our efforts will thank us, even if our names are not known to them and our pains and glories go unremembered. Herein is our motivation: that we know that we have put ourselves, our very bodies, minds, and spirits into the work of movement from a messy *here* to a *there* of new and better messes.

Open Book Editions
A Berrett-Koehler Partner

Open Book Editions is a joint venture between Berrett-Koehler Publishers and Author Solutions, the market leader in self-publishing. There are many more aspiring authors who share Berrett-Koehler's mission than we can sustainably publish. To serve these authors, Open Book Editions offers a comprehensive self-publishing opportunity.

A Shared Mission

Open Book Editions welcomes authors who share the Berrett-Koehler mission—Creating a World That Works for All. We believe that to truly create a better world, action is needed at all levels—individual, organizational, and societal. At the individual level, our publications help people align their lives with their values and with their aspirations for a better world. At the organizational level, we promote progressive leadership and management practices, socially responsible approaches to business, and humane and effective organizations. At the societal level, we publish content that advances social and economic justice, shared prosperity, sustainability, and new solutions to national and global issues.

Open Book Editions represents a new way to further the BK mission and expand our community. We look forward to helping more authors challenge conventional thinking, introduce new ideas, and foster positive change.

For more information, see the Open Book Editions website: http://www.iuniverse.com/Packages/OpenBookEditions.aspx

Join the BK Community! See exclusive author videos, join discussion groups, find out about upcoming events, read author blogs, and much more! http://bkcommunity.com/

CPSIA information can be obtained at www.ICGtesting.com
Printed in the USA
LVOW112342270112

265937LV00002B/3/P